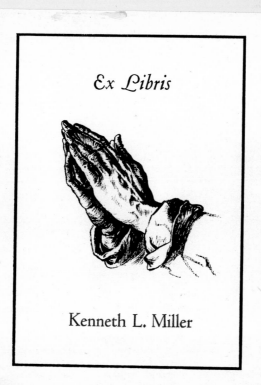

Ex Libris

Kenneth L. Miller

WORSHIP SERVICES
FOR
PURPOSEFUL LIVING

WORSHIP SERVICES FOR PURPOSEFUL LIVING

By

ALICE ANDERSON BAYS

ABINGDON-COKESBURY PRESS

NEW YORK • NASHVILLE

WORSHIP SERVICES FOR PURPOSEFUL LIVING

Copyright MCMXLIX by Pierce & Smith

Library of Congress Catalog Card Number: 49-48227

D

SET UP, PRINTED, AND BOUND BY THE
PARTHENON PRESS, AT NASHVILLE,
TENNESSEE, UNITED STATES OF AMERICA

To
COLONEL AND MRS. CLAUDE S. REEDER

FOREWORD

THIS volume of worship services for youth was written to help young people in making their choices and in selecting worthy purposes for their lives. It is to supplement the planned worship services of the various denominations and is prepared for use in local churches, for morning watch and vesper services in camps, summer conferences, retreats, and other occasions.

The services are complete but may be easily adapted to local needs, or may be simplified by omitting a poem, hymn, or other elements. It is hoped that young people will use this volume as resource material, lifting out a poem, prayer, or story and using it to enrich their worship. It is suggested that they take the stories in Part II and build their own worship services according to their needs. Many of the characters in these stories are young people in situations similar to those of youth today. Some of them are real people, facing modern problems, arriving at Christian decisions, and choosing worthy purposes for their lives.

Young people make choices daily. The following choices made during youth are the major decisions of a lifetime: to accept or reject Christ, to choose a vocation, and to select a life partner. The material in this volume sheds light on these and other choices, and points the way to a Christian solution of the problems involved. It is possible to learn from the experience of others the results to be expected from certain decisions. However, some may learn from their own experience that foolish choices tend to enslave, but wise choices open doors of opportunity.

As young people evaluate and select from the various possibilities the way they shall follow, ideals are formed and character is developed according to the choices made. Certain goals are set, new resolutions are formed, and progress is made through purposeful living.

I wish to acknowledge indebtedness and to express deep appreciation to all who co-operated in the preparation of this volume—to the young people and to the leaders of youth for their suggestions; to Mary Jeff-coat, Lawson-McGhee Library, Knoxville, Tennessee, for valuable assistance; to my brother, Jack Anderson, and to Elizabeth Wray Taylor for reading the manuscript and for helpful criticism; to my son, Robert Bays, for literary criticism; and to Col. and Mrs. Claude S. Reeder, in whose home in Fort Myers, Florida, the manuscript was completed.

Grateful acknowledgement is made to authors and publishers, es-pecially Dr. C. A. Bowen. Every effort has been made to trace owner-ship of all copyrighted material and to give proper credit. I am not conscious of any infringement, directly or indirectly; but should there be questions regarding the use of any material, I shall take pleasure in making proper acknowledgment in future editions.

ALICE ANDERSON BAYS

CONTENTS

WORSHIP SERVICES FOR PURPOSEFUL LIVING

PART ONE

WORSHIP SERVICES

SERVICE 1

TO RENOUNCE SELF

PRELUDE: Hymn tune "Boylston."

CALL TO WORSHIP:

> To serve the present age,
> My calling to fulfill;
> O may it all my powers engage
> To do my Master's will.
> —CHARLES WESLEY

HYMN: "A Charge to Keep I Have," or
"O Young and Fearless Prophet."

SCRIPTURE:

He that loveth father or mother more than me is not worthy of me: and he that loveth son or daughter more than me is not worthy of me. And he that taketh not his cross, and followeth after me, is not worthy of me. He that findeth his life shall lose it: and he that loseth his life for my sake shall find it.

Verily, verily, I say unto you, Except a corn of wheat fall into the ground and die, it abideth alone: but if it die, it bringeth forth much fruit. He that loveth his life shall lose it; and he that hateth his life in this world shall keep it unto life eternal. If any man serve me, let him follow me; and where I am, there shall also my servant be: if any man serve me, him will my Father honour.[1]

PRAYER:

O God, Light of the minds that see thee, Life of the souls that love thee, and Strength of the thoughts that seek thee; enlarge our minds and raise the vision of our hearts, that with swift wings of thought

—13—

our spirits may reach thee, the eternal Wisdom, who art from everlasting to everlasting; through Jesus Christ our Lord. AMEN.[2]

LEADER:

Jesus said, "He that loseth his life for my sake shall find it." In many parts of the world there are those who have taken Jesus literally—doctors, nurses, teachers, pastors, missionaries, and others who have lost themselves in a cause greater than themselves, and have found life. We will hear the story of four chaplains who renounced self to serve others.

STORY:

CHAPLAINS COURAGEOUS

I'M JUST an ordinary guy who's been through a war. I've had my fill of fighting all across France and deep into Germany. I've seen men die like flies around me and heroic deeds were a dime a dozen.

But I'm here to tell you that the finest thing I've ever seen, or hope to see this side of heaven, took place on the troopship that carried me across the Atlantic.

I was a raw replacement then; a little homesick, a little seasick, and more than a little scared. We'd heard a lot about the tin fish that traveled in wolf packs for the kill, and our convoy was steaming slowly through the northern seas. It was bitter cold that February of 1943 and icebergs dipped blue and ominous on the horizon.

Even in peace time the S. S. "Dorchester" was no pleasure boat, and now she was crammed to the gunwales with seasick, shivering GIs and a pile of stores and munitions.

I used to lean over the rail—if I could find an empty spot—maybe give up my last meal to the fishes, and wonder. In those blue-gray, icy waters were Nazi submarines. Suppose one of them connected! It didn't take an expert to guess what might happen with thousands of kids like myself first time out of sight of land, with just a few flimsy lifeboats and some inflated belts to keep us this side of eternity. Sure, those grim gray destroyers that kept circling and sniffing at us were a comfort—but the tin fish sometimes burst through—and then . . .

We had four sky pilots on board—chaplains, you know. Our boys were a mixed lot as far as religion went, and the chaplains who tended to our religious needs were in the same proportions—two Protestant, one Catholic, and one Jewish. They were nice guys as far as I could see. They tried hard to cheer us up.

—14—

They'd come quietly up to you when you were down in the dumps, thinking of your ma back home, and say a few words to you man to man. It wasn't so much what they said as *how* they said it; and you perked up after that. What I liked especially was that they never asked you what church you went to when they did something for you. There was one God, they told you at the Sunday services, and all us GIs who were decent human beings were headed straight for him, no matter what brand of religion we practiced. They left you with a mighty good feeling.

We were getting close to Iceland, our destination, and we all began to feel better. Maybe it was too cold this far north for the tin fish; maybe . . .

It was nighttime, and most of the boys were asleep. I couldn't sleep in the two inches of space they gave me below, so I wandered on deck. It was bitter cold, and the sea was acting up. Way out beyond, a blinker light winked and went out. A destroyer signaling. I went tense. I'd picked up a little code book back in camp, and that blinker was saying: "Warning! Enemy . . ."

Right above me the lookout let out a cry: "Periscope to starboard! Periscope to . . ."

That was all I got to hear; that was all a lot of us ever heard. There was a tremendous crash and the whole world seemed to explode. The sea vomited like a volcano and the sky blazed with light. The ship bucked, groaned, and slanted down toward the water.

At the first torpedo I was knocked flat on my face. I slid down the dark, slippery deck toward the heaving ocean. A hand caught me by the collar, lifted me to my feet just as I was going overboard.

"Are you all right, son?" asked a calm, kind voice. I gulped, looked up into the young, quiet face of Chaplain Goode. "Yeah! I guess so," I muttered, trying to catch my wind. Then I remembered. "Gee, thanks, padre! You saved my life!" Every chaplain in this man's army is called *padre,* even when he's a Jewish rabbi like Chaplain Goode.

He smiled at me. It was a nice, thoughtful smile. "The ship is sinking, son," he said. "The order's to abandon ship. You'd better get to your station."

When I looked again, he was gone. I stared dazed about me. Even a chap who'd never before been out in anything bigger than a rowboat could see that we were done for. The torpedoes had smacked square into the engine room. The whole Atlantic Ocean was rushing into the gaping hole. Half the lifeboats and the rafts had been torn away.

And there were a couple of thousand of shouting, crying, bewildered GIs, just out of sleep, milling and rushing around the listing decks.

"A fat chance any of us got!" I groaned and pushed blindly toward the nearest lifeboat.

But just as I got there a big wave broke over the ship and—the boat was gone. Everyone was pushing and shoving at me, but I just stood there and bawled.

Someone took my arm. "Don't be afraid," said a young voice. "We're in God's hands, my boy. Whatever be his will, let us face it like men of faith and courage."

Ashamed, I wiped my eyes on my sleeve. "Yes, padre," I answered humbly. Here was Chaplain Washington, Catholic priest, a man of peace, comforting *me* in time of danger; me who thought I was tough and a soldier!

"Have you a life belt?" he asked.

"N-no, sir!" I stammered. Like a fool I had left it down below when I came up on deck.

"Go to the forward deck. There's a box full of life belts there."

Then he turned to other panic-stricken, blindly stumbling soldiers. As I ran forward, I heard his deep voice booming balm of Gilead to those scared, bewildered men.

By the time I got to the box there were about a thousand others ahead of me.

Three officers stood before the box, handing out belts as fast as they could—three chaplains—two Protestant and one Jewish. The next moment Father Washington hurried up, took his place beside them.

"Take it quietly, men," said Chaplain Poling, one of the Protestants. "There are enough for everyone."

"Yeah!" I thought kind of panicky. "Not for me. There's too many guys ahead o' me." Yet I didn't try to push some other poor devil out of the way, and I thank God I had sense enough for that.

The four chaplains were working fast and furious. These belts disappeared like magic as trembling fingers buckled them on. When some youngster was too frozen or scared to do a proper job, a chaplain would do it for him with steady, efficient hands.

Finally there were only four of us guys left. Maybe we held back a little, maybe we were last in line. Anyhow, the box was empty. And the ship was going down fast. It was only a matter of a minute or two.

Chaplain Fox, the other Protestant, looked at us four with tragic eyes. "The box is empty, boys."

Then a miracle happened. I'd swear on my Bible that it was a simultaneous act. For each one of those blessed chaplains stripped off his own life belt, held it out to us. Four strong voices lifted. "Here, son, take this."

We had guts enough to fall back. "No-no, sir!" we stammered. "We—we *can't*!"

"Take them!" they said in a single awful voice.

"B-but you . . ."

"God will provide!"

We took them, sheepishly. They even buckled them on for us. It was Chaplain Poling who put mine on.

Next to me was Lt. Mahoney. He was staring down at his bare hands. They were blue with cold. Rabbi Goode saw his look. Without hesitation he pulled off his heavy mittens, handed them to Mahoney. "You can have these, Mahoney," he said. "I have an extra pair." I'd swear those were the last pair around.

It was time to go overboard. There wasn't a lifeboat left, and the sea was dotted with jumping, swimming figures. I went to the rail. Now, I can't swim more than a few strokes and that water was ice. I hung on the broken rail, afraid to jump, afraid to stay.

Father Washington's voice boomed behind me. "You'd better jump, lad," he said. "The ship won't last."

I stared into his smiling face, felt a great wave of courage come over me, and jumped.

I hit the water with a gasp. The life belt buoyed me up. I twisted to look back at the ship. There, on the deserted deck, already awash, stood the four men of God. Their arms were linked together and their heads bowed. Clear, unfaltering voices rose into the din and welter of the night. They were singing. I never heard such singing before, and I never will again. I couldn't make out the words, but afterward I made it my business to learn them.

"Our Father who art in heaven . . ."

"Miserere mei Deus, secundum magnam misericordiam teum . . ."

"Shma Yisroal Adoney Elehenu Adoney Echod . . ."

Then the ship gave a shudder, and plunged down into the waves. Those chaplains were still linked, still singing as the ocean swallowed them up. In my dreams I can hear them yet. . . .

I started to swim away as hard as I could.

Don't let anyone tell you about the bravest feat of the war. This was it. And here are their full names. Rev. Clark Poling, Rev. George

Fox, Protestants; Father John Washington, Catholic; Rabbi Alexander Goode, Jew. Four men of God, whose common faith in their Heavenly Father inscribed them on the tablets of immortal fame. Remember their names, remember their deeds, the next time you start to grouse about the other fellow, whose religion happens to be different from yours. I've *learnt*.[3]

POEM:

> Lord, in the strength of grace,
>   With a glad heart and free,
> Myself, my residue of days,
>   I consecrate to thee.
>
> Thy ransomed servant, I
>   Restore to thee thine own;
> And, from this moment, live or die
>   To serve my God alone.
>
> —CHARLES WESLEY

PRAYER:

O God, cultivate within us the spirit of righteousness, and help us to build thy kingdom here. We would manifest the Spirit of our Lord in every act and thought, and bring thy message unto fellow men. Make us pure within, where no one can see. Help us not to develop virtues merely that they may be seen of men, and help us to remain faithful to our own testimony of thee, and not try to appropriate the experience of others which is not ours. Inspire us to acquire purity of mind, strength of will, and beauty of spirit, that our inmost souls may be temples in which thou wouldst dwell. Help us to seek Christian character and spiritual power without thought of reward or praise. . . . May we live as if thy Son lived within us every minute of every day.[4]

We thank thee for the lives of these chaplains. When we think of their sacrifice, we realize that we have dissipated our energies and have not earned the right to be called thy children. Help us to re-dedicate our lives to thee and learn anew to walk the way of our Master, thy Son. AMEN.

HYMN: "Now in the Days of Youth," or
    "More Love to Thee, O Christ."

BENEDICTION:

May the example of the Master lead us into abundant living. AMEN.

SERVICE 2

TO MASTER SELF

PRELUDE: "Largo" from Dvořák's *New World Symphony*.

CALL TO WORSHIP:
> Worship the Lord in the beauty of holiness,
>   Bow down before Him, His glory proclaim;
> Gold of obedience, and incense of lowliness,
>   Kneel and adore Him,—the Lord is His name.
> > —JOHN S. B. MONSELL

HYMN: "Dear Master, in Whose Life I See," or
"Breathe on Me, Breath of God."

SCRIPTURE:
If we live by the Spirit, let us be guided by the Spirit. Let us not in our vanity challenge one another or envy one another. But if a man is caught doing something wrong, brothers, you are spiritual, and you must set him right, in a spirit of gentleness. Think of yourself, for you may be tempted too. Bear one another's burdens, and in that way carry out the law of Christ. For if anyone thinks he is somebody when he is really nobody, he is deceiving himself. Every man ought to test his own work, and then whatever satisfaction he has will be with reference to himself, and not in comparison with someone else. For everyone will have to carry his own load.

Those who are taught the message must share all their goods with their teacher. Do not be deceived. God is not to be sneered at. A man will reap just what he sows. The man who sows to gratify his physical cravings will reap destruction from them, and the man who sows to benefit the spirit will reap eternal life from the Spirit. Let us not get tired of doing right, for at the proper time we shall reap, if we do not give out. So then whenever we have an opportunity, let us do good to all men, especially to those who belong to the family of the faith.

For our knowledge is imperfect and our preaching is imperfect. But when perfection comes, what is imperfect will pass away. When I was a child, I talked like a child, I thought like a child, I reasoned like a child. When I became a man, I put aside my childish ways. For now we are looking at a dim reflection in a mirror, but then we shall see face to face. Now my knowledge is imperfect, but then I shall know as fully as God knows me.[1]

PRAYER:

Gracious God, in thee we live and move and have our being. In thy presence is fullness of joy. Break the spell of that which binds our minds. Purify our hearts, that we may see thee. Renew our inward life through the unseen and eternal. Visit our spirits and witness with them that we are thy children. AMEN.[2]

POEM:

Lives are in the making here,
Hearts are in the waking here,
Mighty undertaking here.
　Up!—and On!

We are arming for the fight,
Pressing on with all our might,
Pluming wings for higher flight.
　Up!—and On!

Fair before us lies the way,
Time for work and time for play,
Fill the measure while we may.
　Up!—and On!

Life and Time will not delay,
Time is running fast away,
Life is Now—today, today!
　Up!—and On!

Foes in plenty we shall meet;
Hearts courageous scorn defeat;
So we press, with eager feet,
　Up!—and On!

Ever onward to the fight,
Ever upward to the Light,
Ever true to God and Right,
Up!—and On! [3]

—JOHN OXENHAM

OFFERING.

OFFERTORY:

Honor the Lord with thy substance, and with the first fruits of all thine increase: so shall thy barns be filled with plenty.

HYMN: "Rejoice, Ye Pure in Heart," or
"Teach Me, O Lord, Thy Holy Way."

STORY:

THE MIRROR

THERE were many beautiful and costly residences in the suburbs of Jericho, but none so beautiful as the home of Zacchaeus. Because he was utterly friendless, he had endeavored to find compensation in the loveliness and luxury of his exquisite marble house.

The mounting fame of the Galilean carpenter had interested Zacchaeus deeply. Himself snubbed by the priests and scorned by the aristocracy, the revenue collector felt a bond of sympathy with the audacious Nazarene who was reputed to have outwitted the Sanhedrin on their own ground and inveighed against a social system which permitted blind beggars to die of starvation on rich men's doorsteps.

This morning Zacchaeus had roused with something important on his mind. Oh, yes, he remembered; this was the day the carpenter was coming to Jericho. The town had been buzzing with the rumor for a week. About an hour before noon Zacchaeus set off alone and on foot toward the business area. The waiting crowd grew more and more dense as he proceeded. Almost suffocated, for he was less than average height, Zacchaeus wormed to the curb and climbed up in a sycamore tree.

Far up the avenue the commotion in the crowd clearly indicated that the carpenter had been sighted, but the noise died away as he approached. In a moment he would pass directly beneath the tree. The carpenter was near enough now to be seen clearly. The half-patronizing smile that Zacchaeus had assumed on behalf of the foolhardy young Nazarene froze on his own lips. The cries of the crowd below were hushed. It was so quiet now that one could hear the rhythmic plop-plop of their leather sandals as the carpenter's crew strode forward.

The tense heart of Zacchaeus gave a throb. The carpenter was looking up! He seemed about to speak! He paused for the fraction of a second.

"Zacchaeus!"

"Aye, sir?"

"Come! I am dining with you."

Barely conscious of his own movements, such was the turbulence of his mind, Zacchaeus found himself on the street, attempting to measure his short steps to the masterful stride of the self-invited guest from Galilee. For the moment he was both proud and amused over his unexpected distinction. To have been considered the meanest man in Jericho and then, for some mysterious reason, to have been singled out for the honor of entertaining a prophet of such note, was almost beyond belief.

At his gate Zacchaeus turned as they entered and saw, trailing them, a local procession of many hundreds. This might be very annoying. He spoke to his amazed gatekeeper.

"If they insist upon entering, give them welcome to the grounds. See that they do not trample the flowers."

Evidently the fishermen who accompanied the carpenter had brought their own provisions. The foremost of them, a burly, black-bearded fellow, informed his master, in the dialect of north Galilee, that they would await him without.

Detached now from all this miscellaneous rabble, Zacchaeus and his strange guest, with slackened pace, walked side by side on the broad, winding, graveled driveway toward the marble palace. On either side of the road cypress and eucalyptus trees spread an inviting shade over the lawn.

The carpenter stepped aside from the road, lingered for a moment in the arbor, cupped a flower in his hands, bent over it, breathed deeply of its perfume, but made no comment beyond the gesture that carried the value of a caress. Zacchaeus was finding him difficult. It was plain to see, however, that the Nazarene had an instinct for beautiful things. One liked him for that.

Zacchaeus and his guest entered the house, and as they sat at luncheon, a dozen servants moved quietly about the low table. The dinner, thus far, had not proved to be much of a success. It was evident that the carpenter's thoughts were with the common riffraff plainly to be seen through the open bay. At length, thoroughly annoyed over a situation that had overtaxed his ingenuity, Zacchaeus idly toyed with his bracelet, his head bent in bewilderment over what should be his next move.

He heard a slight rustle of his guest's garments, indicating that he had risen from his elbow to a sitting position. Slowly raising his head, Zacchaeus looked for the first time squarely into The Eyes. He endeavored to meet that steady gaze with an insolent stare, but failed of it. He shrugged slightly and made as if to glance away, but found he could not get loose. The Eyes held him fast!

Within a few seconds he realized that he was as thoroughly a prisoner as if he sat there with manacled hands. The house was very quiet. Zacchaeus had never before experienced such deathlike stillness. As the minutes passed he sat transfixed, utterly powerless now to detach himself from the searching gaze that clutched him in a grip he could not shake off. Everything began quietly slipping into complete eclipse—his possessions, his dilemma, his discomfort, his indignation. Now there was nothing left to be conscious of but the calm face of the carpenter.

The Galilean's head was slightly inclined. His elbows were pressed close against his ribs. His hands were clasped under his firm chin. He gazed into the eyes of Zacchaeus. He did not smile or scowl. He searched. His lips were slightly parted as if there were words that might be spoken. From beneath straight, confident brows he gazed into the retreating eyes of Zacchaeus.

The seconds passed, each one emphasized by the savage pounding of the rich man's heart. Zacchaeus shuddered, and his mouth and throat were dry. He swallowed convulsively and tried again to tug away from The Eyes. A gray pallor overspread his face. He felt sick. But he could not turn away. A sudden change came. *He had seen a strange vision!* With a choking sob he woodenly raised both forearms and shielded his eyes against the sight, covered his face, and for a long time sat with his head in his quivering hands.

The carpenter spoke. "My friend," he said gently, "a great salvation has come to your house today."

His eyes suffused with blinding tears, Zacchaeus tremblingly arose and walked unsteadily to the doorway that opened out on the terrace. He stepped outside; and the multitude, brought to attention, scrambled to their feet and ran toward the house, frightened and perplexed, as they drew near enough to see his haggard face. The old bravado and impudence of his carriage had given place to something akin to humility.

He raised his hand for silence; but it was unnecessary, for everything was so still that each man could hear the beating of his own heart.

"I have resolved," said Zacchaeus, brokenly, "to give half of my goods to feed the poor. . . . And if I have defrauded any man, I shall make restitution."

After a long silence the multitude slowly retreated, step by step, without turning, no man venturing to reply. At a little distance they huddled together in awe-stricken groups, and some murmured, "It is a miracle!"

Groping his way back into the banquet hall, the shaken man crumpled into his seat again, opposite his dynamic guest. Once more he ventured to look into The Eyes. Now they were smiling.

"Zacchaeus," said the carpenter gently, "what did you see that made you desire this peace?"

"Good master—I saw—mirrored in your eyes—the face of the Zacchaeus I was meant to be!" [4]

POEM:

> Within my earthly temple there's a crowd;
> There's one of us that's humble, one that's proud,
> There's one that's broken-hearted for his sins,
> There's one that unrepentant sits and grins;
> There's one that loves his neighbor as himself,
> And one that cares for naught but fame and pelf.
> From much corroding care I should be free
> If I could once determine which is me.[5]
>
> —EDWARD SANFORD MARTIN

PRAYER:

Our Father, may we have the ability to see ourselves as thou seest us. As we study the life of Jesus, may there come to us a vision of the person that we can become. Grant us strength to uproot all evil desires and unworthy thoughts. May we build into our lives kindness, goodness, honesty, humility, steadfastness, and consideration for others. Give us courage and fortitude to follow our highest convictions regardless of what others may do, and may we fear nothing except that which is wrong. Keep us ever loyal to the truths which are exemplified in the life of our Master, we pray in his name. AMEN.

TO MASTER SELF

Hʏᴍɴ: "Open My Eyes," or
"Take Thou Our Minds, Dear Lord."

Bᴇɴᴇᴅɪᴄᴛɪᴏɴ:

Now unto him who is able to keep you from falling, and to present you faultless before his presence, be glory and power, now and evermore. Aᴍᴇɴ.

SERVICE 3

TO SHOULDER RESPONSIBILITY

PRELUDE: "Largo" by Handel.

CALL TO WORSHIP:

> Not for the eyes of men
>   May this day's work be done;
> But unto thee, O God,
>   That, with the setting sun,
> My heart may know the matchless prize
>   Of sure approval in thine eyes.[1]
>
> —Thomas Curtis Clark

HYMN: "Be Strong," or
  "Rise Up, O Men of God."

SCRIPTURE:

O Lord our Lord, how excellent is thy name in all the earth! who hast set thy glory above the heavens.

Out of the mouth of babes and sucklings hast thou ordained strength because of thine enemies, that thou mightest still the enemy and the avenger.

When I consider thy heavens, the work of thy fingers, the moon and the stars, which thou hast ordained;

What is man, that thou art mindful of him? and the son of man, that thou visitest him?

For thou hast made him a little lower than the angels, and hast crowned him with glory and honour.

Thou madest him to have dominion over the works of thy hands; thou hast put all things under his feet:

All sheep and oxen, yea, and the beasts of the field;

The fowl of the air, and the fish of the sea, and whatsoever passeth through the paths of the seas.

O Lord our Lord, how excellent is thy name in all the earth! [2]

PRAYER:

O God, by whom the meek are guided in judgment, and light riseth up in darkness for the godly; grant us, in all doubts and uncertainties, the grace to ask what thou wouldst have us to do; that the spirit of wisdom may save us from all false choices, and that in thy light we may see light, and in thy straight path may not stumble; through Jesus Christ our Lord. AMEN.[3]

POEM:

> A life which urges you to take
> From inner self each wrong, and break
> The artful habits that prevent
> Your very best accomplishment.
>
> A life which speaks, if you will hear,
> The answer to each doubt and fear;
> A life to fill each eager youth
> With living love and deathless truth.
>
> A life to lift the life of man
> Above the common caravan;
> That he may climb and guide his kind
> To life eternal—rich, refined.
>
> There is a life above your own
> To lead your life to God's high throne.[4]
>
> —CHAUNCEY R. PIETY

OFFERTORY:

Upon the first day of the week let every one of you lay by him in store, as God hath prospered him. Freely ye have received, freely give.

LEADER:

Let us hear the story of one who did not fail when responsibility was given to her.

THE STUFF SHE WAS MADE OF

BETTY OSGOOD stood by the desk of the superintendent of nurses. "You rang for me, Miss Randall?"

"Yes, Miss Osgood, I wanted to inform you that you are to assist in the operating room two weeks from today."

"Oh, Miss Randall!" There was blank dismay on Betty's face.

"What is the trouble?"

"I don't know how I shall ever do it. It seems that I can't."

"I don't understand you. You certainly knew that this work was in store for you; it's part of your training."

"Yes, Miss Randall," answered the girl with an air of utter discouragement. "I've known it only too well and have been dreading it."

"Why?" asked Miss Randall, as she looked keenly at the girl.

"I've always felt that if I ever had to help in an operation I should make some dreadful blunder, and some patient would lose his life because of it. When I first came in training, something went wrong in the operating room and a patient died. They blamed the nurse and she was sent away."

"But you have been in the operating room already, and you have done good work."

"That's different. But this—you know, I could make a blunder and the patient would die," said Betty.

"Is that your only trouble?"

"No, it isn't. Dr. Joslin, the chief surgeon, doesn't like me. Something happened during my first year, and he's never forgotten it."

"I think, Miss Osgood, that you exaggerate his feeling. Dr. Joslin is rather abrupt, but he's really kind."

"He frightens me so that I make mistakes. Miss Randall, may I leave out that part of my training?"

"Miss Osgood, the operating room is your great fear, and you must conquer it. Now is your time. If you don't, it will hurt your nursing career. I will help you, and you shall practice in advance until it will be impossible for you to make a mistake."

"Oh, I don't think it is possible."

"Will you try?"

"Yes, Miss Randall."

"Then, we will begin tomorrow, and I shall expect you to succeed. I know that you can."

The next morning Betty began studying under the instruction of Miss Randall for the new position. She worked as she had never worked before, and yet her efforts seemed futile. What was the use of thinking that, merely by hard work, she could conquer her fear of the operating room? Success meant hurrying, yet never making a mistake; it meant pleasing the surgeons, yet having exactly right every detail.

At last the day came when Betty and the assistant nurse took charge of the operating room. "An easy morning for your first," Miss Randall said. "Only two minor cases, both for Dr. Minturn, who is very considerate. I shall be here to help you, and you'll have no trouble."

Dr. Minturn was pleasant and wanted nothing out of the ordinary. Everyone treated Betty as if she were merely a part of the hospital machinery.

When the surgeon had gone, Miss Randall came to Betty, saying, "You did all right."

"But it won't be the same when I have hard cases with Dr. Joslin, who asks for several things at once and says 'Hurry up' every minute."

"He won't say 'Hurry up' if you have everything ready to put into his hands before he knows that he needs it."

Miss Randall posted three operations for Dr. Joslin for the next day and remarked that she would be in the operating room herself.

The next morning when Betty met Miss Randall, she said, "I've gone over everything, but it's no use. Dr. Joslin will want something I've never heard of, and I'll get so scared that I'll make some dreadful mistake."

"Betty Osgood, I'm ashamed of you! You've always done good work and been a credit to the hospital. Are you actually planning to fail?"

"Oh, Miss Randall! I didn't mean that! But I'm afraid that I can't . . ."

"Then you are not going to try?"

"Miss Randall, I do mean to try, but Dr. Joslin . . ."

"Annoying Dr. Joslin isn't the worst thing in the world. It's worse to fail people who trust you."

There was a visiting surgeon in the operating room, Dr. Foster of Philadelphia, and Betty quailed before his searching eyes.

The first case started smoothly; the doctors were relaxed and cheerful. Then Dr. Joslin asked for a special retractor. Betty looked among the instruments on the table, but it was not there.

"It isn't here, Dr. Joslin," Betty said timidly.

"Isn't here?" he growled; then he said, "Oh, I remember. I left it at the office."

The second case proved to be a complicated one, and Dr. Joslin worked rapidly. Even Miss Randall seemed to be under a strain. At last they were ready for the third case. As a frail woman was brought into the operating room, Betty caught a glimpse of a man peering anxiously after her. "This woman's life," she said, "may depend upon my knowledge and faithfulness."

An orderly came to the door and beckoned to Miss Randall, saying, "An emergency and they want you."

Panic seized Betty, for her mainstay was gone. A sense of tremendous responsibility came over her. There was no one to help her now, and the work must de done. Setting her lips firmly, she began to think clearly, and her hands became steady. She was no longer a panic-stricken girl; she was a mature person who must keep faith with those who trusted her, and make it possible for a surgeon to do an important piece of work.

"Sponge count," droned Dr. Joslin.

"Seven," said Betty.

"Four," supplemented the assistant.

"Count them again. You probably had only eleven," said Dr. Joslin.

"There were twelve," she replied firmly.

"Have the orderly look again in the waste pail," said Dr. Joslin, as he began to search in the incision for the lost sponge.

"Only seven here." Betty's tone was hopeless; she felt sure the mistake was hers.

Dr. Joslin began to pull a strip of gauze from the wound. "Here it is! How did we happen to lose it? I'm sure I put a clamp on every one of those sponges." He threw it into the waste pail. "Now the closing-up sutures. Quickly."

Betty handed them to him ready for use. Her eyes fell suddenly upon the sponge that had been lost. The end that had been deep in the wound was soaked with bright blood, which mean an artery—and a leaking artery meant death to a patient. This patient must not die. Her husband was waiting for her out there. Betty dared not speak to the surgeon, but in a low tone she said to the assistant, "The last sponge had bright red blood."

Before the assistant could reply, Dr. Joslin looked up eagerly, "What's that?" The assistant pointed to the sponge. The surgeon gave it one glance. "Ligature slipped," he commented and, pulling out the suture he was carefully putting in, drew open the incision and began to search in its depths again.

"There it is! A spurter! Clamp." Betty had the instrument almost in his hand, and as he fastened it she gave him a ligature to stop the bleeding permanently. He tied it securely, sponged thoroughly, and scanned everything intently. "All right. Now we'll try again to close up."

Dr. Joslin was pulling off his rubber gloves when Miss Randall came in.

"You had a hard morning," Dr. Foster remarked, "but things go smoothly in your operating room. Good operating nurse you have. She saved the day this time. She has her wits about her, and she shows her training. How long has she been with you? Where did she graduate?"

"She is a pupil, just getting her experience."

"She is better than most of the graduates. When does she finish?" asked the visiting surgeon.

"In a few months."

"If you don't keep her for yourself, I'd like to put her in charge of my operating room. She's the best that I've seen in a long time."

As the door closed, Miss Randall said to Betty, "Your great fear is conquered. The most exacting surgeon in the city admits that you saved him from a mistake; the best surgeon in the state wants you for his operating room; and the patient owes her life to you."

Betty said to herself, "And I didn't fail the one who trusted me."[5]

PRAYERS

Our Father, we thank thee for every influence which helps us to become responsible persons. Give us patience, courage, and persistence in our struggle to prepare ourselves for our life's work. Increase our confidence in our ability to reach the goals which we have set for ourselves. In our choices and in every decision help us to follow the principles which are taught in thy Word. May the pull of the crowd not lead us astray, nor our own lack of determination hinder us in our effort to keep faith with those who believe in us and expect us to reach our highest development. Forbid that we should ever be satisfied with less than our best. In the name of our Lord we pray. AMEN.

HYMN: "I Would Be True," or
"My Soul, Be on Thy Guard."

BENEDICTION:

May we go from this service with a strong determination to shoulder our share of responsibility. AMEN.

SERVICE 4

TO ACCEPT DISCIPLINE

PRELUDE: Hymn tune "Crusader's Hymn."

CALL TO WORSHIP:

> O let me feel thee near me!
> The world is ever near;
> I see the sights that dazzle,
> The tempting sounds I hear;
> My foes are ever near me,
> Around me and within;
> But, Jesus, draw thou nearer,
> And shield my soul from sin.
> —JOHN E. BODE

RESPONSIVE READING:

Leader: He that is slow to anger is better than the mighty; and he that ruleth his spirit than he that taketh a city.

Group: Teach me to do thy will; for thou art my God: thy spirit is good; lead me into the land of uprightness.

Leader: Keep thy heart with all diligence; for out of it are the issues of life.

Group: Incline not my heart to any evil thing, to practise wicked works with men that work iniquity.

Leader: Put away from thee a froward mouth, and perverse lips put far from thee.

Group: Set a watch, O Lord, before my mouth; keep the door of my lips.

Leader: My brethren, count it all joy when ye fall into divers temptations; knowing this, that the trying of your faith worketh patience. But let patience have her perfect work, that ye may be perfect and entire, wanting nothing.

Group: We glory in tribulations ... : knowing that tribulation worketh patience; and patience, experience; and experience, hope.

Leader: Be strong in the Lord, and in the power of his might. Put on the whole armour of God, that ye may be able to stand against the wiles of the devil.

Group: I can do all things through Christ which strengtheneth me.[1]

PRAYER:

Our Father, open our minds to the impressions coming from thee. May we not become so engrossed with material things that we fail to heed thy guidance. Help us to realize that by appropriating the help which comes from thee and through self-discipline we may develop our capacities so as to be able to face bravely hardships, frustration, adversity, or whatever comes to us. We would not attempt to go in our own strength alone, but would rely upon thee. We do not ask for difficulties to be removed from our path, but for strength to overcome them; we do not ask to be sheltered from adversity, but to be fearless in facing it. If we have given way to anger, help us to control ourselves; if we have been slothful, help us to be more enthusiastic about our work; if we have been self-centered, help us to lose ourselves in the service of others. May we demand of ourselves high thinking, clean living, and right attitudes toward persons of every race and condition of life. Suffer us not to be tempted above that which we are able to bear. In the name of Christ, who is our example, we pray. AMEN.

HYMN: "I Would Be True," or
"Fight the Good Fight."

POEM:

> Self-reverence, self-knowledge, self-control,
> These three alone lead life to sovereign power.
> Yet not for power (power of herself
> Would come uncall'd for) but to live by law,
> Acting the law we live by without fear;
> And, because right is right, to follow right
> Were wisdom in the scorn of consequence.
>
> —ALFRED TENNYSON

LEADER:

We will hear the story of a young man who through self-discipline overcame a handicap which would have been disastrous to a person of lesser courage and determination.

STORY:

THE MAKING OF A CHAMPION

FLOYD and Glenn Cunningham went to school early one morning, for it was their turn to build the fire. When Floyd picked up the oilcan and poured the contents on the wood, he did not know that the can contained gasoline instead of the customary kerosene. In a few moments after he lighted the fire the building was in flames, and both boys were badly burned.

Dr. Harvey Hansen of Plainview, Kansas, was called to attend the boys at their simple farm home in Cimarron Valley. When he arrived Floyd had died, but Glenn, the younger lad, about eight years of age, was still alive. After examining his patient the doctor shook his head, saying, "It will be a miracle if he ever walks again." The physician, looking at the seared flesh and shriveled tendons, was justified in his statement. But he could not see the unconquerable spirit and high courage that were latent in the lad.

For some time Glenn was confined to his bed, unable to move. The toes of his left foot were almost burned off, and he was unable to straighten his right leg. A physician looking at his scarred legs would still contend that he would never be able to use them. When the wounds healed, the members of his family took turns massaging his legs. Eventually he was able to hobble around with the aid of crutches. With fortitude and rare patience he began exercises which were very painful. By these means he stretched the tendons and stimulated the growth of new tissue. After several years he was able to walk, first slowly, but later with more ease. Although he was still far from normal, a miracle had happened.

A greater miracle was yet to come: he became a runner and a champion. The mile is the hardest race on the track. Glenn Cunningham ran the mile faster than anyone in the world, with those same burned legs. After winning his first race at a local fair at the age of fourteen, he became seriously interested in running. He entered every race with a strong determination to win, for he was not content with anything less than his best. Success on a small scale spurred him on to greater endeavor. In spite of his handicap he broke record after record on the track.

In 1932 while a student at the University of Kansas, he was sent to Los Angeles to represent his state in the trials for the Olympic Games. At that time little was known about him outside his own state, but when he ran the mile in 4:14, his name became known throughout the world. On the same day he won the half mile in 1:53.5. In 1934 his outdoor mile was 4:06.7 and his indoor mile was 4:04.4. A man with lesser courage would have remained an invalid, but his determination made him a world champion.

In spite of all the honors heaped upon him as a popular sportsman, Cunningham remained modest and unassuming. On one occasion after he had won a great race the people of his home town honored him with a celebration. They made merry with gay streamers and confetti. His humility is evident in the fact that when the celebration was over he helped his father sweep up the litter. His determination helped him to overcome his physical handicap, and also led to the development of his mental powers. While doing graduate work at New York University in 1938, he was one of the outstanding students.

Cunningham's desire to help young people led him to accept the position of physical director at Cornell College, Mt. Vernon, Iowa. Although a world champion himself, he felt that he had a contribution to make to those who could never attain such heights. He has often remarked that high courage and clean living are qualities which are needed by every person who desires to make the most of his life.

Glenn Cunningham is interested in young people getting the right start in life, in playing the game fairly, whether they win or lose. He urges them to seek relaxation which is free from alcohol, regardless of what their friends may say or do. He asserts that one may have wholesome fun and fellowship without the use of injurious alcoholic drinks. He points out that a boy who is being trained for sports has to accept the discipline of refraining from smoking and using alcohol, for the good of the team. He says that other young people who will not be athletes need to build up clean habits, too.

The world champion remarked: "I know some young people will say, 'I am not an athlete, and I need not be bound by requirements that apply to success in athletics.' I am thankful that I do not come into contact with many young people whose thinking is so shallow and whose purposes for living at one's best are so flabby! It is hard for me to be patient when I meet or hear about boys and girls who do not value themselves highly enough to learn what practices will aid their health and fitness and what practices will injure them." [2]

Playing the game of life demands discipline, also. If we play well, we will accept the principle that immediate pleasures must be sacrificed for the sake of greater ultimate happiness later.

POEM:

We look to you—each one of you—
To make Life better than before,
For God is shaping all things new,
For He has greater still in store.

Be clean—in body and in mind!
Think high, and live up to your thought!
In work well done more joy you'll find
Than all that can by wealth be bought.

Let every thought and word and deed
Be kind and honest, brave and true!
Never refuse another's need,
Do as you'd have him do to you!

Be strong! Be patient! Pray for grace
To bear you steadfast through all ill!
Against all evil set your face,
And bravely do your Master's will.[3]

—JOHN OXENHAM

LITANY OF SUPPLICATION:

Leader: Our Father, thou hast implanted within us high desires and worthy aspirations.

Group: Forgive us when we fail to heed the promptings of our better nature.

Leader: Thou hast promised to be with us in every crisis in life and in every situation.

Group: Help us to be sensitive to thy Spirit and to avail ourselves of the spiritual resources which thou hast provided.

Leader: Give us the proper attitude toward difficulties and handicaps, and in every situation may we look for an opportunity to grow.

Group: In submission to thy will may our lives be creative and abundant.

Leader: Give us strength and determination so that we may not shirk our duty nor fail at the testing time.

Group: Forbid that we should ever falter in doing thy will, or stray from the path into which thou wouldst lead us. AMEN.

TO ACCEPT DISCIPLINE

HYMN: "My Jesus, as Thou Wilt," or
      "Are Ye Able?"

BENEDICTION:

Now unto him who giveth strength sufficient for every experience of life, be glory and honor evermore. AMEN.

SERVICE 5

TO DISCOVER LIFE THROUGH SERVICE

PRELUDE: "Cavatina" by Bohm.

CALL TO WORSHIP:
Once to every man and nation comes the moment to decide,
In the strife of Truth with Falsehood, for the good or evil side;
Some great cause, God's new Messiah, offering each the bloom or blight,
. . . .
And the choice goes by forever 'twixt that darkness and that light.
—JAMES RUSSELL LOWELL

HYMN: "O Young and Fearless Prophet," or
"God of Grace and God of Glory."

SCRIPTURE:
Thus saith the Lord of hosts; Consider your ways.

My son, forget not my law; but let thine heart keep my commandments: for length of days, and long life, and peace, shall they add to thee. Let not mercy and truth forsake thee: bind them about thy neck; write them upon the table of thine heart: so shalt thou find favour and good understanding in the sight of God and man. Trust in the Lord with all thine heart; and lean not unto thine own understanding. In all thy ways asknowledge him, and he shall direct thy paths.

Now therefore fear the Lord, and serve him in sincerity and in truth. . . . And if it seem evil unto you to serve the Lord, choose you this day whom ye will serve; . . . but as for me and my house, we will serve the Lord.

Yet shew I unto you a more excellent way.

Whosoever will be great among you, let him be your minister; and whosoever will be chief among you, let him be your servant.[1]

TO DISCOVER LIFE THROUGH SERVICE

INVOCATION:

Our Father, guide us as we plan our lives. Give us a proper sense of values and help us understand that if we choose the way of service we may become doorways through which thou mayest enter the world. May we be willing to be instruments in thy hand to help bring thy kingdom on earth. In the name of the Master of us all, we pray. AMEN.

HYMN: "O Master, Let Me Walk with Thee," or
"Heralds of Christ."

POEM:

I know that kindness can't be wrong,
    That truth will not betray,
That charity excels revenge
    In this or any day.

I know that verities endure,
    That vanities will fade,
That righteousness exalteth men,
    And makes them unafraid.

I know that knowledge feeds the mind,
    That beauty feeds the heart,
That virtues are the stones of life
    In God's consummate art.

I know goodwill must yield good fruit,
    That honesty is best,
That faith and hope and love abide,
    Supreme in every test.[2]

—CHAUNCEY R. PIETY

LEADER:

We will hear the story of a man who tried two ways of living: his early life was spent accumulating gold; later through the way of service he not only helped the community but discovered an abiding happiness and peace of mind.

STORY:

SILAS MARNER

SILAS MARNER, a weaver, was held in high regard by the Lantern Yard Community. Among the members of the church a young man by the name of William Dale was his closest friend. Sarah, a mutual friend of theirs, did not object to William's presence on their dates, even though for some months she had been engaged to Silas.

Marner took his turn sitting during the night at the bedside of a deacon who was ill. The next morning the deacon's bag of money was missing, and Silas was accused of having stolen it. He declared his innocence, saying that he fell asleep while a robber slipped into the room and stole the money. A search was made and the empty bag was found tucked away in a drawer in Marner's room.

Instead of using legal measures, the deacons decided to draw lots to find out whether or not the young man was guilty. Marner's religious convictions were such that he firmly believed that God would clear him of the charges. But the lots declared that he was guilty, and he decided that it was futile to attempt to prove his innocence. The deacons suspended him from the church and urged that he return the stolen money at once.

Silas was stunned at such injustice. He went to William Dale and said, "You stole that money, and you have woven a plot to lay the sin at my door. You may prosper for all that: for there is no justice."

William replied, "I leave the brethren to judge your guilt. I can do nothing but pray for you, Silas."

Silas muttered to himself, "Sarah will cast me off, too." For a whole day he sat alone at home, grieving without a ray of hope, for he had lost faith in God and in man. It did not occur to him to go to Sarah and prove his innocence. On the next day a message came from her saying that their engagement was broken, and in a little more than a month she married William Dale.

Leaving his home Silas came to Raveloe, where he continued his linen weaving. He wove like a spider, from impulse, and without reflection. He hated the thought of the past because of the unjust charges against him; there was nothing in the present to challenge him; and the future was dark, for he felt that not even God was concerned about him now. All the affection which he had held for people had died under the blow that he had been dealt.

Marner lived on in solitude, his life made up of weaving and hoarding the gold which he received for his work—with no thought of the end in view. Day after day he sat at the loom, his ears filled with the monotonous sound, his eyes fixed on the slow growth of the web before him. But at night it was different. He closed the shutters, made fast the doors, and brought out the gold. Spreading out the coins in heaps he bathed his hands in them, counted and set them in regular piles so that he could feel their outline with his fingers. He handled them until their form and color satisfied his thirst.

Marner had taken up some bricks in the floor underneath the loom and had made a hole into which he hid his gold, covering the bricks with sand when he replaced them. Gradually the coins grew to a heap, and Marner drew less and less for his own needs because the hoarding became an absorbing passion with him.

As Silas withdrew from his neighbors, his isolation became more complete. Anyone looking at his pale face, strange eyes, and meager form would understand why the neighbors regarded him with dread and suspicion. The light of his faith had gone out, his affection had disappeared, but he clung with all the force of his nature to his work and his money. Like all objects to which a man devotes himself, they had fashioned him into a semblance of themselves. His gold, as he hung over it, gathered his power of loving into a hard isolation like its own. No one would have recognized him as the person who had once loved his fellows and trusted in an unseen goodness. Even to himself that past experience had become dim and unreal.

Returning one evening from an errand in the village, Silas found that his gold had been stolen. The sight of the empty hole in the floor made his heart leap violently. Putting his trembling hands to his head, he gave a cry of desolation. As he looked about the room, he saw the loom, the glowing pattern in the web, but the bright treasure in the hole under the loom was gone; the prospect of handling and counting it was gone. The thought of the money he would get in the future for his work brought him no joy; it was only a fresh reminder of his loss. When Christmas came a few days later, Marner spent it in loneliness.

Toward evening the snow began to fall, but he did not bother to close the shutters or to lock the door, for he had no treasure to guard. A mother with her child in her arms was trudging through the snow to Raveloe. As she neared Marner's cottage, the cold and weariness brought on a stupor which made her feel that she must lie down and sleep. She began to sink in the snow, and her arms lost their tension. She did not rise again. The child slipped from her grasp, followed a bright streak of light, and came to Marner's cottage. Coming to the door she walked straight to the warm hearth and fell asleep before the fire.

When Silas returned from his chores, he thought that he saw his gold on the hearth—his own gold, brought back as mysteriously as it had been taken away. He leaned forward to clutch it in his hands, but instead of hard coins, his fingers touched soft curls. As he examined the sleeping child, she awakened and clung to him. At once he thought of the porridge which he had cooked for his supper, and wondered if it would do to feed the child.

The neighbors suggested that Marner take the child to the parish house, but being lonely he begged to keep her. He realized that he would need to learn many things from the women of the neighborhood if he would care for her properly, and he was eager to make any sacrifice that would benefit the child. When one of the women suggested that the child be christened, Marner dressed in his best and appeared at the church the following Sunday for the ceremony.

The little girl created fresh links of friendship between Marner and those about him. Unlike the gold, which needed nothing but to be worshiped in solitude, Eppie was a creature of endless claims and desires. The gold had kept his thoughts in an ever-repeating circle, leading to nothing beyond itself; but Eppie forced his thoughts outward toward others and carried them away to new things that would come in the years ahead. The gold had asked that he sit weaving longer and longer, but Eppie called him away from his weaving, awakened his senses with her fresh life, and brought him happiness because of her own joy.

A great change came over the weaver. His life was linked with the life of the community, and there was love between him and the people he met. He thought of life entirely in relation to Eppie. She must have everything that was good. He listened carefully to the people that he might understand better the life of the community from which he had stood apart for fifteen years.

When summer came, Silas left his weaving and took Eppie to the meadows that she might gather the bright flowers. When he delivered his weaving to the homes, he took her with him, for she was always welcomed because of the joy she brought. The gold which he received for his work had a new meaning now. It was for her. All desire to hoard it was gone. The purpose of his life had changed.

Love for the child continued to draw Marner out of himself, leading him to think of others. No longer was he living for self alone since Eppie had come into his life. She replaced his love of gold and gave him a new purpose. Every thought and action was related to this purpose; his entire life was organized around a new motive of service which was mastering his life.

Years later when Eppie had grown up, an old stone pit near Marner's cottage was being cleaned out, and his gold was found where the robber had dropped it. That evening as Silas and Eppie sat looking at it, he told her how he used to count the coins every night, and that his soul was utterly desolate after he lost the gold until she came to him. He remarked, "If you hadn't been sent to me, I should have gone to my grave in misery. The money was taken away from me in time, and it has been kept until you needed it for your wedding day."

Silas had heard that in the old days angels came and took men by the hand and led them away from the city of destruction. He saw no angels, but he believed that men are still led away from threatening destruction: a hand is put into theirs, which leads them forth gently toward a new country; and the hand may be that of a little child.

PRAYER:

Our Father, help us to organize our lives around a purpose that is in keeping with thy will. Grant us courage and patience as we strive to correct our faults and weaknesses. Help us to uproot selfishness and make service and helpfulness the motive of our lives. Give us that measure of success which thou seest that we need. May thy spirit illumine our hearts and lead us to a better understanding of thy purpose for us. AMEN.

HYMN: "O Jesus, I Have Promised," or
         "Take My Life, and Let It Be."

BENEDICTION:

Now unto him who is able to keep us pure in thought, faithful and diligent in work, kind and considerate in our contacts with others, be honor and glory for evermore. AMEN.

SERVICE 6

TO SEARCH PATIENTLY FOR TRUTH

PRELUDE: "Jesu, Joy of Man's Desiring" by Bach.

CALL TO WORSHIP:

> O God, our spirits greet thy Spirit,
> We hear thy voice in the lovely music,
> We behold thee in all beauty,
> We feel thy love in Christian fellowship,
> We drink thy truth in the worship,
> And thy life renews our lives
> Through Christ, the Way, the Truth, the Life.[1]
>
> —CHAUNCEY R. PIETY

HYMN: "Holy Spirit, Truth Divine," or
"Another Year Is Dawning."

RESPONSIVE READING:

Leader: O send out thy light and thy truth: let them lead me;
Let them bring me unto thy holy hill,
And to thy tabernacles.

Group: Send down thy truth, O God:
Too long the shadows frown;
Too long the darkened way we've trod:
Thy truth, O Lord, send down.

Leader: When he, the Spirit of truth, is come,
He will guide you into all truth.

Group: Send down thy spirit free,
Till wilderness and town
One temple for thy worship be:
Thy spirit, O send down.

TO SEARCH PATIENTLY FOR TRUTH

Leader: To this end was I born, and for this cause came I into the world,
That I should bear witness unto the truth.

Group: Send down thy love, thy life,
  Our lesser lives to crown,
And cleanse them of their hate and strife:
  Thy living love send down.

Leader: Ye shall know the truth,
  And the truth shall make you free.[2]

Group: Send down thy peace, O Lord:
  Earth's bitter voices drown
In one deep ocean of accord:
  Thy peace, O God, send down.

—EDWARD ROWLAND SILL

PRAYER:

Our Father, we believe that thou art calling us to the various professions and that all honorable work has a part in thy plan and purpose. Reveal to us the kind of work for which we are best suited, and grant us the patience and determination to prepare ourselves for the task. Whether we are teaching, ministering to the sick, doing research, or serving in some other capacity, may we feel that we have thy approval in our work. Illumine our souls with a knowledge of thy divine truth that shall lead us to be colaborers with thee.

"O thou who art Heroic Love, keep alive in our hearts that adventurous spirit, which makes men scorn the way of safety, if only thy will be done. For so only, O Lord, shall we be worthy of those courageous souls who in every age have ventured all in obedience to thy call. . . . AMEN."[3]

LEADER:

Let us honor a great man whose faith led him to carry on research in new fields, a scientist who dedicated his life to the benefit of mankind and whose contribution in that field has enriched the lives of countless thousands, a patient searcher of hidden secrets who gave his time, talents, and possessions to the welfare of others, a man of good will whose labors have made life fuller and richer for those who come after him.

Story:

STEINMETZ, THE PATIENT SEARCHER FOR TRUTH

Charles steinmetz is known today as the "Patient Searcher for Truth." With more than two hundred patented inventions to his credit he ranks with Edison as one of the great benefactors of mankind. He did not have a very auspicious beginning. He was born in Breslau, Germany, on April 9, 1865, into a family of moderate circumstances. It was soon discovered that his back was crooked and his legs twisted. Yet in spite of his imperfect physique he was endowed with a keen mind. His father realized this and gave him every opportunity.

Charles finished preparatory school at an early age and entered the University of Breslau. He studied various subjects and finally selected mathematics, chemistry, and electricity as his major interests. In a short while he had learned all that the professors could teach about electricity, so meager was the knowledge at that time concerning this new child of science. Carrying on research in his own laboratory he became convinced that electricity could be made to aid mankind and become one of the world's greatest assets.

While a student he became interested in socialism and joined a secret society. Bismarck, disapproving of the movement, set about to stamp it out. When some of his friends were arrested and thrown into prison, Steinmetz realized that he would have to flee. It was an inopportune time to fall into disfavor with the authorities, for within a short while he would have received the degree of Doctor of Philosophy. However, he dared not remain and did not receive the coveted degree.

Packing his scanty belongings, the young man fled to Switzerland, where he continued his study at Zürich Polytechnic School. Here he met Asmussen, a Danish student, and they became close friends. Learning that his new friend was sailing for America, Steinmetz remarked that he too would go but that he did not have the necessary funds. Asmussen replied that he had enough for both, provided they go steerage. The young men sailed on a French immigrant steamer, unmindful of the discomforts of the trip for they spent most of the time trying to learn English.

Steinmetz' first view of America was from behind the bars of a detention pen. The immigration authorities, seeing the forlorn appearance of the little hunchback, decided that he was a poor risk. They said, "What can a penniless cripple with only a meager knowledge of English do to earn a living in a strange country?" They had no way of knowing that this unimposing immigrant would be the electrical wizard of the future.

Again his Danish friend came to his rescue, saying, "If you will allow us to enter America, we will stay together, and I will personally see that he does not become destitute." The pleas of his friend gained him admittance to the country that he was to adopt as his home.

Steinmetz' deformity, his poor clothes, and his meager knowledge of English were definite handicaps. When applying for work in Edison's laboratory, he was dismissed by a clerk who barely glanced at his letters of introduction. Finally he was able to talk in his native tongue to Rudolph Eichmeyer, a manufacturer of electrical machinery, and he secured a job as a draftsman at twelve dollars per week. His next step was to appear before a naturalization court and take out his first papers for citizenship.

The new position was not enough to challenge the young man, so he began to study electrical engineering. He joined the New York Mathematical Society, where he attracted attention by his skill and knowledge. The other engineers soon realized that the friendly young man had unusual ability. His facility in the use of English improved rapidly, and he was soon able to speak and write correctly.

About this time Steinmetz learned that many engineers were trying to build generators and transformers. Convinced that mathematics could be used to help work out the process, he took the difficult task upon himself. He spent long hours experimenting with all sorts of metals and all kinds of currents. At last he read before the American Institute of Electrical Engineers a paper setting forth his discoveries which eliminated a great deal of uncertainty in designing electrical equipment.

The General Electric company bought the Eichmeyer company and moved the business to Lynn, Massachusetts, with the understanding that Steinmetz woud come with the new company. Later he was transferred to Schenectady, and throughout the remainder of his life this city was his home. Here he built a house and adopted a son. During this time he took out more than two hundred patents for electrical inventions. The one which attracted the widest attention was the arc street light, which was put into use immediately. Honors came to him from many sources. When he received the degree of Master of Arts from Harvard University, the president said, "I confer this degree upon you as the foremost electrical engineer in the United States."

Steinmetz was not thought of as a professor, though teaching was one of his chief joys. While he was professor of electrophysics at Union College in Schenectady, he received no salary, but the college became well known because of his work.

Throughout his lifetime Steinmetz held the socialistic ideas which he had as a youth. He did not believe that one should strive to build up large fortunes, but should make only enough money to live comfortably. The General Electric company would have paid him any amount of money for his inventions, but he asked for barely enough to cover his needs. Instead of working for material gains for himself, he was more concerned about the welfare of others.

The inventor was interested in more than science. His own words reveal his insight and ideas:

"Science has been concerning itself too much with material things. We have been trying to invent all kinds of machines whereby life may be made more comfortable and soft. . . .

"In a day to come, which will be much wiser than our day, I believe science will not simply go on blindly inventing things, presuming that everything new is sure to be good. Science is going to consider a far more important matter . . . ; it is going to try to discover something about the human spirit, its origin, its nature on this globe, and its far destiny, if humanly possible.

"After all, the goal of all human endeavor, and especially of scientific research and effort, should be the spiritual development of the race. . . .

"As soon as we have become sated with gadgets, as soon as we make the really great discovery that they cannot nourish the spirit, then we shall give our time and talent to those things which build character. Then we shall be working in the very noblest field of human endeavor." [4]

Never at any time did Steinmetz indicate that he thought of himself as superior in any way. Instead of trying to show off his knowledge, he was always humble and eager to learn from others. His reply to an inquiry never left the impression that he felt that he had the last word on any subject. He was not fully appreciated by those who did not know him intimately. Because of his deformity he was considered an oddity. He lived quietly, concentrated on the task at hand, and worked diligently for the good of all, dedicating his life to the service of mankind. The world owes much to this patient searcher for truth.

TO SEARCH PATIENTLY FOR TRUTH

How they have learned the secrets of the ether!
   Ships in the clouds, afloat as on a sea;
Voices through miles of distance singing, captured,
   Brought to our homes to gladden you and me.

How selflessly they seek profounder meanings
   Hid in the clump of moss—the iron ore!
How they have found in energy the secrets
   God smiled to know a billion years before.

Counting their lives not dear, so they discover
   Some bit of truth through eons all unguessed,
Something to make the lives to come richer,
   Ere they themselves shall shut their eyes and rest.

Ah, still the Lord God walks with noiseless footfall,
   Visits the workshops of these patient men—
Smiles on the test tubes, the revealing lenses,
   And "It is good," he murmurs once again. [5]

       —BERTHA GERNEAUX WOODS

PRAYER:

We praise thee, O Lord, for that mysterious spark of thy light within
us, the intellect of man, for thou hast kindled it in the beginning and
by the breath of thy spirit it has grown to flaming power in our race.

We rejoice in the men of genius and intellectual vision who discern
the undiscovered applications of thy laws and dig the deeper springs
through which the hidden forces of thy world may well up to the
light of day. We claim them as our own in thee, as members with us
in the common body of humanity, of which thou art the all-pervading
life and inspirer. Grant them, we pray thee, the divine humility of
thine elect souls, to realize that they are sent of thee as brothers and
helpers of men and that the powers within them are but part of the
vast equipment of humanity, entrusted to them for the common use.
May they bow to the law of Christ and live, not to be served, but
to give their abilities for the emancipation of the higher life of man. . . .

But to us who benefit by their work do thou grant wisdom and
justice that we may not suffer the fruit of their toil to be wrested from
them by selfish cunning or the pressure of need, but may assure them

of their fair reward and of the meed of love and honor that is the due of those who have served humanity well. Gladden us by the glowing consciousness of the one life that thinks and strives in us all, and knit us together into a commonwealth of brothers in which each shall be heir of all things and the free servant of all men.[6] AMEN.

HYMN: "Be Strong! We Are Not Here to Play," or
　　　"O Jesus, Prince of Life and Truth."

BENEDICTION:

May thy spirit lead us as we dedicate our lives more fully to serve humanity. AMEN.

SERVICE 7

TO MAKE PRAYER EFFECTIVE

PRELUDE: Hymn tune "Finlandia."

CALL TO WORSHIP:

Speak to Him thou for He hears, and Spirit with Spirit can meet—
Closer is He than breathing, and nearer than hands and feet.

—ALFRED TENNYSON

HYMN: " 'Mid All the Traffic of the Ways," or
"Dear Lord and Father of Mankind."

SCRIPTURE:

And when thou prayest, thou shalt not be as the hypocrites are: for they love to pray standing in the synagogues and in the corners of the streets, that they may be seen of men. Verily I say unto you, They have their reward.

But thou, when thou prayest, enter into thy closet, and when thou hast shut thy door, pray to thy Father which is in secret; and thy Father which seeth in secret shall reward thee openly.

But when ye pray, use not vain repetitions, as the heathen do: for they think that they shall be heard for their much speaking.

Be not ye therefore like unto them: for your Father knoweth what things ye have need of, before ye ask him.

Ask, and it shall be given you; seek, and ye shall find; knock, and it shall be opened unto you: for every one that asketh receiveth; and he that seeketh findeth; and to him that knocketh it shall be opened.

Or what man is there of you, whom if his son ask bread, will he give him a stone? Or if he ask a fish, will he give him a serpent?

If ye then, being evil, know how to give good gifts unto your children, how much more shall your Father which is in heaven give good things to them that ask him?

All things, whatsoever ye shall ask in prayer, believing, ye shall receive.

If ye abide in me, and my words abide in you, ye shall ask what ye will, and it shall be done unto you.[1]

PRAYER:

O God, invisible and eternal, our yearning hearts reach out to Thee; but our feeble faith often fails to find Thee. Our sight for unseen things is so untrained. We are but kindergarten children of the spirit world. We have not practiced the Presence as we should. The heavens declare Thy glory, and yet we so often fail to see. The universe is full of the echo of Thy voice, but we do not listen. But once in a while, in the quiet of a dawning day, or of the evening time, we do have the consciousness of Thy presence and the still small Voice breaks through. . . . As Thy Spirit witnesses to ours there does come the peace and power of heaven.

But why are we not always strong? Oh, why are we so often without the consciousness of Thee? . . . We do the things we ought not to do, and leave undone the things we ought not to leave undone. How weak we are, how great our need, how wonderful Thy patient love! One thing we know: we cannot get along without Thee. We thank Thee for the growing hunger of our hearts. In Christ's dear name we ask for victory this day. AMEN.[2]

POEM:

Sometimes I pray but hurried words
And fling them past my shoulder,
Lest I begin some task when day
Is several minutes older.

But when I kneel and talk to God
And call upon his name,
The wonder of him bends so near—
My heart is filled with shame! [3]

—ESTHER BALDWIN YORK

HYMN: "Jesus, Kneel Beside Me," or
"Lord, for Tomorrow and Its Needs."

TO MAKE PRAYER EFFECTIVE

THE WHITE BIRDS

THERE was once a man who had a waking dream. He dreamed he was in a spacious church. He had wandered in to pray, and after his prayers were finished, he knelt on, his eyes open, gazing round at the beauty of the ancient building, and resting in the silence. Here and there in the great building were quiet kneeling figures. Across the dim darkness of the nave and aisles shafts of sunlight streamed into the church from upper windows. In the distance a side door was open, letting in scents of summer air, fragrant with the smell of hay and flowers, and the sight of trees waving in the breeze, and beyond, a line of blue hills, dim and distant as an enchanted land.

Presently the man withdrew his eyes from the pleasant outdoor world and looked again at the church. Suddenly, close to the spot where he was kneeling, there was a gentle whir of wings, and he saw a little white bird fluttering about in the dim nave; it flew uncertainly hither and thither, and once or twice he thought that it would fall to the ground. But gradually it gathered strength, rose toward the roof, and finally, with a purposeful sweep of its wings, sped upwards, and out through one of the open windows into the sunshine.

The stranger looked down again at the kneeling men and women, scattered throughout the building; and now he saw, what he had not noticed before, that by the side of each worshiper there hovered, close to the stone floor, a little white bird. Just then he saw another bird rise from the floor and try to reach the roof. But it, too, was in difficulties; it flew round and round in circles, occasionally beating its wings in a futile way against the great lower windows, rich with stained glass. Finally it sank down exhausted, and lay still. A little later another bird rose from the ground, with a swift and easy flight; for a moment it seemed that it would reach the open window and the open air beyond; but suddenly, it whirled round, fell helplessly over and over, and came to the ground with a thud, as if it had been shot. The man rose from his knees and went over to see what had happened; the little bird was dead.

He went back to his place and sat down on one of the chairs; then he noticed an ugly little bird, its white feathers dirty and bedraggled, rise from the ground. At first this bird laboured heavily, but it soon gathered speed, for it was strong, and it soared up and out into the sunlit world beyond the walls of the great church. More and more the man wondered what all this might mean. He looked again at the persons at prayer near him, and he noticed one, kneeling very reverently, by whose side lay a very beautiful bird, snowy white and perfectly formed. But when he looked at it more closely he saw that its eyes were glazed, its wings stiff; it was a lifeless shell.

"What a pity!" he murmured under his breath. At that moment, a gentle whir of wings a few feet away attracted his attention: another bird was rising from the ground, steadily and quietly, at first with some appearance of effort, but more and more easily and lightly as it gathered strength; this bird flew straight up, past the carved angels which seemed to be crying "Hallelujah!" to one another across the dim spaces of the church, and out through the open window into the blue sky, where it was soon lost to sight.

Pondering on what he had seen, the man looked round again, and this time he saw standing close to him, an Angel, tall and strong, with a face of great kindness, wisdom and compassion. It all seemed perfectly natural (as things do in dreams), and the man whispered to him: "Can you explain to me about these white birds?"

"Yes," said the Angel, in a low voice, as he seated himself beside him, "for I am the Guardian of this place of prayer. These white birds are the outward sign of the prayers of the people who come here to pray. The first bird, which found it difficult to rise, but then succeeded, is the prayer of a woman who has come here straight from a busy life; she has very little time to herself; in fact she usually comes here in the midst of her shopping. She has a great many duties and claims, and her mind was full of distractions when she first knelt down and tried to pray. But she persevered, for her heart is right with God, and He helped her; her prayer was real and her will good, so her prayer reached God."

"And what about the bird that flew round in circles?" asked the man.

The Angel smiled slightly, with a tinge of faint amusement. "That," he said slowly, "is the prayer of a man who thinks of no one but himself; even in his prayers he only asks for 'things'—success in his business and things like that; he tries to use God for his own ends . . . people think he is a very religious man . . . but his prayer does not reach God at all."

"But why did that other bird fall to the ground as if it had been shot?"

The Angel looked sad as he replied: "That man began his prayer well enough; but suddenly he remembered a grudge against someone he knew; he forgot his prayer and brooded in bitter resentment, and his bitterness killed his prayer. . . . And the ugly little bird," he went on after a moment's silence, "is the prayer of a man who hasn't much idea of reverence; his prayer is bold, almost presumptuous, some people might call it; but God knows his heart, and He sees his faith is real; he does really believe in God, so his prayer reaches Him."

"And the beautiful lifeless bird that never stirred from the ground at all?" said the man.

"That," said the Angel, "is a beautifully composed prayer; the language is perfect, the thought is doctrinally correct; the man offered it with the greatest solemnity and outward reverence. . . . But he never meant a word of it; even as he said the words his thoughts were on his own affairs; so his prayer could not reach God."

"And what about the last bird that flew upwards so easily?"

The Angel smiled. "I think you know," he said gently. "That is the prayer of a woman whose whole heart and will is set upon God. . . . *Her* prayer went straight to God." [4]

POEM:

A small, white cross upon my wall
　Glows through the hours of night,
Reminding me to pray to One
　Who made my darkness Light.

The longer it has stood beside
　The lamp upon my table,
Absorbing light into itself,
　The longer it is able

To shine in darkness. And I know
　My witness will grow dim
In less proportion as my heart
　Has lingered close to him. [5]
　　　　　　　　　　—ESTHER BALDWIN YORK

PRAYER:

Our Father, in whom we live and move and have our being, we humbly pray that thou wilt make us aware of thy presence. If we have become absorbed with petty details, grant us a truer sense of values. If sin in our lives hides us from thee, forgive all our misdoings. If dullness of vision shuts us off from thee, take away the dimness of our eyes. Make us pure in heart that no evil thought or deed may hide thee from our sight. Grant us an open mind to the impressions coming from thee and a willingness to be guided by the still small voice as it speaks to us. We want above all to be true followers of Jesus, and may thy Spirit bear witness with our spirits that we are thy children. Grant us wisdom to meet the problems of each day, and give us courage to live by the teachings of Jesus. May our words and our lives show that thou art abiding with us. We dedicate our lives to thee, through Jesus Christ our Lord. AMEN.

HYMN: "Sun of My Soul," or

"Saviour, Like a Shepherd Lead Us."

BENEDICTION:

Fill our hearts with thy peace and help us to walk in fellowship with thee. AMEN.

SERVICE 8

TO LIVE BY ONE'S CONVICTIONS

PRELUDE: Hymn tune "Festal Song."

CALL TO WORSHIP:

> Our skill of hand and strength of limb
> Are not our own, but thine;
> We link them to the work of him
> Who made all life divine!
> —THOMAS W. FRECKELTON

HYMN: "March On, O Soul, with Strength!" or
"He Who Would Valiant Be."

LEADER:

When we search in the Old Testament for a person who lived by his convictions, Daniel is one who is outstanding. The writer of the book of Daniel says of him that he was one "in whom was no blemish, but well favoured, and skilful in all wisdom." Why was he preferred above the other Hebrew captives in the king's court? It may have been because he had a purpose or plan which gave direction to his life. He had a course mapped out for himself, and for fully seventy years he continued to follow this course.

SCRIPTURE:

Daniel purposed in his heart that he would not defile himself with the portion of the king's meat, nor with the wine which he drank. . . . And Daniel continued even unto the first year of king Cyrus.[1]

HYMN:

> Believe not those who say
> The upward path is smooth,

—57—

Lest thou shouldst stumble in the way,
And faint before the truth.

To labor and to love,
To pardon and endure,
To lift thy heart to God above,
And keep thy conscience pure,

Be this thy constant aim,
Thy hope, thy chief delight;
What matter who should whisper blame
Or who should scorn or slight,

If but thy God approve,
And if, within thy breast,
Thou feel the comfort of his love,
The earnest of his rest? [2]

—ANNE BRONTE

LEADER:

We will hear the story of a young man who had a purpose for his life, and lived by his convictions.

STORY:

DISHWASHER WANTED!

PETER chalked up one on his mental blackboard. Mission practically completed! He had promised himself a trip to the nearest Red Cross blood bank as soon as he changed into civilian clothes. The blood-donating business was about over, and here he was, stretched out on a sheet-draped cot, presumably recuperating from what a nurse in the plasma room called "shock."

"Shock, eh?" Peter grinned. He looked at his watch. Five minutes more. If only he had a pencil he would do a sketch of the nurse from memory. He ought to be out now hunting Wellington Forbes, of Universal Advertising, Inc. That was number two on the list of things to be done. Peter Quinlin, Civilian, had to have a job.

The screen around his cot moved quietly.

"Here's a little something for that all-gone feeling," the girl in white said.

Coffee! The smell was exciting. Peter had almost forgotten that coffee could taste like anything other than ashes, mud, or kerosene. He swung his feet to the floor and reached for the cup.

"Your first visit to the blood bank, Mr. Quinlin?"

Peter nodded slightly, and ignored a nagging inner reminder that his nod wasn't telling the whole truth. For Peter Quinlin, Civilian, it was a first trip to the blood bank. G.I. Pete was somebody else. Involuntarily his mind ticked off a list of names: Hollandia, Tinian, Manila, Okinawa. He wondered if someday he would be able to forget the reason for the urgency that had forced him to haunt every Army hospital from New Guinea to the Philippines, offering to donate blood for fellows who had to have it. "Bloodhound" his company had called him. But they hadn't been around the unloading docks in Hollandia when the colonel from the hospital came for the plasma he had been promised and found only a mountain of boxes—five hundred boxes of whiskey for the officers' club! It was as much for the colonel as it was for the fellows in bandages that he had been donating blood ever since.

"That's what comes with choosing ancestors having rock-ribbed New England consciences," he thought ruefully.

"Swell coffee, nurse," he said aloud. "I'll trade pint for pint any day."

Then the sketch portfolio was under his arm, and Peter Quinlin was just another civilian looking for a job. He hoped there would not be much looking involved. Peter had done a good bit of drawing, and after he entered the Army his talent began to pay off. He had had a series of cartoons in *Yank Down Under,* and six months ago a pictorial magazine had given him a four-page spread—sketches he had done while hanging around hospitals.

Before he left for the States, Major Enders, an executive in an advertising firm, had called him in to ask whether he would consider a job with Universal Advertising when he was a civilian again. Would he! That was where he was going, portfolio under his arm. He was to see Mr. Forbes, art editor of the concern. After that, presumably, he would be sitting down at a drawing board and conjuring up ads for soap and perfume. It seemed fantastic.

This was the place, 1108 Lexington. With a fine tingle of anticipation he swung through the revolving door and pushed a button beside a long row of elevators. Three minutes later a receptionist was saying, "Mr. Forbes will see you."

The art editor glanced through the sketches in the portfolio and talked about his experiences in the last war. "Well, Quinlin," he remarked at last, "there's a desk waiting for you whenever your're ready to dig in."

The salary he named sounded stupendous to an ex-sergeant. Peter blinked. It meant that there would be enough to pay for instruction in oils at the Art Institute. "Would tomorrow be all right?" he asked.

"Make it the first of the week," Forbes suggested. "Have a little fun."

Peter was collecting his sketches when Forbes swung toward him, a sheaf of papers in his hand. "By the way, we're working on a new account. I'd like you to see how the thing's shaping up. Maybe you can give us a slant."

Copy sheets swirled across the desk in a pattern of color. Peter bent over them; his face suddenly tensed. At the bottom of each page was a delicate gilt crown and, in black English lettering, the slogan he had seen on the docks in Hollandia and also a doctor's face turning pinched and gray because of proudly decorated boxes.

"Big boom during the war," Forbes was explaining. "Their sales manager is boosting a gigantic expansion program. They're angling for the ex-serviceman's trade, and that's where you come in."

Peter interrupted. "I can't take it."

"What's this?" A flash of real bewilderment crossed the executive's face.

"The job, sir. . . . I can't take it." Peter could almost hear Forbes saying to himself: *Another case of war jitters. Kid comes home all keyed up; gets himself a job and finds he's not quite ready for it.*

"Well, now," he was saying carefully, "if it's more time you want to get organized—"

"No, Mr. Forbes," Peter went on. "It's this." He motioned toward the liquor advertising display across the desk. "I'm not trying to be dramatic, really. It's just that once I saw this stuff make the difference between life and death for a lot of Marines, and I guess I don't forget easily. Thanks, sir. You've been swell."

He was at the door when Mr. Forbes spoke again. "What shall I tell Major Enders, Quinlin?"

Peter turned. "Maybe I do owe you more of an explanation. It probably won't make sense to anyone but me. About three years ago I saw a doctor crying on a Hollandia dock because the plasma the office of supply promised turned out to be five hundred cases of this brand of whiskey for the officers' club."

"An unfortunate incident, certainly," the older man admitted.

"That's just it," Peter replied. "There are a lot of unfortunate incidents connected with the stuff: like the soldiers who raided a truck convoy headed for the jungle, to get at the medical alchohol; like that mission I saw desecrated by Americans who'd been sampling native liquor; like my best friend who spent a couple of days celebrating in the night spots of San Diego and woke up to find himself with a wife whom he did not know. As far as I'm concerned, the stuff is no good. I won't help sell it."

All the trite, obvious things the art editor was thinking were never said. . . . He wanted to tell Peter Quinlin that a man's private views need not interfere with his business. There was something, however, about the strong young honesty of Peter's face that kept him silent. He liked the young man. He wondered to himself how it would feel to be twenty-two again, to have convictions and live by them.

"Well," he held out his hand, "nice to have met you, Quinlin."

"Thanks for listening, sir," said Peter.

Mr. Forbes sat for a half hour looking out the window.

Peter's fervor for his decision lasted only as far as the door. By that time he was as deflated as an old football. "All right, so you had to be a hero!" he jibed at himself. "What are you going to do now for a job? I'll wager this town needs another Class B pencil pusher like it needs a typhoon."

He was out of doors by this time and halfway down the block. He knew that it didn't pay always, financially, to do the decent, honorable thing. Reluctantly he put aside the thought of lessons in oil.

Flash! the sign loomed up before him in the window of a corner restaurant. "Dishwasher wanted. No experience necessary."

Peter's sense of humor took the situation in hand. He had washed dishes for his board during his two years at the university. He would try now for something in his line at one of the big dailies or in the advertising division of a department store. If no one wanted him, he could always come back to the window and the sign. His long experience should make him a valuable man at any sink!

"Thanks, Doc," he said, mentally saluting the colonel on the docks of Hollandia. "Thanks to you, I may be the world's first sketch artist with dishpan hands!"

Peter Quinlin, Civilian, was whistling as he turned the corner.[3]

POEM:

> Because he, too, was young, he knows each snare
> Along the way. He knows what youth must dare!

He, too, in Nazareth's narrow little street
Found hidden nets to trip the youthful feet;
And such forbidden music as you hear
Fell, strangely luring, on the young Christ's ear.

The broad way—then, as now—was gay with song
And laughter; and the straight way lone, and long.
The same foes lurked beside his humble way
That thwart the golden dreams of youth today;
And all the dark temptations that *you* know
He was acquainted with . . . long, long ago.

Tell him your longings! He will bend to hear.
Bring him your heartaches! And the skies will clear.
And share with him your dreams! He speaks the tongue
Of youth—He, too, was eager, glad, and young!
Tell him! He is a comrade loyal, true,
To whom you can trust all you think . . . or do.[4]

—Jessie W. Murton

PRAYER:

O God of strength and purity, in whose image we have been
made and in whose will is our joy and peace, consider, we beseech
thee, our need of thy grace and guidance. Suffer us not to yield in the
hour of temptation, nor to fail thee in the time of testing. Give us
courage to stand for what is true and right, and strength to live for
the highest and best.

Deliver us, we beseech thee, from the fear of scorn, the favor of the
crowd, and the downward drag of all that is unworthy. Grant us
through discipline of mind and devotion of heart to maintain a con-
tinual openness of life to thee. When we are prone to waver or to
deny thee, may we fix our minds upon him who alone can supply grace
sufficient for any test. May the remembrance of all who have prayed
and sacrificed for us make us strong to resist temptation in public duty
and in private thought. Suffer us not to be tempted above that which
we can bear. In Jesus' name we pray. AMEN.[5]

HYMN: "Take Thou Our Minds."

BENEDICTION:

Now unto him who is able to keep us from falling, be glory and
power, both now and evermore. AMEN.

SERVICE 9

TO CO-OPERATE WITH GOD

PRELUDE: Hymn tune "*Laudes Domini.*"

CALL TO WORSHIP:

> O matchless honor, all unsought,
> High privilege, surpassing thought
> That thou shouldst call us, Lord, to be
> Linked in work-fellowship with thee!
> To carry out *thy* wondrous plan,
> To bear *thy* messages to man;
> "In trust," with Christ's own word of grace
> To every soul of human race.
>
> —AUTHOR UNKNOWN

HYMN: "Lord, Speak to Me, That I May Speak," or
"Breathe on Me, Breath of God."

SCRIPTURE:

I am the true vine, and my Father is the husbandman. Every branch in me that beareth not fruit he taketh away: and every branch that beareth fruit, he purgeth it, that it may bring forth more fruit.

Now are ye clean through the word which I have spoken unto you. Abide in me, and I in you. As the branch cannot bear fruit of itself, except it abide in the vine; no more can ye, except ye abide in me.

I am the vine, ye are the branches: He that abideth in me, and I in him, the same bringeth forth much fruit: for without me ye can do nothing.

If a man abide not in me, he is cast forth as a branch, and is withered; and men gather them, and cast them into the fire, and they are burned.

If ye abide in me, and my words abide in you, ye shall ask what ye will, and it shall be done unto you.

Herein is my Father glorified, that ye bear much fruit; so shall ye be my disciples.[1]

PRAYER:

O Christ, thou hast shown us how to co-operate with thee. Grant that we may know more of thee and of thy plan for the world. Forbid that anything in our lives would hide the true light of thee. May we never be content with less than our best. Give us courage to face new truths and to adventure along new paths of service. Thou hast called us to be workmen with thee and to share the task of bringing thy kingdom on earth. Break down all barriers of selfishness and ignorance which would keep us from dedicating all that we have to thee—our time, talents, and possessions. Help us to realize that if our lives are dedicated to thee, our tasks, however small, are a part of thy plan and purpose in the world. Enlarge our vision of the work we can do in co-operation with thee. In Jesus' name. AMEN.

LEADER:

Many doctors have had a vision of ridding the world of infectious disease. Some of them had better equipped laboratories and greater resources than Dr. Alexander Fleming, but it was he who gave to the world the wonderful drug penicillin. He did not merely dream, but continued his research until his vision became a reality. Courageous persistence is back of every great achievement, and men of action like Dr. Fleming pass on to posterity a great heritage.

STORY:

SIR ALEXANDER FLEMING

SIR ALEXANDER FLEMING, discoverer of penicillin, predicts that eventually the world may be freed of infectious diseases by a drug more powerful than penicillin. He foresees that the span of life will be increased when other bacteria-killers are found and put to use. Deadly scourges, he predicts, will be wiped out, and mankind will be freed of diseases which still take a tremendous toll of lives. Penicillin and the sulfa drugs are only the beginning in the battle against infection.

Alexander Fleming was born near the little town of Darvel in Ayrshire, England, in 1881. He was the seventh child in the home of Hugh Fleming, a farmer. He is so reticent that all he will say about his early life is that he lived on a farm down at the end of the road. He came to London at the age of fourteen and lived with a brother who is a doctor. It may have been his brother's influence that turned his thoughts to medicine; at any rate, he attended St. Mary's Hospital Medical School and in 1906 was awarded his degree in medicine.

Dr. Fleming says that he is a bacteriologist because there was an opening in that department at St. Mary's Hospital at that time and the position was offered to him. Since then he has remained at St. Mary's except for the time spent in the army during World War I. Before the war he did research in the vaccine treatment of disease. While in the army he found that the antiseptics used in the treatment of wounds actually encouraged infection. They destroyed the white corpuscles, which are man's best fighters against infection. It was then that he resolved to find a substance that would kill germs and at the same time not harm human tissue.

With his usual modesty Dr. Fleming says that it was only by chance that he discovered penicillin. "Had my laboratory been as up-to-date and sterile as some, it is possible that I would never have discovered penicillin." He had been experimenting with bacterial cultures which he had placed in covered dishes, and he noticed that when the lid had been left off a spot of mold had formed on one of them. Around the edge of the mold where the spores had fallen the bacteria had completely disappeared, but in other places they had continued to grow. Obviously the mold was making something which stopped the growth of the bacteria. Here was the clue that he wanted.

He touched the mold with a wire and transferred some of it to a test tube filled with meat broth. In this way he obtained a pure culture free from other germs. After many experiments he found that the fluid in which the mold had grown contained an effective antiseptic. He continued the research for several months but was not able to isolate the substance which actually killed the germs, so his discovery lay dormant for almost ten years.

Hoping that others might succeed where he had failed, Dr. Fleming published the results of his research. Like all true scientists he was willing to share his discovery that it might be used for the good of mankind. But the attention of the scientists was focused upon the sulfa drugs, which were considered a panacea, drugs which would stop the growth of germs without affecting living tissue. Later it was found that the sulfa drugs did not work well in infected areas, that they were often irritating, thus retarding healing, and that sometimes they caused severe poisoning when taken internally.

It was at this point that Dr. Florey of Oxford and Dr. Chain, his associate, took up the research. They planted Fleming's mold in a sugar solution and after a few days noticed shining golden droplets on the surface of the mold. When these droplets dried to a yellowish-brown powder, the result was natural penicillin.

In the early stages of the research the new drug was found to be a thousand times more powerful than the sulfa drugs. It was a tedious and complicated process to obtain sufficient quantity of the drug for an experiment. Trying it first on mice, they observed that it killed microbes without destroying the white corpuscles. The first two attempts on man were unsuccessful, for the supply of the drug ran out. The next was made on a seven-year-old girl who had gangrene. Although she had lost her arm up to her shoulder, the new substance saved her life.

At last Dr. Fleming's dream of freeing the world of infectious disease was becoming a reality. By 1940 the fame of the wonder drug had spread throughout the world. Many honors came to him: he was knighted by the king and, together with Dr. Florey and Dr. Chain, awarded the Nobel prize.

Coming to America in 1945, Dr. Fleming visited various hospitals to see who was being done with penicillin and to share what he knew. During his stay the University of Pennsylvania and Princeton University conferred the degree of Doctor of Science upon him. The fifteen manufacturers of penicillin in this country started the Alexander Fleming Fund with a gift of $84,000 to be used for research under his direction at St. Mary's Hospital in London. A more fitting gift could not have been selected, for St. Mary's meant much to him.

Dr. Fleming is pleased with the progress that has been made in the battle against disease through the use of penicillin, but he warns against overrating it. While it is effective against certain organisms, there are others upon which it has no effect. For example, the germs or viruses which cause the common cold, whooping cough, tuberculosis, influenza, cholera, and cancer are apparently immune to it.

The manufacture of this wonder drug is a big business, but Dr. Fleming took no patents and does not profit from his discovery. He says that if it has eased human suffering he is content. In his thinking the first consideration is the welfare of mankind. The many honors that have come to him have not affected him in the least. After having been knighted and having received the Nobel prize he is still modest. He is soft-spoken and looks more like a professor than a world-famous scientist.

Dr. Fleming has always worked hard, but he finds time for some recreation. He likes painting, rowing, and swimming, but he prefers work in the laboratory to any other activity. His life has been organized around research, and it is in that field that he is most at home. He may have stumbled on the new drug by accident, but he has made the most of his discovery. He is regarded today as one of the great benefactors of mankind. The world owes a debt of gratitude to him for his discovery, which has already saved thousands of lives and bids fair to realize the dream of its discoverer to stamp out infectious disease.

POEM:

> Go forth to life, O child of earth!
>   Still mindful of thy heav'nly birth;
> Thou art not here for ease, or sin,
>   But manhood's noble crown to win.
>
> Tho' passion's fires are in thy soul,
>   Thy spirit can their flames control;
> Tho' tempters strong beset thy way,
>   Thy spirit is more strong than they.
>
> Go on from innocence of youth
>   To manly purity and truth;
> God's angels still are near to save,
>   And God himself doth help the brave.
>
> Then forth to life, O child of earth!
>   Be worthy of thy heav'nly birth!
> For noble service thou art here:
>   Thy brothers help, thy God revere!
>   —SAMUEL LONGFELLOW

HYMN: "Go, Labor On!" or
      "Work for the Night Is Coming."

PRAYER:

We praise thee, O God, for our friends, the doctors and nurses, who seek the healing of our bodies. We bless thee for their gentleness and patience, for their knowledge and skill. We remember the hours of our suffering when they brought relief, and the days of our fear and anguish at the bedside of our dear ones when they came as ministers of God to save the life thou hadst given. May we reward their fidelity and devotion by our loving gratitude, and do thou uphold them by the satisfaction of work well done.

We rejoice in the tireless daring with which some are now tracking the great slayers of mankind by the white light of science. Grant that under their teaching we may grapple with the sins which have ever dealt death to the race, and that we may so order the life of our communities that none may be doomed to an untimely death for lack of the simple gifts which thou hast given in abundance. Make thou our doctors the prophets and soldiers of thy kingdom, which is the reign of cleanliness and self-restraint and the dominion of health and joyous life.

Strengthen in their whole profession the consciousness that their calling is holy and that they, too, are disciples of the saving Christ. May they never through pressure of need or ambition surrender the sense of a divine mission and become hirelings who serve only for money. Make them doubly faithful in the service of the poor who need their help most sorely, and may the children of the workingman be as precious to them as the child of the rich. Though they deal with the frail body of man, may they have an abiding sense of the eternal value of the life residing in it, that by the call of faith and hope they may summon to their aid the mysterious spirit of man and the powers of thy all-pervading life.[2]

BENEDICTION:

May thy spirit, O God, open up avenues for service and aid us in a more complete dedication of our lives to thee. AMEN.

SERVICE 10

TO FULFILL GOD'S APPOINTMENT

PRELUDE: "Adagio" from Beethoven's "Moonlight Sonata."

CALL TO WORSHIP:

>Love is an elusive thing
>>When gone directly after,
>Like gossamers on dewy grass
>>Or unexpected laughter.
>The give and take of bartering
>>All matters not a whit;
>Love *asks* for nothing—
>>*Everything* comes back to it.[1]
>>>—EVERETT ARTHUR OVERTON

SCRIPTURE:

Love is forbearing and kind. Love knows no jealousy. Love does not brag; is not conceited. She is not unmannerly, nor selfish, nor irritable, nor mindful of wrongs. She does not rejoice in injustice, but joyfully sides with the truth. She can overlook faults. She is full of trust, full of hope, full of endurance. Lover never fails.[2]

POEM:

>Love will live forever,
>>Brighter than the spring,
>Warmer than the summer,
>>Joyous and comforting;
>Love grows sweeter, stronger,
>>As we toil and plod—
>Love will live forever,
>>Love is life and God.

Love will live forever
With the young and old,
Holding homes together,
Worth far more than gold;
Love my heart will cherish,
Daring every odd;
Love will never perish—
Love is life and God.[3]

—CHAUNCEY R. PIETY

PRAYER:

We invoke thy gentlest blessings, our Father, on all true lovers. We praise thee for the great longing that draws the soul of man and maid together and bids them leave all the dear bonds of the past to cleave to one another. We thank thee for the revealing power of love which divines in the one beloved the mystic beauty and glory of humanity. We thank thee for the transfiguring power of love which ripens and ennobles our nature, calling forth the hidden stores of tenderness and strength and overcoming the selfishness of youth by the passion of self-surrender.

We pray thee to make their love strong, holy, and deathless, that no misunderstandings may fray the bond, and no gray disenchantment of the years may have power to quench the heavenly light that now glows in them. May they early gain wisdom to discern the true values of life, and may no tyranny of fashion and no glamour of cheaper joys filch from them the wholesome peace and inward satisfaction which only loyal love can give.

Grant them with sober eyes to look beyond these sweet days of friendship to the generations yet to come, and to realize that the home for which they long will be part of the sacred tissue of the body of humanity in which thou art to dwell, that so they may reverence themselves and drink the cup of joy with awe.[4] AMEN.

HYMN: "Love Thyself Last," or
"Temper My Spirit, O Lord."

LEADER:

One's happiness and success in life are largely dependent upon a wise choice in the selection of a life partner. We will hear a story which illustrates the importance of clear thinking and good judgment in this important choice.

TO FULFILL GOD'S APPOINTMENT

LISTEN TO THE HEART

TED BRUCE opened the door into the waiting room. There he heard Miss Gallagher, the receptionist, saying to a shabby lady holding a sick boy, "I'm sorry, Mrs. Medders, but Dr. Westfield's appointments are all full."

"I can see her," Ted interrupted. "I'll take all responsibility," he continued, realizing full well that Dr. Westfield would be angry because of his taking another charity case.

Fifteen minutes later, the woman and child gone, Ted listened to Dr. Westfield, "I've told you, Ted, not to take these charity cases. Two months ago you had an M.D., but not enough money to buy a stethoscope. You were about to take a starvation job as missionary doctor in China. I saved you from all that by taking you in as my partner, equipping you even with a car."

"You've been extremely kind, Dr. Westfield, but you did it with the understanding that if in two months I so decided, I could take that China job."

Dr. Westfield's face grew concerned, his voice softer. "Surely, Ted, you've given up that ridiculous notion about China. Evelyn's a rich man's daughter and . . ."

"Yes," Ted said, "I know that, and she's a fine girl. This town can do very well without another doctor, but over there in China millions of people are dying."

"You're talking nonsense again, Ted. You're doing wonderful here. So well, in fact, I can raise you from $250 a month to $400.

"I'll let you know in the morning."

"Ted, you aren't serious!" Ted went out and Miss Gallagher entered. "He really might do it, Miss Gallagher, if I don't stop him, and he means a lot of money to me. Get Evelyn on the phone."

Ted drove home, trying to shake off the uneasiness that he felt. Why was he so dissatisfied with himself? Hadn't he always dreamed of coming back and helping the people who had no money? That, of course, was before he had heard the missionary talk of the people in China and their great need. That night a resolution had formed that he would spend his life in China. After the missionary's talk he had gone up to him and asked, "How do you go about going to China?"

"Son, let's sit down. It's easy enough."

When the missionary had taken his name and address, Ted received letter after letter from the religious organization that would sponsor him.

But he had started working for Dr. Westfield because his father was in debt. He drove home, tossed his hat on the divan where his father sat smoking a cigar behind the evening paper.

"Hi, Dad," Ted said. "Any mail?"

From behind the paper Mr. Bruce answered, "Haven't seen any. You're not still looking for a letter from those missionary people?"

"Yes, I wrote them last week."

"Son, you're doing so well. You're just getting started, and your mother and I are getting old. Thomas will be ready for college next year, and your mother, she ought to take things a bit easier."

"I know." Ted stared at him and went into the kitchen where his mother was basting a roast. He nodded and said, "I won't be home for supper. I've got to see Evelyn tonight. You've cooked especially for me, haven't you?"

"Oh, Thomas can eat it."

"Tell me something, Mother. You haven't had a very easy life. I know it was the money you made sewing that kept me in school and not anything Dad did. You must have had many chances when you were a girl. Do you regret. . ."

She sat down facing him. Her face showed no resentment, and her voice was soft. "I did have many chances. But if I had it to do over again, I wouldn't change one bit. Don't ever tell your father, Ted, but I almost didn't marry him. There was a young man, extremely wealthy, who hounded me. I nearly married him."

"Why didn't you?"

"Well, for one thing, I loved your father, and besides he needed me. It was what my heart told me to do. Some men just don't get along as well as others. You know, Ted, there's not much purpose in life unless you're needed, unless you are giving instead of taking. By the way, did you get your letter?"

Already he had guessed its contents: he must let them know by return mail whether or not he would accept the offer. "I'd better get on over to Evelyn's."

The restaurant where they ate was one of those quiet places. Finally Ted said, "I was just thinking about you and my mother. How both of you seem to know exactly what you want."

"Don't you know what you want, Ted?"

"Do you love me enough to go to China?"

There was a frown on her brow. "That again! Ted, I've told you over and over that's not a fair question to ask any woman. If you're going to start that, I'm going home."

"Suppose, though," he continued, "I decided to go."

"There's so much for you to do here. You'll be famous in a few years."

Ted felt that she was displeased with him. But knowing whether she would go seemed important, a kind of test of her love for him, a proof that it was he she loved and not the fact that he might be famous some day.

"Dr. Westfield told me tonight that he was worried about that foolish notion of yours, that it would be a tragedy for a brilliant young doctor like you to bury yourself in China when you could do so well here."

The waiter touched Ted's shoulder. "There's a mountaineer outside waiting to see you, Dr. Bruce. Says it's important."

"Ted!" Evelyn commanded. "Dr. Westfield has asked you not to treat cases like this, and you have an engagement with me."

But Ted went out. This, of course, was another charity case, and Dr. Westfield had forbidden it. But suppose Ted didn't go? Could he live with himself and not listen to his heart's reproachings? Yet he had to decide, and his choice was somehow deeper than this one decision; it was somehow tied up with what he would do with his life. His mother's words about one having to be needed and to give and to listen to the heart suddenly came to his mind, and all at once he understood the source of her complete happiness. But Thomas? How would he get through college? What about his father and mother? They'd come out all right. And Evelyn? Well, Evelyn was for men who had time for things like fine cars and the country club.

He went back into the restaurant. Evelyn's face was white. "You can call a cab, waiter," she said, meaning that this was the end.

Somehow as Ted left the restaurant he felt wonderfully and strangely at ease and happy for the first time in two months. He knew that at last he had found the source of his mother's happiness.[5]

PRAYER:

We know, O God, that love comes from thee, and that he who loves is born of thee. Forbid that we should ever act from selfish motives, forgetting the welfare of others. May we never exploit another person, or take advantage of anyone for our own benefit or selfish pleasure. Grant that we may always be mindful of the sacredness of human personality and demand honesty, purity, and chastity of ourselves at all times. Help us to think clearly and to channel our affections rightly so as to beautify and ennoble life. May we live daily in such manner as to be worthy of the love which should come to us. In the name of the Master we pray. AMEN.

HYMN: "O Love Divine and Golden," or
"Love Divine, All Loves Excelling."

BENEDICTION:

The Lord bless you and keep you; the Lord make his face to shine upon you and be gracious unto you; the Lord lift up his countenance upon you and give you peace; both now and evermore. AMEN.

SERVICE 11

TO ANSWER THE CALL OF CHRIST

PRELUDE: Hymn tune "Felix" by Mendelssohn.

CALL TO WORSHIP:

> O Father, deign these walls to bless;
> Fill with thy love their emptiness;
> And let their door a gateway be
> To lead us from ourselves to thee.
> —JOHN GREENLEAF WHITTIER

HYMN: "Draw Thou My Soul, O Christ," or
"Go Forth to Life."

THE CALL OF CHRIST:

First Reader: During his earthly ministry Jesus had a purpose in life, and it gave meaning to everything that he said or did. Let us hear the words of Jesus as he spoke of his purpose:

Second Reader: I came not to call the righteous, but sinners to repentance. I am come that they might have life, and that they might have it more abundantly. To this end was I born, and for this cause came I into the world, that I should bear witness unto the truth.

First Reader: Let us hear Jesus' call to his disciples:

Second Reader: And Jesus, walking by the sea of Galilee, saw two brethren. . . . And he saith unto them, Follow me, and I will make you fishers of men.[1]

POEM:

First Reader: The road dust stirs in the April heat
And settles down on his strong, brown feet;

Second Reader: (*Lay down your nets and follow me*)

First Reader: The lark skirls into the sun at dawn
And burly Peter bestirs his brawn,
Strides through the shadows of Galilee.

Second Reader: (*You will fish for men, who follow me*)

First Reader: Andrew and James and grave, young John
Have heard a voice and followed him on. . . .
They have seen a man in a dusty cloak,
With sweat on his face
And a voice that spoke
In the twanging tongue of the common folk. . . .
A trumpet call that has made them free.

Second Reader: (*There'll be rougher roads if you follow me*)

First Reader: They've looked in his eye and they've seen his humor,
Here is no strolling saint with a rumor
Of holy riddles and puling fable,
But a man of men with a look that is able
To study a man in his silent soul. . . .
Or rest on a leper
And make him whole.

The months go by and the seasons change.
They have walked with the Man
From the distant range
Of the limestone hills
To the narrow valley where Jordan spills
Its pushing course in a long-dead Sea.

Second Reader: (*You'll have found your lives when you've followed
me*)

First Reader: They have seen his black eyes flame
With a righteous and blistering anger,
They have seen him tired and worn with hunger;
They have seen him resolute, unafraid,
Stalwart, on a course a star has laid;
They have known the Father, friended his Son.

Second Reader: (*Not my will, but thine be done*)

First Reader: They have known his laughter and seen his tears
And his vibrant voice has stilled their fears.

A journey is finished, a course is run.

Second Reader: (*Father, my work with these is done*)

First Reader: The truths they have heard will make men free,

Second Reader: (*Lord, I gave them the words which thou gavest me*)

First Reader: And death is not death for he walks the sands.

Second Reader: (*Reach hither thy finger, behold my hands*)

First Reader: The road dust stirs in the April heat
And settles down on his strong, brown feet. . . .

Second Reader: Leave your nets, throw down your past,
(*I am the first and I am the last*)
Follow a light no dark can mar. . . .
I AM THE BRIGHT AND MORNING STAR.[2]

—RICHARD S. BATTLE

First Reader: Let us hear the words of Jesus as he calls us to follow him:

Second Reader: If any man will come after me, let him deny himself, take up his cross, and follow me.[3]

First Reader: We will hear the story of Jesus' call to Nicodemus:

STORY:

THE HILL ROAD

GOD had a song he wanted to sing, and when he had finished it he created a man to sing it. You see, it was a mighty song and needed a godlike singer. And the man was Jesus, a carpenter of Nazareth. He went up to Jerusalem, and as he walked up and down its narrow, crowded streets, God's song swept across the hearts of people.

Some ran to meet it, it was so full of strength and beauty. But others ran *from* it, trembling with fear. And these were they who dreaded lest it rend the hate and uproot the falsehood in which their lives were so comfortably grounded.

When the rulers of Israel—priests, scribes, and Pharisees—heard it, they shuttered the windows of their souls and barred the gates of their mind against it; that is, all of them except Nicodemus and one or two others who, when they heard it, stopped to listen.

Nicodemus was no longer a young man, and at first he listened with the gentlemanly indifference of one who is tired of life. But a day came when the swift, clean words cut through the mist of indifference and with a lightning flash revealed Nicodemus to himself.

That night he took the hill road to the Mount of Olives. He had heard that Jesus was in the habit of spending his nights there. In his eagerness he hurried. But it was not long before his footsteps faltered, heavy with weariness. He swayed with fatigue, caught hold of a rock, and sat down to rest. His hands trembled as he wiped the sweat from his face. But his soul's need was more urgent than that of his body, and it was not long before his determined tread fell softly upon the silence and Nicodemus was on his way again.

The road became a friendly path, ending abruptly among a clump of olive trees, as though it knew that Nicodemus could not possibly take another step. As he stood looking down upon Jerusalem, he felt the presence of long-forgotten memories, and dreams of his boyhood seemed to rise from the city of pinnacles and towers, lying there so quiet and clean in the white radiance of the Eastern night. Unconsciously he lifted his face toward heaven and stretched out his hands, palms upward, in prayer. In the light of the moon and stars his thin, tired face was like an exquisite cameo of old ivory, carved against the onyx shadows of the olive trees.

Jesus saw him thus. The beauty and pathos of the old man tugged at his heart, and quietly, lest he break in upon the prayer, Jesus came and stood beside him. He watched the labored rise and fall of the old man's breathing, the throbbing pulse in the thick veins on his forehead, and at once sensed the courage and endurance it had cost Nicodemus to come out alone and by night on the hill road.

Nicodemus looked up. "You are here. I am so glad."

"Yes, during the time I am in Jerusalem I almost always spend my nights up here. Wide, unwalled places are good to refresh oneself in after being jostled the whole day long in the narrow crowded streets. But you are very tired." Jesus put out his hand to steady Nicodemus and, suiting his pace to that of the older man, led him to a spot under an olive tree.

Several minutes passed before either of them spoke. Now that he was face to face with the young teacher, Nicodemus was at a loss for words. How could he tell Jesus that for an old man to seek the comradeship of a younger, and for a ruler of Israel, a Hebrew of the Hebrews, a member of the Sanhedrin, to have any dealings whatsoever with a Sabbath-breaking Nazarene was not only flagrantly undignified, but dangerously unconventional. But Jesus came to his relief, sensing with instinctive kindliness the older man's difficulty.

"I understand perfectly. It is a bitter experience to be scorned by one's own, an experience from which we may well shrink unless we live so near to God that we are filled with his life."

No sooner had the word "life" been spoken, than Nicodemus found the words for lack of which he had been unable to make his need known. Now he spoke slowly, hesitatingly: "You are a teacher come from God."

"Are you sure, Nicodemus?" And there was both sadness and a smile in the Master's voice, which Nicodemus was quick to catch.

"You may well ask that. We priests and Pharisees have so often tried to bait you with those very words, but I speak them in all sincerity. Only *you* can tell me, and my need is too great to be denied—how I, an old man, may find life, *eternal* life."

Jesus put his hand on that of the old man. "By knowing the God within you, by catching a vision of his Kingdom."

"But it is so long since I have felt God within me—and the eyes of my soul have grown too dim to see so divine a thing as his Kingdom. Surely you realize that I cannot do these things. And if I could—how?"

"There is only one way; you must be born anew."

Nicodemus shook his head and answered with bitter irony: "How can a man be born when he is old? Can he enter his mother's womb over again, and be born?"

"Do not wonder, Nicodemus, at my telling you that you must be born again, spiritually. The wind blows wherever it chooses, and you hear the sound thereof, but you do not know where it comes from or where it goes. This is the way with everyone who owes his birth to the Spirit."

"How can that be?" Nicodemus asked, bewildered.

"You are a teacher of Israel and yet ignorant of this? I speak of that which I know, and of that which I have seen. You remember how it is told that Moses in the desert lifted the serpent up in the air—even so the Son of man must be lifted up, so that everyone who believes in him may have life. Don't you see, Nicodemus? You said your soul seemed to you like a barren, hemmed-in plain. Break down its barriers, widen its horizons, let God's light flood it, and even as the spring sunshine makes the fields blossom, so his light will make your soul alive with new interest, new hope, new joy, new life, life in its fullest sense. Lift up the Son of man within you, and this new life will be life eternal.

That's what it means to be born again, Nicodemus, not once, but every day and every hour."

As Jesus spoke these words, night gave place to dawn. The song of a lark swept over the hillside and lost itself in the immensity of life waking everywhere.

"It is as though that song had come out of my heart," Nicodemus began. He wanted to say more, to make some expression of gratitude, but he could not find the right words. "I came to you in the night," he hesitated, "a soul seemingly without life; now in the dawn I go back— reborn."

They arose and walked arm in arm to the edge of the hillside and stood looking down in a sky of rose and amber. Nicodemus turned thoughtfully homeward to march forward in an ever-broadening spiritual experience.[4]

POEM:

> O Master! when thou callest,
>   No voice may say thee nay,
> For blest are they that follow
>   Where thou dost lead the way;
> In freshest prime of morning,
>   Or fullest glow of noon,
> The note of heavenly warning
>   Can never come too soon.
>
> O Master! whom thou callest,
>   No heart may dare refuse;
> 'Tis honor, highest honor,
>   When thou dost deign to use
> Our brightest and our fairest,
>   Our dearest—all are thine;
> Thou who for each one carest,
>   We hail thy love's design.
>
> They who go forth to serve thee,
>   We, too, who serve at home,
> May watch and pray together
>   Until thy Kingdom come;
> In thee for aye united,
>   Our song of hope we raise,

Till that blest shore is sighted
Where all shall turn to praise.
—Sarah Geraldina Stock

PRAYER:

Our Father, thou hast revealed to us thy commandments and hast given us minds to judge between right and wrong, but at times we have disregarded thy Word and failed to follow thy commandments. Continue to illumine our hearts with the light of thy truth, increase our understanding, and help us correct our weaknesses. Thou hast given thy commandments to guide us, thy prophets to inspire us, thy teachers to instruct us, and finally thy Son to be our example. Yet at times we walk in our own way and go contrary to thy revealed will and purpose. Forgive us the sins of pride, egotism, prejudice, indifference, selfishness, and all other faults. Banish them from us and help us to live according to thy will concerning us. Give us strength to resist temptation and lead us into ever broadening experiences as we rededicate our lives to thee. Help us to follow thee wholeheartedly in every relationship of life and acknowledge thee as our Lord and Master. AMEN.

HYMN: "Just as I Am, Thine Own to Be," or
"Give of Your Best to the Master."

BENEDICTION:

May the Spirit of the Master lead us into faithful and devoted service from this day forward. AMEN.

SERVICE 12

FEAR NOT
(*Christmas*)

PRELUDE: Hymn tune "Kings of Orient."

CALL TO WORSHIP:

Holy Father of the holy Christ-Child,
Cause him to be reborn today in our world,
Make each heart a cradle for his nativity,
Each life a temple for his glory,
Each home a worship for his Spirit,
Each church a sanctuary of his Kingdom,
Until his Presence shall master all mankind.
In his Spirit of Love, Amen.[1]
—CHAUNCEY R. PIETY

HYMN: "While Shepherds Watched Their Flocks," or
"As with Gladness Men of Old."

SCRIPTURE:

And it came to pass in those days, that there went out a decree from
Caesar Augustus, that all the world should be taxed.

And Joseph also went up from Galilee, out of the city of Nazareth,
into Judaea, unto the city of David, which is called Bethlehem; . . . to
be taxed with Mary his espoused wife, being great with child.

And so it was, that, while they were there, the days were accomplished
that she should be delivered. And she brought forth her firstborn son,
and wrapped him in swaddling clothes, and laid him in a manger;
because there was no room for them in the inn.

And there were in the same country shepherds abiding in the field,
keeping watch over their flock by night. And, lo, the angel of the

Lord came upon them, and the glory of the Lord shone round about them: and they were sore afraid. And the angel said unto them, Fear not: for, behold, I bring you good tidings of great joy, which shall be to all people. For unto you is born this day in the city of David a Saviour, which is Christ the Lord. And this shall be a sign unto you; Ye shall find the babe wrapped in swaddling clothes, lying in a manger.

And suddenly there was with the angel a multitude of the heavenly host praising God, and saying, Glory to God in the highest, and on earth peace, good will toward men.[2]

Poem:

> I wonder if sometimes His heart goes back
> Beyond the glory of that other World,
> Beyond His triumph, and beyond the rack
> Of human agony, to where He curled
> In infant sleep one night, when angels hovered?
> Do vague, nostalgic dreams of starry light
> On quiet hills, of palms whose shadows covered
> A manger roof, return to Him tonight?
>
> If so, the Son of God must love these hills
> Soft-clothed in chaparral, these palms outlining
> Their graceful fronds in black, where starlight spills
> A silver glory of its own designing.
>
> And He must smile and lean down close to them,
> Remembering a night in Bethlehem.[3]
>
> —Esther Baldwin York

Story:

CHRISTMAS EVE IN BETHLEHEM

CHRISTMAS EVE I went to Bethlehem. It had always been my dream to spend a Christmas Eve there. With a Swedish missionary friend I went to the Damascus gate where we took a dilapidated taxi and asked the driver to take us to the Church of the Nativity in Bethlehem. We had covered about three quarters of the distance from Jerusalem to Bethlehem when we ran into the worst traffic jam I have ever been in. There were jeeps, ambulances, private cars, busses, and four-wheeled vehicles of every description trying to make their way to and from Bethlehem on the narrow road. For an hour we waited, unable to move. Finally my friend suggested that we walk.

I shall always be thankful that we walked to Bethlehem that night. Instead of being whirled up to the door of the Church of the Nativity in true American style, we made our way up the winding narrow streets of Bethlehem. Children thrust their heads out the doors and windows to see the crowd. Passing some of the houses one heard the donkey bray and saw the camel beside the door resting from his travels of the day. Arab merchants were on the street selling sweets. We mingled with the crowd. Young men and women in the uniforms of many nations were there. Some spoke strange tongues.

Men and women of all races mingled in Bethlehem that night. Among others were several Jews who had come from one of the large concentration camps, sent by their fellow Jews to see what the Christians do in Bethlehem on Christmas Eve. They were there because they were curious, and so was I. Many of the folks were far from home and were lonely and needed a Friend. I was far from home and lonely, and I too needed a Friend. Some were there who had recently lost loved ones, whose hearts were broken, and who needed a Comforter. Such an experience had been mine only a few days before, and I too needed a Comforter. We met a Moslem doctor who had sat next to me at dinner about three hours earlier. To him Jesus was a Prophet. To me he was the Christ. All on the streets of Bethlehem that night had sinned and needed a Saviour, and so did I.

Then I looked to the left and saw on the shepherd's field a fire still glowing. A service had been held earlier in the evening for the men in the armed forces. I thought of that first Christmas Eve when the angels announced to the shepherds there the birth of Jesus. How significant that announcement was! I had visited in various countries, and everywhere I was finding some kind of fear—fears of all descriptions and some beyond description. How significant then the words of the angels, "Fear not, for I bring you good tidings of great joy which shall be to all people, for unto you is born this day in the city of David a Saviour who is Christ the Lord."

Mingled in the streets of Bethlehem were the curious, the lonely, the broken-hearted, the sin-sick. All of us needed the Christmas message of the angels, and I realized again that only in him could all these needs be satisfied.[4]

FEAR NOT

Above a world entrapped by fear
   There shone a silver Star.
The doubters saw it not, nor cared;
   The men of faith, from far,
Knew that the Lord of Love looked down,
And followed it through field and town.

Through desert lands they found their way,
   Past mountains, bleak and wild;
They came to humble Bethlehem
   And found a little Child.
Their hearts rejoiced—their feet had trod
Through desert wastes to learn of God.

Our hearts are broken by the years,
   But still there shines the Star
Above a little manger home.
   O that we might, from far,
Retrace our steps from fear and night
To faith and hope, and Bethlehem's light![5]

—THOMAS CURTIS CLARK

HYMN: "O Little Town of Bethlehem," or
       "It Came upon the Midnight Clear."

MEDITATION:

Joy unspeakable fiilled the hearts of faithful and expectant souls
when Jesus was born in Bethlehem. Shepherds watching their flocks on
the quiet hillsides were startled into ecstasy as the heavenly choir sang,
"Glory to God . . . on earth peace." Wise men in the east, seeing a new
star in the western sky, bestirred themselves and made haste to go in
search of the newborn King. Both shepherds and wise men, coming
to the place where Jesus was born, worshiped him with adoration of
heart and with material gifts. It seems that everywhere, save in the
minds and hearts of tyrannical rulers and unseeing religious leaders,
there was joy and hope.

It is not strange, therefore, that the observance of Christmas has been
surrounded with the spirit of gladness and good will. True happiness
begets good will and a desire to share. Not only does this result in gifts

to children and other loved ones, but giving to the needy in one's community and to projects of relief throughout the world. The hope and expectation of peace and happiness for the whole world are central in the celebration of Christmas. For the true spirit of Christmas is creative good will. And creative good will leads inevitably to self-giving.

Jesus came into a world of need but also a world of hope. His people longed for deliverance and looked forward to the coming of the Messiah. It was the promise of a new day. The Messiah would deliver them from their conquerors and masters. He would sit on the throne of David and the golden age of Israel would return.

Into the midst of the Jews' deep needs and into the atmosphere of their hopes Jesus came as a little child. Those who recognized him as the Promised One rejoiced. He grew through boyhood "in wisdom and stature, and in favor with God and men," until the time arrived for him to assume and perform his divine mission. The simple story of Jesus as he grew from infancy through childhood and youth to mature manhood illustrates the patience and long-range view of God. He waited for his Son to grow. The simplicity surrounding that growth inspires patience and devotion.

Jesus came to reveal God the Father and to lead in the way of life at its best. He was the Way, the Truth, and the Life. He was misunderstood, opposed, and maltreated. But he went all the way in privation, in sorrow for those about him, in suffering for the evil deeds of others, even to death on a cross.

An understanding of the life and death of Jesus contributes to worthy motives and experiences in the celebration of his birth. Not only so, but Christmas joy becomes empty and vain and pagan if it is not related to the hope and expectancy of victorious living through good will and self-giving service.

The way we celebrate Christmas has a significance far greater than the temporary delights surrounding the occasion. We are responsible agents through whom the hope of a better world, a world of peace and good will, must be realized. Christmas, then, should evoke and encourage true Christian joy. More than unselfish, it should be a positive expression of self-giving. Herein lies the basis of developing good will. Through the experience of being Christian at Christmas we learn and practice the central law of the Christian life: we are "not to be ministered unto, but to minister." We catch the spirit of Christmas as we view the cross; we understand the cross as we comprehend the miracle of birth and the promise of life at its best through self-giving.[6]

FEAR NOT

LITANY:

Leader: O thou who didst reveal thyself in him who was born in Bethlehem,

Group: Grant that in our lives thy Spirit may be made known to the world.

Leader: Thou who didst show thy love for mankind in the giving of thy Son,

Group: Grant that our lives may demonstrate his love of self-giving.

Leader: As thou didst send a song at midnight to the shepherds watching their flocks,

Group: Grant that our songs may bring messages of good will to the world.

Leader: As we celebrate the birth of thy Son at this season,

Group: May his spirit be ever new and transforming in our hearts.

Leader: As at his birth thou didst declare tidings of great joy to a saddened world,

Group: May his spirit, still alive in our hearts, awaken hopes for international peace in the world that now is, and eternal peace and joy in the world to come. AMEN.

HYMN: "O Come, All Ye Faithful."

BENEDICTION:

May the peace of God remain with you evermore. AMEN.

SERVICE 13

ACCEPTING CHRIST AS MASTER
(*Easter*)

PRELUDE: "The Palms" by Faure.

CALL TO WORSHIP:

> Joy dawned again on Easter Day,
>   The sun shone out with fairer ray,
> When, to their longing eyes restored,
>   Th' Apostles saw their risen Lord.
>
> O Jesus, King of gentleness,
>   Do thou our inmost heart possess;
> And we to thee will ever raise
>   The tribute of our grateful praise.
>
> —AUTHOR UNKNOWN

HYMN: "Sing, Men and Angels, Sing," or
    "Come, Ye Faithful, Raise the Strain."

SCRIPTURE:

When the Sabbath was over, Mary of Magdala, Mary the mother of James, and Salome, bought spices, in order to come and anoint His body. So, very soon after sunrise on the first day of the week, they came to the tomb; and they said to one another,

"Who will roll away the stone for us from the entrance to the tomb?"

But then, looking up, they saw that the stone was already rolled back: it was of immense size. Upon entering the tomb, they saw a young man sitting at their right hand, clothed in a long white robe. They were terrified. But he said to them,

"Do not be terrified. It is Jesus you are looking for—the Nazarene, the crucified one. He has come back to life: He is not here: this is the place where they laid Him. But go and tell His disciples and Peter that He is going before you into Galilee: and that there you will see Him, as he told you."

So they came out, and fled from the tomb, for they were trembling and amazed; and they said not a word to any one, for they were afraid. Now when He rose to life early on the first day of the week, He appeared first to Mary of Magdala, from whom He had expelled seven demons.[1]

POEM:

> They bowed beside Him as He prayed,
>   The flower bells in the grass,
> And watched close by Him till they felt
>   Grim Roman sandals pass.
>
> And when the Lord was led away,
>   Weary and comfortless,
> Along the path they touched His robe
>   In gentle, shy caress.
>
> They stood beside the sepulchre,
>   Against impassive stone,
> And drooped to see the Master laid
>   There, lifeless and alone.
>
> But in the world's first Easter dawn,
>   An ancient legend tells,
> The flowers voiced their joy in sounds
>   Like little chiming bells;
>
> And "Allelujah" pealed their song
>   In music silver-sweet,
> While from their petals danced the dew
>   Like jewels at His feet.
>
> The last star faded from the sky;
>   The east was rosy red.
> The risen Christ paused in His walk
>   And bent His shining head,

And with a blessing in His eyes,
He smiled to hear them play,
He said that bells should ever speak
His love on Easter day.[2]

—ESTHER BALDWIN YORK

PRAYER:

O Lord and giver of life, who dost renew the face of the earth
with singing and joyful loveliness, renew in our hearts an unconquered
faith in the power of righteousness. Even as the spirit of Christ rose
triumphant over the bitter pain of the cross and darkness of the tomb,
enable us to look beyond the things of earth which pass away to find
our joy and peace in thine infinite and eternal love. Give us such
trust and confidence in thy love that we may know ourselves to be
ever in thy hand, and uplift our souls to worship thee in spirit and in
truth, at one in heart and voice with the great company of those who
have walked in thy light and who stand in joy before thee. AMEN.[3]

HYMN: "Life Is Good, for God Contrives It."
"Spirit of Life, in This New Dawn."

LEADER:

A story will be told of a young person, a friend of Jesus, to whom
he first appeared after his resurrection.

STORY:

MARY OF MAGDALA

MYSTERY had always mingled freely with life for Mary, the beautiful
daughter of Ezra, the rich fig merchant of Magdala. Ever since the
first day she could remember, some strange force had seemed to shut
her off from the companionship of other girls. There were times when
the big house had seemed a prison, and she had sobbed out her heart
in uncomprehending grief.

It all went back to those terrible spells of illness, when she would
fall suddenly without warning in horrible convulsions, bloody froth
streaming from her mouth, and her eyes rolling back in gruesome
fashion. Her father had visited every physician in Galilee, but to no
avail. There was no cure, they said.

The fact of her affliction was supposed to be a secret; but servants
will talk, and ugly rumors circulated through the town. One day,
returning from her father's shops, she was seized by a spasm and fell,

writhing and tortured, in the street. Thereafter the village said she was possessed of a devil. A few weeks later she fell under another attack on the very steps of the synagogue, after which it was openly declared that she was possessed of not one but seven devils.

Poor Mary was never able to understand why other children avoided her, but her sensitive soul felt their aversion like something deadly. And as she grew older she withdrew upon her own resources until, in time, she learned to live almost entirely alone. Even her sisters shared her life only in commonplaces.

Matters might have gone on thus indefinitely except for a circumstance, quite trivial, that occurred late one afternoon. Mary was engaged about some small task as two servants were conversing excitedly in the court below her window. One of them, just returned from Capernaum, was full of the news of a wonder-working Prophet who was preaching to great multitudes. Mary listened indifferently at first, for the tales of servant girls could hardly be of interest to the rich merchant's daughter.

Suddenly, in the midst of the recital, Mary's ear caught some amazing words. Instantly her face went white, her body became tense, and her breathing almost stopped. "They say he heals the sick," the woman was saying. "He makes the lame to walk, he causes the blind to see, and he restores hearing to the deaf. A fisherman even told me that he casts out devils."

In a few quick steps Mary was beside the open window, listening breathlessly. That night, at the evening meal, she appeared normal except for a bright red spot that glowed on each cheek. There was nothing to indicate the daring plan upon which she had determined.

It was sometime before sunrise the next morning that the heavy gate swung back and Mary, with a great coat thrown about her, slipped out of her father's house and into the street. Keeping close to the wall, and making all possible speed, she was off to Capernaum in search of the Prophet.

It was still early morning when she arrived at the gate of the city, just as a party of young men were coming out, chatting as they came. None of them would have given more than a passing glance at the girl at the side of the road if she had not suddenly cried out with a piteous little cry. Instantly all eyes were upon her, and as she fell in the dust of the road, twitching and twisting in ghastly convulsions, they shrank back in horror. All save the Leader. With one quick stride he was at her side. Stooping over her in compassion, he laid his hand upon her shoulder ever so gently and spoke in a low tone of voice. As he did so, the stricken girl grew quiet, and as he continued to speak her body relaxed, her eyes opened, and her countenance lighted up as if she had seen the face of God.

Helping the girl to her feet and brushing the dust of the road off her great coat, the Master then warned her in seriousness to say nothing of the meeting to anyone. But, assuring her that she would never again suffer so, he directed her to return home. As he rejoined his companions and took up his journey again, Mary stood in the roadway, watching, until they turned off toward the mountains and were lost to sight. With a glad cry that came leaping up out of a heart suddenly set free from a terrible fear, she raced away toward home like some wild thing given its liberty.

From that day the house of Ezra, the fig merchant, rang with song. Gone was the terrible fear; gone was the horror that clutched at all hearts; gone was the shame that attended them all because of Mary's illness. That which her father's great wealth had not been able to accomplish had been wrought by the single word of the Prophet. The girl, whose slightest wish had been the law of the home when she was stricken, now was free to do as she pleased. Being healed, and attended by the mother of two of the Prophet's disciples, she joined the company of his friends and traveled the countryside with him, drinking in his wonderful words.

One day he was dining with some friends, Mary watching from a distance. Suddenly overcome with the realization of her vast indebtedness to him, and in a delirium of gratitude, she pushed her way up to the couch on which he was reclining and, kneeling, broke the seal of an exquisite alabaster box of precious perfume, and anointed his unshod feet. Then, while the fragrance filled the room, she wiped them with her long raven-black tresses, and sobbed out a prayer of thanksgiving. It was a daring thing to do, but love like hers knows no conservatism.

He who had given her back her life was the center of her universe. It was as if he had all at once become God to her. It never occurred to Mary that she would ever again live in a world without him, for there was something eternal about him. He who had given her life must be the Master of Life—death could not touch him.

When, therefore, months afterwards, a wild and disheveled messenger arrived at the door of her hired room in Jerusalem one morning with the news that the high priests and Pharisees had browbeaten Pilate into ordering his execution as a seditionist, the very universe trembled under her feet. Following her guide as fast as feet and fear would permit, she soon found herself at the bottom of "the Skull," just in time to see Roman soldiers raise the cross to which he was nailed. With a wild cry, Mary raced to the side of his mother, who crouched, sobbing, at the edge of the crowd. There she took up her station and waited, throughout the awful day. Once the Prophet turned to his mother and said, "Woman, behold thy son," indicating one of the disciples with his look. To the disciple he said, "Behold thy mother." But for Mary of Magdala he had no word!

They took his body down from the cross as the sun was slipping behind the western hills. It was Mary who wiped the blood from his brow; she it was who bound up his wounded hands; and it was Mary who stood at a distance and watched the soldiers affix the seal of Caesar to his tomb. Then she set out, alone, for the city and for the blackest night she ever lived through. Her own death would have been sweet in comparison with the tragic death of her dreams.

All that Sabbath she waited. Her heart was in the tomb with her Lord. The lamp of life which he had lighted for her so lately was gone out, leaving her with numbness of soul. He had opened unto her the heart of God. He had seemed the essence of life itself. *Now he was dead!*

Very early in the morning on the first day of the week, long before the slanting rays of the sun had tinted the eastern sky, Mary was down in the streets of Jerusalem, picking her way through the shadows in the direction of the rich man's garden, where her Lord's body lay. Spices for his burial she carried in a bundle next to her heart.

As she turned through the gate of the garden her heart suddenly went cold. The great stone was rolled away, and the tomb appeared empty! Rushing up and peering in, her worst fears were confirmed, and, with a dry sob, she sank, trembling, in a heap before the open grave.

How long she crouched there she never knew. And when she heard a footfall behind her, she did not look up, for she supposed it was only the gardener. Speaking to him, she said: "They have taken away my Lord, and I know not where they have laid him."

There was a moment of sacred silence, and then a voice she had learned to know as she knew her own thoughts said simply, *"Mary!"* It was the Prophet, her Lord, her Master, arisen and alive!

As Mary lifted her eyes and beheld the face of him who had broken her bonds and had given back her life, she knew but one word. It was the cry of the soul that surrenders everything unto God. And with that single word she hailed her risen Lord:

"Master!" [4]

POEM:

> I have seen Christ stand
> With hate on each hand
> And believe and love and die;
> I have seen Him alone
> Make the cross His throne,
> And hate and death crucify;
> And He lives in love victorious,
> Yes, He lives above all glorious,
> Christ lives forevermore.
>
> I have seen the gloom
> Of the garden tomb
> Where my Lord's form used to be;
> I have seen Him rise,
> Shaking earth and skies
> With His immortality!
> And because He lives we too shall live,
> Yes, because He lives we too shall live.
> We'll live forevermore.[5]

—CHAUNCEY R. PIETY

PRAYER:

Our Father, we become so involved with the complexity of living that we tend to lose perspective and confuse the purposes of life. We become so concerned with time that we forget eternity. Help us to see that the fullest meaning of this life is realized in the wider purposes of thy eternal kingdom. Increase our understanding of the relation between our present life and that life to come. May we see life today as more than meat and drink, and eternal life as more than duration.

Grant that thy thought and purpose may so permeate our being that we may discover thy will in personal matters, in social relations, in racial attitudes, and in economic problems, so that we shall build into our lives those qualities that are worthy to endure. Increase our determination to live as sons and daughters of thine, and may we finally grasp the significance of Christ's statement that eternal life consists in knowing thee, the only true God, and Jesus Christ, thy Son. Grant that we may find the deepest meaning of our lives in the eternal principles of goodness and truth, and may our hope in the world to come rest upon our faith in thee, and in a complete dedication to thy kingdom upon earth. We ask in Jesus' name. AMEN.

HYMN: "March On, O Soul, with Strength," or
      "Jesus Christ Is Risen Today."

BENEDICTION:

May we go from this service with a firmer faith in the unseen and eternal. AMEN.

SERVICE 14

HONORING A GREAT MOTHER
(*Mother's Day*)

PRELUDE: "Ave Maria" by Bach-Gounod.

CALL TO WORSHIP:

> From homes of quiet peace
> We lift up hands of prayer,
> And those thou gavest us to love
> Commend, Lord, to thy care.
>
> Let thine almighty arm
> Be their defense and shield;
> And whatsoever cause is thine
> To them the victory yield.
> —WILLIAM HENRY DRAPER

HYMN: "Rejoice, Ye Pure in Heart," or
"O Perfect Love."

SCRIPTURE:

Who can find a virtuous woman? for her price is far above rubies.

The heart of her husband doth safely trust in her, so that he shall have no need of spoil.

She will do him good and not evil all the days of her life.

Strength and honour are her clothing; and she shall rejoice in time to come.

She openeth her mouth with wisdom; and in her tongue is the law of kindness.

She looketh well to the ways of her household, and eateth not the bread of idleness.

HONORING A GREAT MOTHER

Her children arise up, and call her blessed; her husband also, and he praiseth her.

Many daughters have done virtuously, but thou excellest them all.

Favour is deceitful, and beauty is vain: but a woman that feareth the Lord, she shall be praised.

Give her of the fruit of her hands; and let her own works praise her in the gates.[1]

PRAYER:

> Good Father,
>> Parent of us all:
>>> Hear our prayer.
>
> For our rich heritage—
> For our pioneer parents—
> For Thy abounding love—
>> We give Thee thanks.
>
> Be ours—
>> With seeing eye,
>> The knowing mind,
>> And understanding heart—
> To build us homes
>> Where Thy grace rules,
>> Homes—
>>> After Thine own pattern.
>>>> Amen.[2]
>>>>> —EVERETT ARTHUR OVERTON

LEADER:

Thomas A. Edison said, "My mother was the making of me. She was so true and so sure of me. I felt that I had someone to live for—someone I must not disappoint. The memory of my mother will always be a blessing to me."

We will hear the story of a great mother who reared a family of unusual children whose influence reaches to our day.

STORY:

SUSANNAH WESLEY, A GREAT MOTHER

SUSANNAH WESLEY was a great mother, not only of her age but of any age. She was the favorite child of her father, Samuel Annesley, a noted clergyman of London. He taught her to read widely, to make up her mind, and to express herself on the questions of the day. Consequently at the age of twenty, when she married Samuel Wesley, an Oxford graduate, she continued to think for herself. She had poise, dignity, and courage, and on many occasions dared to disagree with her husband.

Eight years after their marriage the Wesleys moved to Epworth in Lincolnshire, where they lived for thirty-eight years. Samuel Wesley was a gentleman and a scholar, the author of a number of books. His many duties as minister of a large country parish kept him from giving much time to the rearing of their children. Susannah took care of the nineteen children born into their home, and managed to clothe and feed them on an income of about seven hundred dollars a year. Since she was the twenty-fifth child in her family, perhaps nineteen did not seem a large family to her.

Mrs. Wesley used firm discipline in bringing up her children. When they were one year old, they were taught to cry softly, if at all, and they learned this lesson so well that the noise of crying was seldom heard in the home. Their table manners were watched closely; they were not allowed to leave food on their plates or to eat between meals.

Mrs. Wesley considered the village schoolmaster crude and ignorant, so her children were not sent to public school. Her home was turned into a school for six hours every day except Sunday, and she was not only the teacher but also the writer of most of their textbooks. As soon as a child could speak, he was taught the Lord's Prayer, and later his own prayers were added, together with verses of Scripture. Mrs. Wesley took the education of her children seriously.

The fifth birthday was a great occasion in the life of each child. On that day the house was put in order, a task was assigned to each, and her attention was given to the new pupil. A child was expected to learn the entire alphabet on his first day in school, and all except two of them were able to do it. A child spent six hours daily in school after he passed his sixth birthday. She often remarked that it was incredible the amount a child could learn in three months if he was in good health and applied himself.

Mrs. Wesley has been criticized for the rigid rules which she set up for her household. Some have wondered if there was any fun in the Epworth parsonage. Time was set aside for play, but theirs was not a carefree childhood. It has been said that Methodism began when Susannah planned the rigid schedule of daily living which molded the lives of her children. She was the patient teacher and wise counselor of her children, for her husband's mind was occupied with the work of his parish. One day he remarked to her, "I wonder at your patience. You have told that child the same thing twenty times."

She replied, "Had I satisfied myself with only nineteen I should have lost all my labor. It was the twentieth time that crowned the whole."

Mrs. Wesley was as careful in the nurture of their religious life as in other aspects of their training. She set aside one hour each week for private conversation concerning the deeper things of the Spirit with each child. The success with which she carried out this part of their education may be seen in the pleasant memory that John had of these hours. While a student at Oxford he wrote asking her to keep for him that hour which had been his during his boyhood.

During family worship it was Samuel Wesley's custom to pray for the reigning king. One morning when his wife did not say "Amen" as she usually did when he reached that part of the prayer, he demanded the reason. She replied that her sympathy was with the absent Stuarts. With that he rushed out of the house, leaped upon his horse, and rode to London, where he remained until the death of the king nearly a year later. Trusting that they could agree upon the new queen, he returned home.

During her husband's absence on this occasion and at other times, Susannah Wesley gave religious instruction to the children of the parish, and also helped the women with their problems. Long before nursery schools and women's clubs had been thought of, she was conducting both in an efficient manner.

On a February night when fire destroyed their home, all of the children had been brought out safely except John. In the confusion he had been left on the second floor, and it was some time before his absence was noticed. Men stood on each other's shoulders, thus making a ladder, by means of which he was rescued. Susannah believed that his escape was miraculous, and, therefore, a sign that God had taken care of him because of special work which he would do later. She resolved to see that he was well prepared for this work.

Because she believed that he was destined for a divine mission, his mother followed John every step of the way. A scholarship enabled him at the age of ten to enroll at the famous Charterhouse School, where he prepared for college. Later when he was graduated from Christ's Church, Oxford, he was offered a professorship which enabled him to support his parents in their old age.

Mrs. Wesley's success in the training of her children gives her an enviable place among the great mothers of the world. Her children were among the most remarkable in England, and their prominence may be attributed to their early training, which firmly built their characters. It was her sacrifice and planning which enabled her sons to secure an education equal to that of the most favored of their times. The daughters, educated at home, numbered among their friends Samuel Johnson and other literary personages of their day.

It may have been Mrs. Wesley's love for the simple country folk of Epworth and her efforts to help them that inspired John to spend his life ministering to the laboring people of England. Her courage may have helped him to make the decision to go to America to serve as a minister in Oglethorpe's colony in Georgia. When John inquired of her whether he should put the ocean between them, she replied, "Had I twenty sons, I should rejoice that they were all so employed, though I never saw them more."

At her husband's death Mrs. Wesley made her home with John in the tall red-brick parsonage beside City Road Chapel in London. Her wisdom may be seen in many instances when John sought her counsel as he channeled the religious movement for which he was largely responsible. The early class meetings, so valuable in the beginning of Methodism, were similar to the meetings which she held in the Epworth parsonage. When John returned from his preaching tours, he frequently found her in the little six-by-ten prayer room seeking guidance from a higher source, and doubtless her prayers helped him to become the great leader that he was.

She made this request of John during her last illness, "When I am released, sing a hymn of praise to God." John committed her body to the soil of England upon which she had lived so eagerly and labored so zealously. She lived long enough to see the religious movement which he had started spread over Great Britain and finally reach America.

Susannah Wesley was a pioneer of her day when the contributions of women were considered to be of little value. She directed the energy that she found in her nursery and used it to send messengers to every hamlet of her land, to light the slums of every city with a shining light, and to make a hundred thousand lives that had seemed cold and lifeless glow with the warmth of a new fire. Her place in history is secure, for few women of the eighteenth century rendered greater service than she.[3]

HONORING A GREAT MOTHER

For others she may not be fair—
Her furrowed cheeks, her faded hair;
To me she is a treasure rare,
  My Mother.

Her charm how can I but confess!
For there's no other face can bless,
And keep my heart from loneliness,
As that dear face
  Of Mother!

So long ago for Mother, young,
The wedding bells were gaily rung;
So long ago glad songs were sung
  For Mother;

And still, to me, she's worthy quite
Of all that's lovely, sweet, and bright.
She's queen today, by her own right,
Queen of my heart,
  My Mother.[4]

—THOMAS CURTIS CLARK

LITANY OF THANKS:

Leader: For the great mothers of all ages and of all men,

Group: We give thee thanks, our Father.

Leader: For the patience and understanding of our own mothers,

Group: We return our thanks to thee, O God.

Leader: For their love which never failed,

Group: We are indeed thankful.

Leader: For their vision which they shared with us, their faith in our accomplishments, and their encouragement in all our undertakings,

Group: We give thee thanks.

Leader: For their sacrifice and all the benefits which have come to us because of their self-denial,

Group: We are grateful.

Leader: Help us to live so that every motive and action of our lives shall honor thee and our mothers,

Group: In Jesus' name we pray. AMEN.

HYMN: "Happy the Home When God Is There," or
"Lord of Life and King of Glory."

BENEDICTION:

May we in every thought and deed of our lives honor those whom we love. AMEN.

SERVICE 15

ATTEMPT GREAT THINGS FOR GOD
(*Mission Sunday*)

PRELUDE: Hymn tune "Tidings."

CALL TO WORSHIP:

> O Master of the waking world,
>> Who hast the nations in thy heart—
> The heart that bled and broke to send
>> God's love to earth's remotest part:
> Show us anew in Calvary
> The wondrous power that makes men free.
>> —FRANK MASON NORTH

INVOCATION:

Our Father, we thank thee that all people of every race are included in thy plan of salvation. We are grateful that we have heard the gospel message and are eager to share these truths which have enriched our lives. Inspire us to give of our time, our talents, and ourselves to advance thy kingdom throughout the earth. In Jesus' name. AMEN.

HYMN:

> Far through the night when nations groping blindly
>> Long for the morning of another day,
> Only the radiance from a living Savior
>> Glows in the darkness on our broken way.

Refrain:

> Bringing the weary light and release,
> Waking the nations unto the God of peace.

Not of despair shall be the final story.
Lo, from thy hearts must rise a mighty shout!
Eternal Love will lift His wings victorious
When men shall cleave the chrysalis of doubt.

Lift up thine eyes. Behold the risen Jesus
Walking today where only Hope has trod.
Dare to proclaim an ever-living Savior!
Call ye the world unto the Christ of God.[1]

—LUCILE SHANKLIN HULL

RESPONSIVE READING:

Leader: Jesus saith unto his disciples, The harvest truly is plenteous, but the labourers are few;

Group: Pray ye therefore the Lord of the harvest, that he will send forth labourers into his harvest.

Leader: Other sheep I have, which are not of this fold: them also I must bring, and they shall hear my voice; and there shall be one fold, and one shepherd.

Group: They shall come from the east, and from the west, and from the north, and from the south, and shall sit down in the kingdom of God.

Leader: And Jesus came and spake unto them, saying, All power is given unto me in heaven and in earth.

Group: Go ye therefore, and teach all nations, baptizing them in the name of the Father, and of the Son, and of the Holy Ghost:

Leader: Teaching them to observe all things whatsoever I have commanded you:

Group: And, lo, I am with you always, even unto the end of the world.[2]

HYMN: "We've a Story to Tell to the Nations."

LEADER:

Jesus called a group of men to leave all and follow him. As he lived with them, they were filled with his spirit and felt compelled to tell the good news of the gospel to those who did not know about it. Having been with Christ, they had something in their hearts to pass on to others.

The early missionaries had a message to tell, and they overcame much opposition in order to carry on their work. We will hear the story of one of the early leaders who did not allow anything to keep him from carrying out the great commission.

STORY:

ATTEMPT GREAT THINGS FOR GOD

"ATTEMPT great things for God; expect great things from God," was more than a vague kind of motto for William Carey; it was his daily challenge and constant inspiration. His life revealed how closely related were this faith and courage. One could not have dared to do such great things, except for God; nor could one have accomplished them, except through his help. The events in Carey's early life bore striking testimony, and were prophetic of days to come.

When Carey was ordained a minister at the age of twenty-six, he was already employed as a shoemaker. He continued his trade for six years to support himself, because his salary as a minister was so meager. During this time he became interested in the Great Commission of Jesus, "Go ye into all the world, and preach the gospel to every creature." While he worked at the cobbler's job, he kept an open Bible on the bench before him and a map of the world on the wall.

When people came into Carey's shop, he talked to them about the people of the world and his hope of taking the gospel to them. He taught himself Latin, Greek, and Hebrew, and studied the Bible in the original languages. So thorough was his job of self-teaching that he was given still another job—that of teaching school. Though he had three jobs—teaching school during the day, working at the cobbler's bench at night, and preaching on Sunday—his one all-consuming desire was to interest Christians in a plan to "preach the gospel to every living creature."

Carey was able finally to interest twelve Baptist ministers in missions, and in 1792 organized the Baptist Missionary Society. It was such a personal thing with him that the next year he offered himself as a missionary. After overcoming incredible difficulties, he and his family sailed to Bengal. There was only one place in India open to missionaries—Serampore, an inland village about twelve miles from Calcutta. It was here that he settled and began his work.

Still other obstacles and difficulties confronted Carey. At the end of the first year his son had died, his wife was ill, and his money was gone. The people he had come to help were still afraid of him, and the East India Company ordered him either to leave India or to make his stay legal by working for them. Undaunted, Carey took a job in an indigo factory.

This seeming obstacle was a blessing in disguise. It offered him a means of supporting himself and also gave him a chance to study Bengali, the language of the people. He was surprised to discover that this language, so expressive in many ways, when spoken by the laboring class contained no such words as love, mercy, and kindness. He later discovered that their contact with him was their first experience of kindness at the hands of a white man.

At the close of seven years the result of Carey's labor was only one convert, but during this time he had translated the Bible into Bengali. A secondhand press was donated to him, but after he put it in condition the East India Company forbade him to use it. Yet he could not give up his plan of making the Bible known to the people of India. While he was debating what to do, a ship from England brought him the message that two recruits, Ward and Marshman, were coming to assist him. One was a printer and the other a schoolmaster. Carey took hope again. Before the East India Company could take action against his printing program, the assistants had come and they had begun their work.

At the turn of the century new hope was born and a new program was inaugurated. Carey secured permission from the governor of Serampore to set up a Christian community. On a dramatic date, January 1, 1800, Carey and his assistants set up a co-operative home. They lived as one family, had one purpose, one common goal—the printing of the Bible in the tongues of the East. To support themselves Marshman and his wife opened a paper mill and a printing press, while Carey worked on the translations. Within fifteen months the first New Testament in Bengali came from the press.

Carey was appointed professor of the Bengali, Mahratta, and Sanskrit languages in the government college at Fort William, near Calcutta. He held this position for thirty years, and it gave him a marvelous opportunity to win for Christ the young men who were destined to be the future leaders of India. The Christian community prospered in spite of the ban against missionaries. Within five years there were eight families in the group.

In a short while the Marshmans were earning annually five thousand dollars. Out of this two hundred dollars was spent for living expenses; Ward kept out a like amount from the earnings from the press, and Carey a similar amount from his teaching. The remainder of their combined earnings went into the expansion of the mission, enlargement of the press, and the employment of translators and language teachers.

Scholars sent their works to Carey for printing, and type was cast in the various tongues of the East. He published the first newspaper in any Oriental language, and an English magazine entitled *Friends of India*. He printed over 200,000 copies of the Bible in nearly forty different languages and dialects.

Up to this time the Bible was read by only the middle and lower class Hindus. The high caste Brahmans seemed to think that Sanskrit, the literary language of India, was the only appropriate language for a sacred book. One day while looking over the Mahratta and Gujerati languages, Carey noticed their similarity to Sanskrit, and it seemed to him that he had discovered the key to the fifteen major languages and dialects of the East. He appealed to the Baptist Missionary Society for $5,000 a year to translate and print the Bible into these languages. At once $6,500 was raised in Great Britain and $3,500 in the United States. Later the British Foreign Bible Society was organized and donated $100 per month for the work.

About this time, during Carey's absence from the city, a fire destroyed the printing press, all equipment, and the translations of the Bible in ten different languages. The loss was estimated at $50,000. When Carey returned, his fellow workmen expected him to be utterly discouraged. But he said, "We shall improve the translations lost. Traveling a road the second time is done with greater ease and certainty." As the news of the disaster spread, sympathy arose in England, and within fifty days they raised $50,000 to rebuild the plant. Within a year the press was running more efficiently than ever.

The next blow came when Ward was stricken with cholera and died. Carey and his associates were saddened, but they went ahead and accomplished an amazing amount of work. With their earnings they built a Christian college at a cost of $75,000. In the college they trained the first Indian ministers, introduced medical science to the Orient, and provided the first school for Indian girls.

When Carey died, June 9, 1834, government flags of British India were at half mast in honor of the man the British had tried to banish from their country forty-one years before. This humble workman's motto, "Attempt great things for God; expect great things from God," had carried him through many trying situations and brought marked success. He is credited with establishing a total of 126 schools, 26 churches, and 30 missions. He and his associates contributed over $450,000 in their attempt to carry out the Great Commission, "Go ye into all the world, and preach the gospel to every creature." He was buried with royal honors and mourned by princes, high officials, scholars, and people in every walk of life, not only in the country he served, but throughout the world.

POEM:

> Use me, God, in Thy great harvest field,
> Which stretcheth far and wide like a wide sea;
> The gatherers are so few; I fear the precious yield
> Will suffer loss. Oh, find a place for me!
> A place where best the strength I have will tell:
> It may be one the older toilers shun;
> Be it a wide or narrow place, 'tis well
> So that the work it holds be only done.
>
> —CHRISTINA G. ROSSETTI

PRAYER:

Our Father, we thank thee for the inspiration that has come to us from the dedicated lives of the workers in thy vineyard, especially for the missionaries today who are carrying the teachings of our Lord to those who are still in darkness. May the same spirit of courage, patience, and faith which dominates them be in our lives. Make us eager to have a part in sharing the gospel with the people around the world. Inspire us with the urgent need for more laborers in the mission fields, and may we be more zealous in our efforts to support them with our means and our prayers. In the name of thy Son we pray. AMEN.

HYMN: "The Voice of God Is Calling," or
"The Morning Light Is Breaking."

BENEDICTION:

May thy Spirit, our Father, guide thy children and unite them in their effort to carry the gospel to all persons of every country. AMEN.

SERVICE 16

SPREAD THE LIGHT
(*Mission Sunday*)

PRELUDE: "Evening Song" by Schumann.

CALL TO WORSHIP:

> O thou, by whom we come to God,
> The Life, the Truth, the Way;
> The path of prayer thyself hast trod;
> Lord, teach us how to pray.
> —JAMES MONTGOMERY

SCRIPTURE:

These twelve Jesus sent forth, and commanded them, saying, Go not into the way of the Gentiles, and into any city of the Samaritans enter ye not: but go rather to the lost sheep of the house of Israel. And as ye go, preach, saying, The kingdom of heaven is at hand.

From the rising of the sun even unto the going down of the same my name shall be great among the Gentiles; . . . for my name shall be great among the heathen, saith the Lord of hosts.

The Lord hath made known his salvation: his righteousness hath he openly showed in the sight of the heathen.

The Gentiles shall come to thy light, and kings to the brightness of thy rising.[1]

POEM:

> There is darkness still, gross darkness, Lord,
> On this fair earth of Thine.
> There are prisoners still in the prison-house,
> Where never a light doth shine.

There are doors still bolted against Thee,
There are faces set like a wall;
And over them all the Shadow of Death
Hangs like a pall.

Do you hear the voices calling,
Out there in the black of the night?
Do you hear the sobs of the women,
Who are barred from the blessed light?
And the children—the little children—
Do you hear their pitiful cry?
O, brothers, we must seek them,
Or there in the dark they die!

Spread the Light! Spread the Light!
Till earth's remotest bounds have heard
The glory of the Living Word;
Till those that see not have their sight;
Till all the fringes of the night
Are lifted, and the long-closed doors
Are wide forever to the Light.
Spread—the—Light!

O then shall dawn the golden days,
To which true hearts are pressing;
When earth's discordant strains shall blend—
The one true God confessing;
When Christly thought and Christly deed
Shall bind each heart and nation,
In one Grand Brotherhood of Men,
And one high consecration.[2]

—JOHN OXENHAM

HYMN: "Heralds of Christ," or
        "O Zion, Haste."

LITANY OF SUPPLICATION:
Leader: O thou who art the Father of us all,
Group: Help us to realize that men of all races are thy children.
Leader: O thou who art the Light of the world and of all men,

Group: Shine in the dark places of our lives that we may see every man in his true light, as a brother.

Leader: O thou Spirit of Truth,

Group: Help us to banish the hatred and prejudice which separate us one from another and divide us as races and nations.

Leader: O thou who didst make of one blood all nations of men,

Group: Unite our hearts in one great brotherhood that we may live together in peace.

Leader: O thou our elder Brother,

Group: Help us to rid ourselves of complacency toward wrongs and injustices from which others suffer.

Leader: O thou Spirit of God,

Group: Hasten the day when Christlike thoughts and brotherly deeds shall bind all races and nations in perfect peace as one great family of thy children. We pray in the name and spirit of Jesus Christ our Lord. AMEN.

LEADER:

We will hear the story of Judson, one of the first missionaries to Burma, who made the Bible known to those who were in darkness and lifted from slavery those who were oppressed. "They that be wise shall shine as the brightness of the firmament; and they that turn many to righteousness as the stars for ever and ever."

STORY:

ADONIRAM JUDSON, MISSIONARY TO BURMA

ADONIRAM JUDSON, the son of a Congregational minister, was a precocious child. He could read at three years of age, and was graduated from college at nineteen. While in college he became interested in French deism, a popular belief at that time on American campuses. According to this belief there is a God—or some ultimate cause—who set the universe going, but who is too far removed to have any significance for the individual. It denies that the Bible is a special revelation or that the Christian religion is valid. Eaton, a student at college, was active in promoting this belief, and Judson, attracted to him, spent many hours discussing the advantage of deism and the folly of the Christian religion.

After finishing college Judson set out to live in his own way, free from any restraint by his parents. After teaching one year, he joined a company of traveling players and fell in with their irresponsible way of living. They contrived somehow to get away from each place where they played without paying for their lodging. Judson was not satisfied with this manner of living, and after a few weeks left them and headed west, still with no definite plan in view.

On the first night he stopped at a country inn. The landlord showing him to his room, apologized for placing him next door to a man seriously ill. While lying awake listening to the groans from the adjoining room, Judson wondered about the sick man. Was he a Christian, calm and strong in his faith, or was he an unbeliever, facing a dark, unknown future? The next morning Judson learned that the young man had died, and when he inquired as to his identity, he found that it was Eaton, his freethinking classmate.

Following this, Judson spent some time thinking about his manner of living. It was evident that he was trying to be something that he was not, and to believe something that he knew to be false. He became convinced that the Christian way was the only satisfactory way of living. He had known this all along but for some reason had fought against it. Returning home he discussed the matter with his father and entered Andover Theological Seminary as a ministerial student.

Shortly afterwards Judson volunteered as a missionary to the Far East. At that time the Protestant churches in America had no mission work abroad. At a conference at Bradford, Massachusetts, young Judson told of his dedication and inquired, "Should I appeal to the London Missionary Society for support, or look to my own denomination?" The ministers were so impressed by his earnestness that immediately they organized the first foreign mission society in America.

In February, 1812, Judson married Ann Hasseltine and sailed for Calcutta. On the voyage they discussed baptism and decided to join the Baptist Church. Upon their arrival in India they were baptized by William Ward, the English missionary. This led the American Baptists to organize a Foreign Mission Society and agree to support the young missionary.

The Judsons had expected to work in British India, but instead were sent to Burma in a slow sailing vessel, the voyage lasting for nearly a year, during which time their first child died. Landing in Rangoon at the rainy season, it seemed to them a swamp surrounded by a jungle teeming with snakes and wild beasts.

Judson began his study of the Burmese language under trying conditions. Not only was he persecuted, but those who helped with the translation of the Bible were threatened with death. After working six years he had only three converts and the translation of the Gospel of Matthew to show for his labor. The slow progress led him to decide to appeal directly to the king; for royal favor, however capricious it might be, was highly desirable for his work.

The trip to the residence of the king by inland waters took thirty-five days. Judson entered the palace grounds through an alabaster gate, climbed marble stairs, walked through doors set with jewels, along corridors of ebony, and into a throne room with pillars covered with gold. He was impressed by the wealth in the king's palace as compared to the poverty of the people.

The king, seated on a cushioned dais, inquired, "Who is this?"

Before the interpreter could reply, Judson answered, "A teacher, great king."

The king inquired, "You speak Burmese? Are you a teacher of religion?"

Judson replied, "Yes," and asked for the privilege of teaching. He handed a tract to the king, who read, "There is one eternal God; besides him there is no other." He ordered Judson dismissed.

Returning to Rangoon, Judson decided to move his mission as soon as he had ten converts and a native teacher to leave with them. He completed the translation of Ephesians and sent it with the Gospel of Matthew to Serampore, India, to be printed.

When Dr. Jonathan Price came to assist Judson, the king ordered them to report to him at Ava. While there Judson preached to the people and Dr. Price healed the sick. The king became interested enough to grant them a tract of land for a new mission. Judson built a church in Ava, started a school for girls, and completed his translation of the New Testament.

Judson took no part in the British-Burmese war which broke out, but was seized as an enemy alien and sent to prison. Fearing that his translation of the New Testament would be destroyed by the enemy, he asked that it be brought to him. To hide its identity his wife wrapped it with palm leaves and made it into a pillow. When removed from the prison eleven months later, Judson begged so for the pillow that the jailor concluded that he had lost his mind.

Judson was sent to the death house, where he spent seven months, daily expecting to be executed. At last an order came from the king for him to report to the Burmese camp, where he woud act as interpreter in the peace negotiations.

At the close of the war Judson and his wife returned to Rangoon to find their mission destroyed. The faithful converts gathered around Judson, grateful that he had been spared. One of them told of visiting his prison, only to learn that he had been removed. However, he begged for any article which the missionary had used and was given the dirty pillow which he returned to Judson, who was delighted to find his translation in good condition.

At last Judson was with his wife and his child, but his troubles were not ended. Shortly afterwards while he was in Ava on business for the mission, his wife and child died of fever. In his sorrow he turned to the Psalms for comfort and found that he could translate with a keener understanding because of his recent experience.

During his thirty-five years as a missionary, book after book poured from his pen. He translated the entire Bible in Burmese and compiled an English-Burmese dictionary. He lived to see the Christian religion spread in Burma until there were over 7,000 converts, 183 pastors, and 63 churches. At his death the story of Judson's patience as he worked for converts and his faithfulness in trying situations was made known throughout the English-speaking world, with the result that many workers were inspired to take up the work which he had laid down.

LEADER:

The offering will be used to carry on some of the mission projects in which our church is engaged.

OFFERTORY:

> We give thee but thine own,
> Whate'er the gift may be:
> All that we have is thine alone,
> A trust, O Lord, from thee.
> —WILLIAM W. HOW

HYMN:

> The gleaming wings that cleave the sky,
> The mighty planes that roar
> On errands over seven seas
> Shall carry fear no more,
> But bring the bonds of brotherhood
> From shore to shining shore.

Glad voices too will hasten out
 Upon the waiting air
When hearts are filled with faith and hope,
 When souls are brave to dare
Proclaim the tidings of good will
 To all men everywhere.

As eagles rise to meet the sun
 So let our spirits prove
That Christ the Lord alone can lift
 The souls of men above
Conflicting clouds of human life
 To serve the God of Love.[3]
      —LUCILE SHANKLIN HULL

PRAYER:

O Christ, thou hast bidden us pray for the coming of thy Father's kingdom, in which his righteous will shall be done on earth. We have treasured thy words, but we have forgotten their meaning, and thy great hope has grown dim in thy Church. We bless thee for the inspired souls of all ages who saw afar the shining city of God, and by faith left the profit of the present to follow their vision. We rejoice that to-day the hope of these lonely hearts is becoming the clear faith of millions. Help us, O Lord, in the courage of faith to seize what has now come so near, that the glad day of God may dawn at last. As we have mastered Nature that we might gain wealth, help us now to master the social relations of mankind that we may gain justice and a world of brothers. For what shall it profit our nation if it gain numbers and riches, and lose the sense of the living God and the joy of human brotherhood?

Make us determined to live by truth and not by lies, to found our common life on the eternal foundations of righteousness and love, and no longer to prop the tottering house of wrong by legalized cruelty and force. Help us to make the welfare of all the supreme law of our land, that so our commonwealth may be built strong and secure on the love of all its citizens. Cast down the throne of Mammon who ever grinds the life of men, and set up thy throne, O Christ, for thou didst die that man might live. Show thy erring children at last the way from the City of Destruction to the City of Love, and fulfil the longings of

—115—

the prophets of humanity. Our Master, once more we make thy faith our prayer: "Thy kingdom come! Thy will be done on earth!" [4]

BENEDICTION:

Grant that we may go from this service with a strong determination to consecrate our time, our talents, and our gifts to the spread of the good news of salvation to all people everywhere. AMEN.

SERVICE 17

NOT WHERE YOU LIVE BUT HOW
(*Race Relations Sunday*)

PRELUDE: Hymn tune "Germany."

CALL TO WORSHIP:

> All men are my kin,
> Since every man has been
> Blood of my blood;
> I glory in the grace
> And strength of every race,
> And joy in every trace
> Of brotherhood.
> —AUTHOR UNKNOWN

HYMN: "O Jesus, Master, When Today," or
"Where Cross the Crowded Ways of Life."

SCRIPTURE:

God that made the world and all things therein, seeing that he is Lord of heaven and earth, dwelleth not in temples made with hands; neither is worshipped with men's hands, as though he needed any thing, seeing he giveth to all life, and breath, and all things; and hath made of one blood all nations of men for to dwell on all the face of the earth, and hath determined the times before appointed, and the bounds of their habitation; that they should seek the Lord, if haply they might feel after him, and find him, though he be not far from every one of us.

And they shall come from the east, and from the west, and from the north, and from the south, and shall sit down in the kingdom of God.

There is no difference between the Jew and the Greek: for the same Lord over all is rich unto all that call upon him.

As ye would that men should do to you, do ye also to them likewise.

Inasmuch as ye have done it unto one of the least of these my brethren, ye have done it unto me.[1]

PRAYER:

O God, Thy love unites men in brotherhood and common purposes. In love for Thee we would draw closer to youth of all races, creeds, and lands, and we would study the problems of life together and jointly seek for truth and light. . . . As we prepare for leadership in the days that are to come, may we do our part to banish war and strife and hate. May we settle our differences with calmness and love, and may we strengthen each other for the tasks that lie ahead. Make us worthy of friendships everywhere, and may these help to make our communities, our state, and our nation better. May this spirit of friendship dominate our churches and societies that we may better serve Thee and hasten the coming of Thy kingdom, for Jesus' sake. AMEN.[2]

POEM:

> Brother is a dangerous word
>   When planted in your heart,
> 'Twill flame and burn with terror
>   Until you dare your part.
>
> Brother is a dangerous word
>   Where hate and envy rule,
> 'Twill make a peaceful Christian
>   Become God's fighting fool.[3]
>
> —CHAUNCEY R. PIETY

HYMN: "O Master Workman of the Race," or
   "Lord, for Tomorrow and Its Needs."

LEADER:

Our church helps to support schools and colleges for the education of Negroes. On Race Relations Sunday we have an opportunity to contribute to this worthy cause.[4]

OFFERTORY:

We bring our gifts to thee, remembering the gift of thy Son, and as we offer our gifts we offer our lives in consecration to thy Cause. AMEN.

Poem:

> If every Christian were Christlike
> And none were biased or blind,
> We would follow but truth and adventure
> On the trail of the Infinite Mind.
>
> If every Christian were Christlike,
> Without injustice or hate,
> Our love and good will would be mighty,
> Rebuilding mankind and the state.
>
> If every Christian were Christlike,
> All the evil could not divide
> One Lord, one faith, one Spirit,
> One kingdom built world-wide.[5]
>
> —Chauncey R. Piety

Story:

BOXCAR NUMBER 9

Ted and George were taking a short cut across the railroad tracks. It was the quickest way to get to the athletic field at Jefferson Junior High.

"Look!" grinned Ted, calling attention to something that was happening in front of a line of boxcars that stood beside the tracks farther down.

"Boxcar Number 9," smiled George, as he recognized the boy with flying black hair who was springing over the line of improvised hurdles made by stacking dry-goods boxes.

It was Manuel Serrano, the Mexican boy, who sat in the same classroom at Jefferson High that Ted and George did. It was in that room that the black-haired Mexican boy got his nickname. When Miss White, the teacher, asked for the home address of each pupil, Manuel gave "Boxcar Number 9" as the place where he lived. The queer address surprised the class, and there was a sudden giggle. The nickname lasted. Everyone referred to Manuel now as "Boxcar Number 9."

"Shucks!" said George, looking up the long line of boxcars where the Mexican families lived. "I'd hate to have to live in a boxcar, wouldn't you?"

"Yeah, I suppose I would," Ted answered slowly. "But where a person lives isn't so important either. It's what a person is that really

—119—

counts. Well . . . isn't that what the speaker said at convocation the other day?" demanded Ted defensively.

"Oh, that fellow," said George, remembering. "But he wasn't talking about boxcars, was he? He said that someone who was born in a little log cabin might become great. Like Abraham Lincoln, you know."

"Yes, but he said, too, that . . . say, we'll be late for practice if we don't hurry."

Jefferson Junior High had a field meet each spring with Slayton School and Blake Junior High, competing with them for a pennant. The meet was only a week off now. Practice time was getting short. Coming in sight of the athletic field, Ted and George saw Max Thornton springing over hurdles. Practice had begun.

While waiting for their turn to run in the short dashes, Ted and George started thinking about the Mexican boy again. Manuel should really be in the hurdle race at the meet, they said. He could run like a streak and was a whiz at sailing over hurdles.

"Guess he didn't have a track suit at first and that's one of the rules," remarked Ted.

"There's another reason, too," nodded George wisely. "Everyone wants Max to have the hurdle race this year. He made second place last year, you know, with Brown of Slayton getting first."

"What's that?" broke in a voice. It was Max, coming to the benches where the boys waited for turns at practice.

"We were talking about Boxcar Number 9," grinned George. "We came across the tracks and saw those old boxcars where the Mexicans live. Do you know that . . ."

"Sure, I know where Manuel lives," broke in Max. "But what difference does that make? The Mexicans had to move into those boxcars when they came here to work in the beets. There wasn't any other place. But you should see the inside of the boxcar where Manuel lives. It's fixed up like a real home with Mexican pictures on the wall and the American flag high up in front. Oh, Manuel is a swell guy," emphasized Max. "And it makes me mad when . . ."

A voice interrupted. The coach was calling the boys for the next race.

"Boy!" exclaimed George half to himself as he started off. It was a queer thing though, he thought. Max Thornton lived on the lakeshore road in a big house with a stone front. Yet Max went to see the Mexican boy in a boxcar, and he was even insisting now that it didn't make any difference where a person lived.

"I didn't know that Max and Boxcar Number 9 were pals," George called across to Ted.

"Evidently," smiled Ted. "And Manuel must be a great guy if Max thinks so. For Max is a square shooter."

"Of course," admitted George. "If Max weren't, the whole school wouldn't be counting the way it is on having him win the hurdle race."

Two days before the field meet Max landed in a heap as he sprang over one of the hurdles in practice. He turned his ankle in landing. But it didn't appear to be a serious injury. The coach tied up Max's ankle and said it would probably be as good as new by morning.

The next afternoon there was a surprise. Coming out to practice at the athletic field, Ted and George saw a tall boy with flying black hair sailing over a hurdle.

"Well, if it isn't Boxcar Number 9," exclaimed George.

The news flew everywhere. Max's ankle showed evidence of a sprain, and the Mexican boy was to take his place in the hurdle race on Saturday.

"The only trouble is that practice time is too short," said a senior who had been talking with the coach.

"Anyway I'll say the Mexican boy is a good sport," put in another. "He knows we didn't want him to have Max's place in the hurdles in the first place. Now he's willing to do the best he can for the school . . . with only a half chance."

With blaring of horns and waving of banners, the three schools gathered for the field meet on Saturday. The girl cheer leaders, in gay sweaters, gathered in groups in front of the school sections.

When the time came for the last race, the hurdle, Jefferson High and Slayton were far ahead of Blake, and the two schools were leading with a tied score. The hurdle would decide which school would carry home the pennant. Brown of Slayton went over the first line of hurdles with Norman of Blake. The Mexican boy was close behind. But at the second line Manuel struck a hurdle and went down on his knee. Brown of Slayton went over the third line of hurdles ahead. The crowd was breathless. Then in going over the last line of hurdles, Manuel passed Norman of Blake. The Mexican was only a little behind Brown of Slayton now. Suddenly there was a great roar of applause from Jefferson High. Manuel, going like a streak now, was a step ahead of Brown of Slayton.

"Manny! Manny! Manny!" cried Jefferson School, making up a new nickname as the Mexican boy crossed the line first and won the pennant for his school. In a matter of minutes Manuel was being carried off on the shoulders of the boys.

"Do you know what a fellow from Slayton School said?" asked a boy in the group where Ted and George and Max had been cheering with the rest. "He'd heard what a good sport the Mexican boy was and he said he wished they could persuade him to go to . . ."

"No chance!" broke in Max. "Manuel has made a place for himself here at Jefferson."

On the way home that night a small boy from a lower grade joined Ted and George and Max. "I know the name of the fellow they carried around," boasted the boy wisely. "Boxcar Number 9. He lives in an old boxcar over there."

"Well, what difference does that make?" George stopped abruptly. He was remembering something. For a minute George whistled meditatively. Then, turning to Ted and Max, he said with a wise grin, "Where a person lives is not so important, after all, as some people think it is." [6]

POEM:

It is not so much *where* you live,
As *how,* and *why,* and *when* you live,
That answers in the affirmative,
Or maybe in the negative,
The question—Are you fit to live?

It is not so much *where* you live,
As *how* you live, and whether good
Flows from you through your neighbourhood.

And *why* you live, and whether you
Aim high and noblest ends pursue,
And keep Life brimming full and true.

And *when* you live, and whether Time
Is at its nadir or its prime,
And whether you descend or climb.

It is not so much *where* you live,
As whether while you live you *live*
And to the world your highest give,
And so make answer positive
That you are truly fit to live. [7]

—JOHN OXENHAM

NOT WHERE YOU LIVE BUT HOW

Our Father, we thank thee for the light of thy truth which illumines our way. Help us to learn from the example of Jesus the importance of friendliness and full respect for personality of every person we contact. Help us to think of persons of every race as brothers and to show them the same consideration that we would expect. If we have neglected or failed to be friendly to anyone, or if we have caused any member of a minority group to suffer, forgive us. If there be pride, egotism, prejudice, hatred, or selfishness, banish these faults from us, and enable us to live by the best that we know. We realize that it is not where we live, or what we possess, but it is our attitudes, motives, and desires that are important. May thy Spirit guide us as we strive to strengthen the bonds of friendship between races and nations. In the name of our Master. AMEN.

HYMN: "Truehearted, Wholehearted, Faithful and Loyal," or
      "We May Not Climb the Heavenly Steeps."

BENEDICTION:

Guide us as we strive to build into our lives the Christian qualities which are worthy to endure. AMEN.

SERVICE 18

MAKING THE BIBLE KNOWN
(*Universal Bible Sunday*)

PRELUDE: Hymn tune "Burlington."

CALL TO WORSHIP:

> We search the world for truth. We cull
> The good, the true, the beautiful,
> From graven stone and written scroll,
> And all old flower-fields of the soul;
> And, weary seekers of the best,
> We come back laden from our quest,
> To find that all the sages said
> Is in the Book our mothers read.
> —JOHN GREENLEAF WHITTIER

HYMN: "O Word of God Incarnate," or
"Wonderful Words of Life."

RESPONSIVE READING:

Leader: Thy word is a lamp unto my feet, and a light unto my path.

Group: Lord of all power and might,
  Father of love and light,
Speed on thy Word!
  O let the gospel sound
All the wide world around,
  Wherever man is found!
God speed his Word.

Leader: Thy word have I hid in mine heart, that I might not sin against thee.

—124—

Group: Lo, what embattled foes,
   Stern in their hate, oppose
God's holy Word!
   One for his truth we stand,
Strong in his own right hand,
   Firm as a martyr-band:
God shield his Word!

Leader: I will meditate in thy precepts, and have respect unto thy
ways. I will delight myself in thy statutes: I will not forget thy
word.

Group: Onward shall be our course,
   Despite all fraud and force;
God is before.
   His words ere long shall run
Free as the noon-day sun;
   His purpose must be done:
God bless his Word![1]

—HUGH STOWELL

PRAYER:

Our Father, we thank thee for the gift of thy Word and for the
privileges which have come to us because of its message. Forgive us
for our slowness in sharing the Bible with those who are still in darkness. Speak to each of us at this time and reveal to us ways in which we
can help to make the Bible known throughout the world. In Jesus'
name. AMEN.

READING:

I am Your Bible.

I am a book for young people.

Youth marches across my pages. Young blood surges in my words.
Only the hopes of youth could keep in step with the limitless reach of
my dreams.

My heroic characters were young—Adam and Eve in the garden;
Moses, lifting his hand in angered enthusiasm for his people; David,
springing from his shepherd's task to the throne; Jesus, my central
figure, maturing his life purpose at twelve and carrying it to its supreme climax at only thirty—these were the age of you.

The vast movements portrayed in my pages are akin with the spirit
of youth—migrations of whole peoples in search of a better life and a

purer religion; prophetic and sacrificial campaigns for purging a na
tion's life; the launching of a new religion by a group of a dozen men
still young, under a leader younger than most of them; the dream of a
new Jerusalem where sorrow and crying are to be no more—these are
the enterprises that young people dream and dare.

Thus I am your book.

And so upon you I stake my best chance for changing the life of
your world.

I am Your Bible.[2]

HYMN: "Book of Books, Our People's Strength."

STORY:

GET ME THAT BOOK!

BISHOP OLDHAM, a native of India, related this incident at a student
conference at Silver Bay, New York:

I, a Christian, living in India, a surveyor employed by the government, was sent to survey the desert of Rajputana in the Northwest. I
entered the desert with the necessary equipment. When night came on
I would send a message to the little oases; my servants would go and
say, "Our master will be here and after the evening meal he wants to
see you."

They knew that I was an official of the government, and perhaps
there was a suspicion that I had a government message.

When the time came I stepped out of the tent, and there were the
people. There was a silvery moon, dropping such light as is seen nowhere else as in the tropics. And there were the people, all men. Looking out on that company I was strangely moved. I was six weeks out
in the desert, 180 miles from a town in any direction. Those who were
listening to me had probably never once heard the name of Jesus.
There is a certain high tension of spirit, a certain sense of tremendous
responsibility, accompanied with a certain profound gladness, when
you feel that those who are listening are absolutely hungry, famine-
stricken without the Word of God.

I talked to those men that night. I spoke their language. At the close
of that earnest and perhaps somewhat long address this happened:

An old man came forward. He was the son of a king, his long beard
flowing down to his waist. He came up to me, leaning on his staff. The
young men courteously made way for him. He stood there looking up
at me, his strong face alert in that bright moonlight. He said: "You

are a young man, and yet the things you have been talking about—how do you know these things? How do you know them?"

I answered, "Father, I have not known these things because of my own personal righteousness or wisdom. But these questions which have troubled your heart and all human hearts—our Great Father has written down the answers in a Book, given to men of olden time who struggled with these questions. And the answers to these questions were written in a Book."

"Do you mean there is a book with all these things you have been telling us about—about a love that is good, and all the rest of it?"

Then I said, "There *is* a Book. It is God's Book, and the answers are in it."

"Young man," said he, "is that book in my language? You speak my language. Did you read it in my tongue?"

"Yes, I have the Book."

I wish you could have seen that old man. He straightened up, and pointing his long finger at me, I shall never forget it as he said:

"Get me that book!"

I ran back to my tent and brought back two copies of the Bible in their language. Forty brown hands were stretched out for them as I returned. I put one into his hand, and when I told him that the answers to the questions were in that Book, the old man looked up and said, "Sir, how long has this book been in the world?"

"It has been here for hundreds of years; for hundreds of years."

"Did your people have it?"

"Yes."

"And I am an old man. All my friends have died hopeless. I am nearly gone myself. And all this time the book was here and nobody brought it to me. *Why didn't someone bring us the book long ago?*"

The question of the old man rings in my ears constantly, and I pass this question on to you. I pass it on to Christendom. Why has not that Book been put into every language in the world? Nineteen centuries after Christ came, and two thirds of the human family still say, *"Why have you not brought us the Book?"* [3]

POEM:

> Light up thy Word; the fettered page
>   From killing bondage free:
> Light up our way; lead forth this age
>   In love's large liberty.

> O Light of light! within us dwell,
> Through us thy radiance pour,
> That word and life thy truths may tell,
> And praise thee evermore.
>
> —WASHINGTON GLADDEN

STORY:

BIBLE PEDDLER EXTRAORDINARY

A BEWHISKERED Arab, with a white cloth over his head like a sheik, must hold the world's record for Bible-selling. At least, he has surely sold more Bibles than anyone in the Holy Land and the surrounding country.

Moussa Majadi is eighty-four years old, and he has been selling the world's best seller since he was twelve. For the last sixty-two years he's been the best-known peddler of the Amercian Bible Society throughout the Near East.

This unusual traveling salesman was born in the Syrian city Hauran, to parents who belonged to the Greek Catholic church. When he was still a small boy, an Englishman offered his father a Bible, but the father refused it because he was forbidden to have a copy in his possession. At last the Englishman prevailed, and the father took the book to the priest, and together they read it. Both decided to become Protestants!

The result was that, when he was still a boy, Moussa started selling Bibles for a representative of the Irish Presbyterian Church in Damascus, a Major Crawford, grandfather of the Archie Crawford who today is acting president of the famous American University of Beirut. After ten years of that, Moussa went with the American society. Virtually all of the thousands of Bibles he has sold since have been printed in Arabic script on presses of the Presbyterian Mission at Beirut.

"The Bible was as if buried in the ground," Moussa mused as he sat on a low rock wall among the date palms in Beirut during a visit to pick up more Bibles. "The Americans came along and dug it up for us."

Maybe it's just an old man's rosy recollection of youth, but he thinks people were more eager half a century ago to buy the Bible. In those days he used to start his rounds on horseback, with the saddlebags jammed with books, and buyers crowded around to take them.

In these lands the sons of Mohammed sometimes make the selling difficult. Many have bought Bibles in the face of reprisals from the Moslems. That fear was great yesterday, and it still is today. Though he has never been beaten, Moussa has taken many a tongue-lashing for selling Christian books. Through the years he has sold perhaps as many as a quarter million Bibles. Even at his age, in the first eight months of 1947 he sold over a thousand. When he is in the crowded, dusty market, with people in from all the countryside, he may sell fifty a day.

All over Trans-Jordan, Palestine, Syria, and Lebanon, Moussa Majadi has carried his bundle of books. He stops in the village a few days—as long as the Bibles are being taken—and then moves on. Today he travels by bus, then tramps along the village streets with his worn shoes and a cane. All over his area he has friends, and sometimes he passes the nights with them, or in tiny hostels too primitive to be called hotels. Then, when the sun is bright again, he goes from door to door, or takes his post along with the other sellers in the marketplaces.

Hauran, his birthplace, is still home. Moussa's wife lives there. They have two sons and three daughters. One daughter is the wife of an evangelist. One boy works for the British army in Palestine; the other son is a farmer at Hauran. There Moussa owns a bit of land—"as much as a yoke of oxen can plow in a day and a half."

But Moussa, though he gets a small pension from the Bible Society, has no intention of retiring and settling down on his farm, even at eighty-four. As through almost three quarters of a century, he still packs his Bibles in the morning and moves out to distribute them in the noon-day heat.

"I'll not stop working till I die," he says firmly and simply.[4]

LEADER:

In the countries where the Bibles have been destroyed the need for the Scriptures is very great. There is not much need to talk of rebuilding war-torn countries if we do not send the gospel along with other gifts. Putting the Bible in the hands of the people will revive their spirits and brighten their hopes more than anything else, and help to put them back on the road to recovery.

For over 131 years the American Bible Society has been the agent of the churches to supply the people the Bible in their own languages. This society has the plates, the presses, the paper, and the organization to distribute the Bible, but it needs $2,000,000 to meet present demands. Recent requests for Bibles and scripture portions total 8,000,000. The largest call is for 1,875,000 copies for Germany; Japan asks for 1,725,-000; and Russia, 1,712,000.

The offering today will be sent to the American Bible Society to aid in this worthy cause.[5]

OFFERTORY:

Every person according as he purposeth in his heart, so let him give; not grudgingly, or of necessity: for God loveth a cheerful giver.[6]

LITANY:

Leader: For the Bible, which is a lamp unto our feet and a light unto our pathway,

Group: We are indeed grateful, our Father.

Leader: For the insight and inspiration which comes to us from the Bible,

Group: We are thankful.

Leader: For those who have translated the Bible into the languages of the people and for all who have helped to print and distribute it,

Group: We are grateful.

Leader: For those who have labored and sacrificed that copies of the Bible in their own tongues may be sent to people everywhere,

Group: We are grateful, our Father.

Leader: Touch our hearts and make us eager to do our share in making the Bible available to all people everywhere,

Group: We pray thee, O Lord.

Leader: Hasten the time when thy Word shall be made known to the entire world and every tongue shall confess thee as Lord and Father of all.

Group: In the name of thy Son we pray. AMEN.

CLOSING HYMN: "A Glory Gilds the Sacred Page."

SERVICE 19

HE BUILDED BETTER THAN HE KNEW
(*Church School Day*)

PRELUDE: "Morning Mood" by Grieg.

CALL TO WORSHIP:

> We are builders of that city,
>   All our joys and all our groans
> Help to rear its shining ramparts;
>   All our lives are building stones:
> Whether humble or exalted,
>   All are called to task divine;
> All must aid alike to carry
>   Forward one sublime design.
>   —FELIX ADLER

HYMN: "Where Cross the Crowded Ways of Life," or
"We Gather Together."

RESPONSIVE READING:

Leader: Teach me thy way, O Lord; I will walk in thy truth: unite my heart to fear thy name.

Group: Give those that teach pure hearts and wise,
    Faith, hope, and love, all warmed by prayer:
  Themselves first training for the skies,
    They best will raise their people there.

Leader: Study to shew thyself approved unto God, a workman that needeth not to be ashamed, rightly dividing the word of truth.

Group: Give those that learn the willing ear,
    The spirit meek, the guileless mind;

Such gifts will make the lowliest here
Far better than a kingdom find.

Leader: So teach us to number our days, that we may apply our hearts
unto wisdom.[1]

Group: O bless the shepherd, bless the sheep,
That guide and guided both be one;
One in the faithful watch they keep,
One in the joy of work well done.

—JOHN ARMSTRONG

PRAYER:

Give us, O Lord, a steadfast heart, which no unworthy affection may
drag downwards; give us an unconquered heart, which no tribulation
can wear out; give us an upright heart, which no unworthy purpose
may tempt aside. Bestow upon us also, O Lord our God, understanding
to know thee, diligence to seek thee, wisdom to find thee, and a faithfulness that may finally embrace thee; through Jesus Christ our Lord.
AMEN.[2]

HYMN:

We would be building; temples still undone
O'er crumbling walls their crosses scarcely lift;
Waiting till love can raise the broken stone,
And hearts creative bridge the human rift;
We would be building, Master, let thy plan
Reveal the life that God would give to man.

Teach us to build; upon the solid rock
We set the dream that hardens into deed,
Ribbed with the steel that time and change doth mock,
Th' unfailing purpose of our noblest creed;
Teach us to build; O Master, lend us sight
To see the towers gleaming in the light.

O keep us building, Master; may our hands
Ne'er falter when the dream is in our hearts,
When to our ears there come divine commands
And all the pride of sinful will departs;
We build with thee, O grant enduring worth
Until the heavenly Kingdom comes on earth.[3]

—PURD E. DEITZ

HE BUILDED BETTER THAN HE KNEW

STORY:

THE RAGGED SCHOOL OF ROBERT RAIKES

ON A dark evening in 1780 Robert Raikes, a wealthy printer and editor of the *Journal* in Gloucester, England, picked his way gingerly along Sooty Alley, a muddy street in the slum district of his city. A servant walked ahead with a lantern. Groups of dirty, ragged children played on their doorsteps or loitered along the walks. Some shouted obscene remarks at this upper-class intruder. Others jostled about him, begging for coins. One large lad scooped up a handful of mud and hit him squarely in the back, to the howls of delight of the other ragamuffins who observed it.

Seeking shelter in a doorway, Raikes roundly reproached a thin, tired woman who came to see what the commotion was about. He told her the parents of those children should feel ashamed of their conduct. She answered:

"Yes, sir. But the children work all day. At night they have nowhere to go, nowhere to play, nothing to do. And you should see how it is on Sundays!"

Back at his home the editor sat pondering. Those tattered, uncouth children! He wondered if he could do something for them. He was the leader of a committee to aid men sent to prison. Perhaps he would have to add another philanthrophy—gifts for working-class children.

Raikes went back to Sooty Alley the next Sunday afternoon. What he saw appalled him. Older boys were cursing and fighting among themselves, and setting little boys one against the other. Younger girls and boys were standing about watching, or lolling listlessly on the ground, now a sea of caked mud and dust. A half-clad man, club in hand, was chasing some boys who had broken a windowpane. Everywhere was the squalor of poverty.

Half of that slum's population was doomed the minute it was born, Raikes knew. The children were put into the factories and apprentice shops at six years of age. Most of them worked twelve hours a day. Eight out of ten of the boys were in jail before they were tweny-one. The hangman got about one out of four. None could ever hope to find more in life than hard work and perpetual hunger.

It was evident to Raikes that the children were allowed to follow their lowest inclinations without restraint. What else could be expected when one considered the homes from which they came? The parents could not instill in their minds principles to which they themselves were strangers. He disagreed with those who believed in severely punishing the children for minor offenses without taking into consideration the causes of such conduct. When they told him that the masses of the people were incapable of improvement, he flatly contradicted them and said that the state had no right to punish people unless it did something to instruct them in right living.

Raikes decided that it would take more than gifts of money to help those children. They needed something to do on Sunday—that one day of the week they were permitted to spend in "idleness." He decided to bring some of them together for religious instruction. That afternoon he talked with a clergyman, and together they planned a school on Sunday for the slum children. Neither of them had any idea that they were beginning a movement which would spread over the world and influence countless millions of people of all ages and races.

Raikes went to Sooty Alley and talked with a Mrs. Meredith, who had a private school in her kitchen, and offered her a shilling a week to teach the boys who would come. Tactfully he won the consent of several parents. By offering candy and coins he rounded up a dozen boys one Sunday morning and led them to Mrs. Meredith's home. The only condition imposed upon these boys was that they have clean hands and faces and have their hair combed. Many had no comb or brush. He supplied combs and showed them how to use them.

Later Raikes secured the help of Mrs. Mary Critchley, a strong-willed, capable woman who he hoped woud be able to handle the restless boys. He explained his plans to her, and she moved into a larger house which was more adequate as a meeting place for a Sunday school. Here Raikes carefully organized the first Sunday school. During the first year he added three other teachers and paid them one shilling per Sunday. It occurred to him that it would be easier to instruct these boys if they could read and write. Since education was for only the upper classes, he knew that slum children could never go to school; so he would bring the school to them on Sunday. He printed small booklets with the alphabet and Bible verses—the first Sunday-school literature.

The children came on Sunday morning at 10 o'clock, and were instructed until noon. They went home for lunch, returned at one o'clock, and were conducted to church. After church they came back to classes and repeated the catechism until half past five. They were rewarded with small cakes and pennies. The first time they were taken to church they stuck pins in each other and behaved so badly that the minister asked them to leave. At length they learned to listen and to enter into the service.

Sunday by Sunday the crowd grew, as word spread about Raikes's school and how there were sweets and pennies to be had just by sitting and listening. Girls begged to come, and Raikes defied the taboo against "mixing the sexes" and welcomed them. His friends thought he had gone mad, as every Sunday morning he could be seen, dressed in his velvet coat, silver-buckle shoes, and tall hat, leading a mob of rowdy children to their class. Someone derisively called it "Raikes Ragged School."

Gloucester's editor could not have foreseen that he was starting a world-wide movement, but he did see immediate results among the children. Many times he heard words of gratitude, such as, "We don't have to beat our Tom near so much now." The movement to organize Sunday schools spread rapidly. At Stockport churches of various denominations buried their differences to erect the first building especially for Sunday-school teaching. More than 1,000 children attended here in relays throughout Sundays. By 1785 Raikes estimated from reports that there were 250,000 children attending Sunday schools over England and Scotland.

Raikes's Sunday schools helped to bring about education for all and to abolish child labor. The greathearted editor advanced the idea that every child, however poor, should have some schooling. He said, "Learning goes with morality, and these will save the child to useful life. The future strength of our country depends upon what we make of our children." The leaders of the Sunday schools continued to work for education, and in 1870 Parliament passed the Education Act, compelling local authorities to provide day schools for all children in the British Isles.

At the age of seventy-five Raikes wrote, "Perhaps what we have started will someday far exceed our first expectations." Like many other men, he builded better than he knew.[4]

PRAYER:

Our Father, we thank thee for the inspiration which comes from the lives of great leaders who helped the oppressed, shared the burden of poverty, and brought about better living conditions for the poor. We thank thee for the influence of Robert Raikes, who gave his time and possessions that the children of the poor might have a chance for a more abundant life. We are grateful for the Sunday-school movement that he started, which has blessed thousands and is still enriching the lives of many today. Since we reap where others have sown, help us to pass on to others the values which have come to us. May we have open eyes and willing hands to grasp every opportunity to serve in our community and throughout the world. When we become discouraged, help us to realize that thy purposes are eternal, and that nothing is done in vain when it is done in thy name, and that thou canst take our gifts and our efforts and use them to great ends. Grant us wisdom to meet the problems of life, strength to face whatever the day sends, and at all times an abiding sense of thy presence. We pray in the name of Christ, thy Son and our Lord. AMEN.

POEM:

> Fair knights of justice and of good,
>   They gave to evil battle gage;
> Bearing their souls in rectitude,
>   They left a goodly heritage—
> God of the righteous, grant that we,
> Their sons, do follow righteously!
>
> Guards of the sacred altar flame,
>   Bringers of learning and of faith,
> They illumined life in the blessed Name
>   And hope they flared in the day of death—
> God of the faithful, grant that we,
> Their sons, do follow faithfully!
>
> Theirs was the Presence ever sure,
>   Theirs was the all-abounding grace,
> Theirs was the passion ever pure
>   To honor the Lord in all their ways—
> God of the Christlike, grant that we
> Do follow, follow worthily![5]

—ROBERT FREEMAN

CLOSING HYMN: "O Master Workman of the Race," or
    "We Thank Thee, Lord, Thy Paths."

SERVICE 20

REMEMBERING JESUS
(*The Lord's Supper*)

PRELUDE: Hymn tune "Eucharist."

CALL TO WORSHIP:
> God is a Spirit.
> Let us worship him in spirit and in truth.
> Seek ye the Lord while he may be found;
> Call ye upon him while he is near.
> Let the wicked forsake his way and the unrighteous man
>   his thoughts.
> And let him return unto the Lord, and he will have mercy
>   upon him:
> And to our God, for he will abundantly pardon.

HYMN: "Break Thou the Bread of Life," or
> "Beneath the Cross of Jesus."

AFFIRMATION OF FAITH:

We believe in the one God, Maker and Ruler of all things, Father of all men; the source of all goodness and beauty, all truth and love.

We believe in Jesus Christ, God manifest in the flesh, our teacher, example, and redeemer, the Saviour of the world.

We believe in the Holy Spirit, God present with us for guidance, for comfort, and for strength.

We believe in the forgiveness of sins, in the life of love and prayer, and in grace equal to every need.

We believe in the Word of God contained in the Old and New Testaments as the sufficient rule of faith and of practice.

We believe in the Church as the fellowship for worship and for service of all who are united to the living Lord.

We believe in the Kingdom of God as the divine rule in human society, and in the brotherhood of man under the fatherhood of God.

We believe in the final triumph of righteousness, and in the life everlasting. AMEN.[1]

THE COLLECT FOR PURITY:

Almighty God, unto whom all hearts are open, all desires are known, and from whom no secrets are hid, cleanse the thoughts of our hearts by the inspiration of thy Holy Spirit, that we may perfectly love thee, and worthily magnify thy holy name, through Jesus Christ our Lord. AMEN.

THE LAST SUPPER:

On the first day of the festival of Unleavened Bread, on which it was customary to kill the Passover lamb, Jesus' disciples said to him, "Where do you wish us to go and make the preparations for you to eat the Passover supper?"

So he sent away two of his disciples, saying to them, "Go into the city, and you will meet a man carrying a pitcher of water. Follow him, and whatever house he goes into, say to the man of the house, 'The Master says, "Where is my room where I can eat the Passover supper with my disciples?"' And he will show you a large room upstairs, furnished and ready. Make your preparations for us there."

When it was evening he came with the Twelve. And when they were at the table eating, Jesus rose from the table, took off his outer clothing, and fastened a towel about his waist. Then he poured water into the basin and began to wash the disciples' feet, wiping them with the towel that was about his waist. So he came to Simon Peter. He said to him, "Master, are you going to wash my feet?"

Jesus answered, "You cannot understand now what I am doing, but you will learn by and by."

Peter said to him, "I will never let you wash my feet!"

Jesus answered, "You will have no share with me unless I wash you."

Simon Peter said to him, "Master, wash not only my feet but my hands and my face too!"

When he had washed their feet and put on his clothes and taken his place, he said to them again, "Do you understand what I have been doing to you? You call me Teacher and Master, and you are right, for that is what I am. If I then, your Master and Teacher, have washed your feet, you ought to wash one another's feet too. For I have set you an example, in order that you may do what I have done to you. I tell you, no slave is superior to his master, and no messenger is greater than the man who sends him."

"I tell you, one of you will betray me!"

They were deeply hurt and began to say to him one after another, "Can it be I, Master?"

He answered, "The man who just dipped his hand in the same dish with me is going to betray me."

As they were eating Jesus took a loaf and blessed it, and he broke it in pieces and gave it to his disciples, saying, "Take this and eat it. It is my body!"

And he took the wine-cup and gave thanks and gave it to them, saying, "You must all drink from it, for this is my blood which ratifies the agreement, and is to be poured out for many people, for the forgiveness of their sins.[2] This do in remembrance of me.[3]

HYMN: "When I Survey the Wondrous Cross," or
"Above the Hills of Time the Cross Is Gleaming."

SERVICE OF REMEMBRANCE:

Let us remember Jesus, who went out from the upper room into the garden of Gethsemane. There he poured out his soul to God, saying, "Father, anything is possible for you! Take this cup away from me! Yet not what I please but what you do!" The answer to his prayer came not in the removal of the cup but in the strength to drink it. What seemed at the moment to be a terrible evil worked out for good.

Let us remember Jesus, who healed men's diseases but never spared himself. It is difficult for us to picture the physical and mental strain under which Jesus spent his last days. Coming into Jerusalem after the long climb from Jericho he chose to ride on an animal because of the pressure of fatigue. He had not slept on the previous night; his body had been scourged with cruel thongs; he fell under the load of the cross and another had to be pressed into service. He died on the cross long before the usual time because of the physical strain to which he had been subjected. It was not for himself that he braved his foes, but for the cause to which he had given his life. He lived a life of self-denial and of devotion to the will of God. He said, "This is my body, which is broken for you."

Let us remember Jesus, who said, "This is my blood of the new covenant which is shed for you, and for many, for the remission of sins." Divine foregiveness awaits upon one thing—the forgiving spirit in the hearts of men. Jesus taught us to pray, "Forgive us our trespasses, as we forgive those who trespass against us." We are invited to the Lord's table when we are in love and charity with our neighbors, and intend to lead a new life. We come to the Lord's table with no merits of our own, with no hatred or anger, but with humility and with gratitude for the forgiveness of our sins. If we confess our sins, he is faithful and righteous to forgive us our sins, and to cleanse us from all unrighteousness.

In Knut Hamsun's masterpiece, *Hunger,* we read of the struggle of a young writer with direst poverty. For days at a time the hero has not a morsel of food. The description of his attempt to eat raw meat off a bone which he had got ostensibly for his dog is gruesome. His empty stomach casts off each bit, and hunger continues to gnaw unmercifully.

Most remarkable of all was how the lust for food in the face of imminent starvation never drowned out the deeper hungers. His unappeased hunger for human fellowship went on; when he had not eaten a meal for three days, and a breakfast was to be had at the police station for the asking, he walked proudly out, for he determined to keep his self-respect, at the cost of his life. His hunger for righteousness was undiminished; direst want could not tempt him to dishonesty. Deepest of all was his longing for mental achievement as he penned the imaginings of his fevered brain.

The gospel has sometimes been presented as medicine for sick souls; a much better figure is that of food for starved lives. The true, imperishable food was the bread of life which Jesus offered unto men. It is at the Lord's table that worshipers are to feed on the true bread of life. To eat the flesh and drink the blood is a symbol of the fullest appropriation to ourselves of the Lord of life. In this ancient symbol we are invited to feed on him in our hearts by faith. We believe that God is present; but whether we rise from this table filled or empty depends upon the inner receptiveness with which we come.

It is a very old custom of the church that worshipers should come to the Lord's table before they have eaten other food. Physical fasting is no longer required, but it is true that the Lord's table is for those who hunger and thirst after a better life. It it not for the full, but for those who are conscious of need. It is not for the satisfied, but for those who yearn for the living bread that comes down out of heaven. Jesus said, "Blessed are they that hunger and thirst after righteousness." Hunger is the condition of true blessedness, and only the hungry can be filled. His promise is, "I will come in and sup with him and he with me." [4]

POEM:

> Drink ye all of it, all, not just a sup—
> Drink my faith, my love, said Jesus,
> Drink the fulness of my cup.
>
> Drink ye all of it, all, not just my peace—
> Drink my dangerous living, dying—
> Drink my fearless, glad release.
>
> Drink ye all of it, all, not just the sweet—
> Drink my bitter tears of anguish—
> Drink the dregs of my defeat.
>
> Drink ye all of it, all, not just my pain—
> Drink my joy of life abundant—
> Drink my triumph, drink my reign! [5]
>
> —E. DENT LACKEY

SERVICE OF CONFESSION:

We are in the presence of God, who knows our thoughts, our desires, and our motives. He knows whether we have confessed our sins, asked for forgiveness, and determined to lead a new life. He knows whether we have forgiven others. He would not have any of us come to the Lord's table in an unworthy manner.

PRAYER OF CONFESSION:

Our Father, we thank thee for thy church, for the missionaries, and for all who labor to bring thy kingdom on earth. We thank thee for the light and liberty that has come to us because of thy revealed Word. Forgive us for the times when we have failed to live by thy commandments. Cleanse us of prejudice and selfishness and help us to think of people of every race as our brothers and as being one with us in faith. Fill us with thy Spirit so that our lives may be in harmony with thy will. Strengthen us for the tasks which seem too great for us, and give us faith to attempt even greater things for thee. May we dare to follow the teachings of thy Son at all times and in all places. Help us to come to thy table with humble and contrite hearts. Make us conscious of thy sustaining presence, and forgive us of all our sins. In the name of Jesus we pray. AMEN.[6]

HYMN: "In the Cross of Christ I Glory," or
"My Faith Looks Up to Thee."

THE SACRAMENT OF COMMUNION (by the minister).

BENEDICTION:

> Father, give thy benediction,
>   Give thy peace before we part;
> Still our minds with truth's conviction;
>   Calm with trust each anxious heart.
> Let thy voice with sweet commanding,
>   Bid our grief and struggles end;
> Peace which passeth understanding
>   On our waiting spirits send. AMEN.
>
> —SAMUEL LONGFELLOW

PART TWO

STORIES FOR WORSHIP

STALWART SON OF SCIENCE

DR. SIMON FLEXNER raised his head in annoyance at the sound of the knock on his laboratory door. "Another idle caller to waste my time," he frowned. "Just when I'm in the middle of a delicate experiment, too."

The knock was repeated. With a sigh Simon Flexner put the test tube back in the rack, wiped his stained fingers on his lab apron, and went to the door.

A tall, thin, stooped man dressed in a baggy suit came in. "Dr. Simon Flexner?" he asked in a high, thin voice.

"That's my name."

The strange visitor's sharp, gray eyes darted keenly around the tiny lab with its meager equipment. Flexner's annoyance deepened. The solution in the test tube was already thickening. "Well, sir," he demanded, "what do you want?"

The caller turned. His seamed and withered face broke into a smile. "Don't you recognize me, Dr. Flexner?"

"No, I don't."

The elderly man shook his head. "That's fame for you," he murmured. "I'm John D. Rockefeller."

Simon Flexner gulped. Even he, immersed as he was in scientific work, had heard of John D. Rockefeller, the richest man in the world, Nevertheless he cast a reluctant glance toward the test tube. The solution had turned to a hard mass. The experiment was ruined.

Mr. Rockefeller noted the glance. "I'll be brief," he promised. "I came to you, Dr. Flexner, for advice. Everyone I asked said you were about the best medical researcher in the world."

"Oh, no, there are many better," Flexner protested.

Mr. Rockefeller smiled. "We won't go into that." Then he hesitated. "I notice that you work alone." His eye took in the shabby lab again. "Do you prefer it that way? I mean, do you find your genius strikes out more sparks when there aren't a lot of other researchers to help you, when you haven't too much money to spend on elaborate apparatus? I've been told .."

Simon Flexner's eyes flashed. "They've been telling you utter nonsense, Mr. Rockefeller. *No* scientist is better when he works alone, or when he works with insufficient tools. Oh, I know there are some pretended researchers that like to talk that way. It feeds their pride. They think that if they make some discovery they won't have to share the glory."

The medical scientist paced up and down his small lab. "*True* science," he went on vehemently, "is a community effort. It's a democracy. No one man makes a full-blown discovery all by himself. He uses the work that others have done before him. Of course, great things have been done in a garret and with a few test tubes. But how much more could be done with many fine brains engaged on a common problem, using proper equipment . . ." He stopped short, looked embarrassed. "I must apologize, Mr Rockefeller, but you started me off on my pet topic."

The millionaire smiled. "I came here for that purpose, Dr. Flexner. I was hoping you'd say just that. Many people I talked to tried to discourage me. You see," he explained, "I'm only a businessman, not a scientist. In business you can't get very far without help and equipment. But in science . . ."

"It's the same."

"Good. Then I'm sure you'll approve of my idea, Dr. Flexner. I want to give some money—a *lot* of money—to establish a medical foundation. I want to see a place where the best medical brains of the world can get together and fight the diseases that afflict humanity. What do you think of it?"

Simon Flexner's face glowed. "Why, it's marvelous, Mr. Rockefeller. Research on a community pattern, everyone working for the common good, exchanging ideas, encouraging each other—sir, that's my idea of paradise!"

The elderly millionaire beamed. "Then it's settled. I'll *do* it." He turned toward the door, stopped. "By George, I almost forgot! Dr. Flexner, I want you to be the director of my foundation."

Flexner stared incredulously. "I? But I haven't the talent, the . . ."

"Let me be the judge of that."

"And . . . and . . ." Simon Flexner's face suddenly clouded. "Look here, Mr. Rockefeller. You're a Baptist, are you not?"

"I am. Why do you ask?"

"Because I follow the Jewish faith. If—if I *should* say yes, I'd want it distinctly understood that I pick my fellow workers with one sole qualification in mind—that they are the best in the field. There must be no other standard."

"That is the only test there should be," the old man said quietly. "I am a good Baptist, I hope. I am sure you are a good Jew. Our particular form of faith doesn't matter so long as we are sincere and godly. Take on anyone you want, Dr. Flexner—Baptist, Methodist, Catholic, or Jew—provided only he can contribute to human knowledge."

Simon Flexner bowed formally. "Mr. Rockefeller, you have hired yourself a director."

Under Flexner's guiding hand the Rockefeller Institute for Medical Research soon became the leading center for great medical discoveries in the world. He gathered about him the keenest and most adventurous minds in the field. The great scourges of mankind were attacked, one after another. Ardent young men, filled with the idea of service to suffering humanity, flocked to Dr. Flexner's standard. The bounds of knowledge were steadily advanced. Disease after disease succumbed to the test tubes and experiments of these brilliant men.

But Simon Flexner was not content with mere guidance and organization. In spite of the tremendous demands on his time and energy, he threw himself into the work of original research with the ardor of his youngest assistant.

One of the deadliest of human ills was cerebrospinal meningitis. It attacked children chiefly, and those who didn't mercifully die were usually left crippled and twisted for life. In the year 1905 an epidemic swept New York. Thousands took sick; hundreds died. The doctors shook their heads despairingly at the pitiful pleas of frantic parents. No, there was nothing they could do. There was no known treatment. Even the cause of the dread disease was unknown.

Simon Flexner called on Dr. William H. Park, world-famous pathologist. "Dr. Park," he said, "I want you to help me."

"In any way I can, Dr. Flexner. What is it?"

"Cerebrospinal meningitis. I can't sleep nights, thinking of all those poor children. Let us work together on the problem."

Dr. Park picked up his hat. "Lead the way, Dr. Flexner."

The two men worked day and night. They hardly ever left the laboratory. They barely ate or slept. Every moment wasted meant more deaths, more twisted cripples. The entire resources of the institute were at their disposal. It was not long before they discovered the germ and developed a serum to fight the disease. The serum was injected into children suffering from meningitis, and one after another was restored to health.

Dr. Flexner took Dr. James W. Jobling to Kentucky, where a new epidemic of meningitis had broken out. From hospital to hospital, from home to home they went. "You'll be all right," Flexner assured the frightened patients, while he injected the precious serum. But out in the corridor he would groan to Jobling: "Their pitiful eyes haunt me. They have such faith in us."

"I am certain it will work," said Jobling.

Flexner's shoulders sagged. "We can only wait and pray," he murmured.

As time passed the epidemic subsided. When the reports came in, Jobling rushed into Flexner's office, flourishing a sheaf of statistics. "You've won, Simon. You've won!" he cried. "Read these figures."

Simon Flexner's hand trembled. His eyes misted so he could hardly read. But the figures were figures of fire. Instead of three out of every four dying from meningitis, his serum had cut down the mortality to one in five. He had subdued one of the greatest scourges of the human race!

Simon Flexner did not rest on his well-earned laurels. Year in, year out, he worked unceasingly on cures for suffering humanity. He found the virus that causes infantile paralysis. He helped develop a cure for the sleeping sickness that laid large sections of Africa wholly waste. He isolated the bacillus that is responsible for acute dysentery. He rendered important services in World War I.

Simon Flexner died only recently at the age of eighty, active to the last, laden with honors showered upon him by grateful governments and institutions of learning. The world has been a richer and better place because of him. During his long career he served his fellowman. What better epitaph can there be for anyone? [1]

PADEREWSKI, PIANIST AND PATRIOT

IGNACE JAN PADEREWSKI, world-renowned composer and concert pianist, stood at the window in his home in Morges, Switzerland. His back turned to the piano, he sought strength from the Alps which towered above him, separating him from his native Poland. On this day, August 1, 1914, he faced the greatest decision of his life.

The great musician was depressed because of the plight of his country. War had been declared, and Poland, though neutral, faced certain destruction at the hands of the conflicting powers. Situated as she was, armies would trample her land, kill and starve her people, and wreck her industries. Poles in German uniform would fight Poles in Russian uniform. Men, food, and money would be poured into a cause in which Poland had no heart. It was a tragic day for his country, part Russian, part Austrian, but all Polish in heart and hopes.

Thinking of Poland—and she was constantly in his thoughts—he realized that his devotion to her had made him what he was. Early in life, music and patriotism had merged to become a controlling passion which directed the course of his life. In childhood he had learned the meaning of tyranny. At three years of age, when his father had been taken a political prisoner, the lad had felt the lash of a Russian whip because he dared to ask a question. His mother, born in exile, had transmitted to him her love of freedom.

During the year that his father was a prisoner, the lad began to discover the music within him. In spite of unskilled teachers his music became an outlet for his intense emotions. He recalled his decision at the age of twelve to devote his life to music. That decision was almost as great as the one he now faced. Many tried to discourage him, but he could not be shaken. When he entered the Warsaw Conservatory, all the stress of adolescence and the urge for freedom found outlet in his music. To be something for Poland—he could not remember when his heart had not burned with that desire.

Paderewski married Antonina Korsak, who shared his devotion to music. A year later she died, leaving a son. Thinking of her in his reveries, he realized that during that year he had known the heights of happiness and the depths of sorrow. The dreams and hopes of that beautiful, brief experience had been shattered. Three years later the child was stricken with paralysis and became a helpless invalid until his death at twenty-one.

Paderewski had to go forward alone, but he found relief in his work. In spite of the promise of success as a composer, he dreamed of being a concert artist. He was twenty-four when he decided to study with Leschetisky, the world's greatest piano teacher. But the teacher declared that it was too late, that past mistakes in training could not be corrected. But Paderewski was determined, and three years later when success, born of hard work and God-given talent, came to him, the great man was humble before it.

The first triumph of the struggling musician was at Paris when he was twenty-seven. After playing in many centers in Europe he came to America. His heart warmed as he thought of America, now so much a part of his life. How he cherished the memory of his many concerts! His music linked his heart with the hearts of people everywhere, but he always identified himself with the people of his own country. "I must be something for Poland," he said to himself.

A feeling of frustration swept over the great musician as he thought of the events which were forcing upon him a decision which would lead him away from his music. He had always been an active patriot, but he was a musician and not a statesman. Patriotism now beckoned him away from his art. He had money and friends, and he spoke French and English fluently. In a neutral country he would be free to travel as he pleased. It was clear to him now. His people needed him in their fight for freedom, and his role would be that of a politician.

Standing at his window, his eyes resting on the Alps, the great artist made his decision. To be something for Poland in this emergency meant giving up his music for the role of the patriot. Acting immediately he organized the Polish Relief Committee and came to America, where he established other branches. Lecturing in many cities he made his appeal, saying, "I speak to you about a country which is not yours, and in a language which is not mine." Eventually he led the American people to forget him as a musician and to think of him as a statesman, and thus laid the groundwork for a new Polish republic.

The great artist recruited 100,000 Poles in the United States and sent them to Poland. At the close of the war he was made Premier and Minister of Foreign Affairs of Poland. Through his influence red tape was set aside and his country was given immediate relief. Food and supplies poured in from America. His talents and his private fortune were dedicated to the cause, and Poland was saved from disaster.

When a dissenting group came into power, Paderewski resigned as premier, but he remained the delegate to the Supreme Council of the Allies, to the Peace Conference and the League of Nations. Finally, when the mistakes of the new group were brought to light, Paderewski could have returned, but he was not willing to endanger the lives of others. His decision to stay out of power when he could have gone back was unique.

The great leader did not live apart from people. He learned of men and of nations, of politics and of diplomacy. He weighed the ideals of one nation against another and understood the motives back of the actions of the people. In every contact he practiced justice and brought prestige to Poland. It was said of him: "In a story like Paderewski's one truth surely is brought home to us: that art is life, that the artist is not remote from life nor antagonistic to it, but a living and illuminating part of it. Better still, we learn another truth: that life itself is an art, a fine art which we may all practice, in which every one of us may perfect ourselves no matter what our work or station may be." [1]

To be something for Poland had been a driving force in Paderewski's musical career. When his country needed him as a leader, he laid aside his career as a musician, shared the burdens and identified himself with his people. Now it seemed that he could serve Poland best by returning to his music. When he turned again to his art, it was found that the new role as a patriot had changed him, had made him an integrated person. Through the giving of himself to his country, he had found life. Thus his music had become enriched with an added power and a new inspiration which seemed a miracle to all who heard him. His desire to be something for Poland had brought him fame as a pianist and a patriot.[2]

STORY 3

WALTER REED, DOCTOR IN UNIFORM

AT THE beginning of the twentieth century Walter Reed gave to medical science one of the most significant contributions that had been made up to that time. After his graduation at the University of Virginia, and until his untimely death at the age of fifty-one, his dominant desire was to relieve human suffering wherever he found it. To gratify this desire fully he was willing to risk his life, if necessary.

Walter Reed was born in a Methodist parsonage in Belroi, Gloucester County, Virginia, September 13, 1851. Too young to practice when he graduated from college at the age of seventeen, he entered Bellevue Medical College, New York, and took another degree. At twenty-four he enlisted in the Medical Corps of the United States Army and served for a quarter of a century. Studying later in Baltimore under the world-famous William Welch, Dr. Reed became one of the foremost bacteriologists of this country.

When the Spanish-American war broke out, Dr. Reed was chosen to head the fight against typhoid fever. His greatest opportunity came at the close of the war when he was asked to direct a commission to rid Cuba of yellow fever. Dr. Reed began this work with a determination to get rid of this scourge which had killed more men than the enemy's bullets.

Upon his arrival in Havana he found the epidemic at its height. Dr. Finley, a Cuban physician, insisted that the anopheles mosquitoes were the carriers of the germ. To prove his theory he pointed out that the fever existed only during the mosquito season and died out when cool weather killed the insects.

Dr. Reed was impressed but decided to make his own experiments to test the theory. Since animals could not be inoculated with yellow fever, men had to be used. Dr. Reed reasoned that he would be justified in risking the lives of a dozen men in order to save thousands of lives annually. The doctors employed to assist him were James Carroll, an Englishman; Jesse W. Lazear, a malaria expert; and Aristides Agramonte, a Cuban educated in New York.

Reed and his assistants were unwilling to expose others to a danger which they themselves did not take. Consequently they were the first to volunteer, but the assistants declared that Reed was the key person in the experiment and should not take the risk. The research had barely begun when Reed was called to the United States on business. Lazear, taking over the project, carried the mosquitoes to the hospital almost daily and allowed them to feed on yellow fever patients.

William Dean, a soldier who declared that he was not afraid of a little gnat, volunteered along with eight other men. Carroll and Dean were the first to become ill with fever, and Lazear came down with an acute case from which he died a few days later. Deeply distressed by the death of his colleague, Reed returned to Cuba.

Reed was convinced that they were on the right track. One thing puzzled him: Why had only three of the men come down with the fever? Studying the records he found that the three men who were victims of the fever had been bitten by mosquitoes that had fed on patients in the second day of illness and twelve days had been allowed for the germs to mature.

General Wood, military governor of Cuba, set aside ten thousand dollars for the experiment and established a camp about a mile from Camp Columbia. Dr. Reed offered one hundred dollars to those who would be inoculated, and if the fever developed another hundred would be given. The volunteers must be young men in good health and without dependents.

One morning two volunteers came. Delighted and surprised by their offer, Dr. Reed explained the danger and mentioned the cash reward. One of them explained, "Major Reed, we're not interested in being paid. The money isn't the point. It's the opportunity to do something for humanity and for science."

Dr. Reed looked at the two boys about the age of his own son and said, "I am proud to accept your brave offer." [1]

At Camp Lazear, as the station was called, one of the shacks, hot and poorly ventilated but carefully screened from mosquitoes, was the scene of the first experiment. In relays for two months seven men slept there in linens that had been used by yellow fever patients, and at the close of the time all of them were in perfect health. In another shack two men were exposed to infected mosquitoes, and both of them took

—153—

yellow fever. When the men recovered, Dr. Reed announced that the difference between the infected and uninfected shacks lay in the presence of the germ-filled mosquitoes. The plan which he set forth for controlling the fever was to get rid of the breeding places of mosquitoes.

Sitting at his desk on New Year's Eve, Dr. Reed wrote to his wife, saying, "The prayer that has been mine for twenty years that I might in some way do something to alleviate human suffering has been granted." As he wrote, twenty-four bugles sounded taps for the old year. There was a moment's silence; then reveille was sounded for a new year, and a new century, to which yellow fever would not be a scourge, but a fading memory.[2] Within three months Havana was rid of yellow fever, and within a few years the civilized parts of the world were free of the deadly scourge.

In November, 1902, at the Washington Barracks Hospital where he had so often brought healing to others, Dr. Reed died, following an appendectomy. He who had saved humanity from a cruel plague could not himself be saved. His last words were, "I leave so little," and it is true that he did not leave much in material possessions, but to the world he left a priceless heritage—freedom from a dread plague.

The world is slow in expressing gratitude to great men who serve humanity. Not much recognition was shown to Dr. Reed during his lifetime, but since then his childhood home has been made a national shrine, a research fund has been established in his name at the University of Virginia, and a great Army hospital in the nation's capital has been named for him. This man who had only one ambition—to help relieve human suffering—was able to realize it fully.

STORY 4

HE GAVE THEM WINDOWS

LOUIS BRAILLE, the French boy with the brown sparkling eyes, was playing in his father's pungent-smelling workshop. Suddenly he clutched in his hand two sharp awls and ran off with them. Then he stumbled. His father, the saddlemaker of the village of Coupvray, hurried to him, but it was of no use. In that accident the boy lost the sight of one eye, and the injury affected the nerves of the other eye. Louis was totally blinded for life.

His father never got over his remorse for the accident and could not do enough for the boy. He took him to Paris, where he spent most of his savings on treatment for his eyes, but the doctors held out no hope. "When the nerves are mutilated, we can do nothing," they said.

The villagers were kind. "There comes Louis," they would say when they heard the tapping of his cane. So many taps to the big tree where he would sit and rest. So many more to the pond where he could hear his friends at play.

At ten, Louis went to the National Institute for the Blind at Paris. Valentin Hauy, its founder, taught Louis the alphabet by guiding his fingers along the twenty-six letters, fashioned from twigs. When the boy learned the alphabet, he read the few books created by Hauy from letters cut out of cloth and pasted on pages. Each letter was about three inches high and two inches wide. A long word would spread across two to three lines. Thus, only short stories, essays, or poems were available to the blind.

When Louis was fourteen, another pupil noticed the ridges on a printed card into which the type had cut. Hauy quickly saw the point and began to turn out embossed letters from movable type. But the letters had to be at least an inch high; a book was still clumsy and tedious to read. It was heartbreaking to Louis, who was eager to learn.

On a visit home he said to his father, "The blind are the loneliest people in the world. Here I can distinguish one bird from another by its call; I can know the entrance to the house by the lintel. But am I never to learn to know what lies beyond the confines of hearing and feeling? Only books can free the blind. But there are no books for the blind that are worth anything."

One day the idea came to him to devise a code with symbols for words and phrases. He begged his father for bits of leather and through the summer he snipped and cut until his hands were raw. He tried codes based on triangles, squares, and circles, each bearing variations representing different letters, but none of them was practical.

After becoming a teacher at the Paris school for the blind, Braille learned of a system of "night writing" developed by a French Army captain named Barbier. A message, he was told, could be written in dots and dashes to another post, where it could be read by touch without striking a light. One evening while he was talking with a friend in a cafe the significance of this development came to him.

"My friend," said Braille, "I have solved the problem of the blind. I can now give them windows."

The following day he sought out Captain Barbier, saying, "I come to you on an errand of mercy. If you will explain your system of 'night writing,' the blind for all time will honor you. Now they are shut away from the light and friendliness which reading would give to them."

"Of course," said the captain, "I had never thought of it." Then he explained how, with an awl, he punched impressions into thick paper so that when it was reversed the small ridges could be felt on the other side. A simple army code had been set up: one dot might mean "advance," two dots "retreat," and so on. "It is possible to build a code for the entire language."

"It is possible!" cried Braille. "Let me be the first one to thank you."

From that day until 1837, when the first book for the blind using the Braille System was published, Braille never rested. Ironically, his system used the same instrument that had blinded him, the awl. It was perfected after five years of trial and error. Using a key of six holes in an oblong, Braille developed sixty-three possible combinations which, besides the letters of the alphabet, supplied symbols for punctuation, contractions, and so forth.

When Braille offered his gift to the world in a lecture at the Institute, he showed how he could "punch-write" almost as rapidly as one could read to him. Then he read back what he had written at almost the same pace as a seeing reader. But jealousy kept his method from being accepted at once.

Braille petitioned the French Academy for a hearing, but was turned down on the grounds that the embossing system, then in use, was the best and that "the blind received sufficient training and education through it." The pupils from the Institute begged Braille to teach them his methods secretly. He not only taught them to read and write, but worked out mathematical symbols and showed them how to solve equations.

Not until he was suffering from his last illness at the age of forty-three did he know that his system had been accepted. One of his pupils, a girl, gave a piano recital before a fashionable audience. At the close the listeners rose to their feet and applauded. She held up her hand, saying, "Your applause is not for me. It belongs to a man who is dying." Then she told of Braille's having taught her his system of sightless reading of books and music, and that his system was being blocked by jealousy and by those who held contracts for embossing books. She said, "He has not only given the blind windows, but he has given them music to enjoy."

The story was carried by the French press, and the heads of the Institute gave in to the demands of the people. Friends came to Braille bringing the news that his system had won. "This is the third time in my life that I have wept," he said. "First when I was blinded. Second when I heard about 'night writing.' And now because I know that my life is not a failure. God works in mysterious ways . . ."

Before long Braille's system swept the civilized world, and by the close of the nineteenth century most of the nations in Europe and the Western Hemisphere passed laws making education for the blind compulsory. Today the system has been adapted to the Chinese, and a number of magazines around the world are published in Braille each month.[1]

STORY 5

AVOIDING THE BEATEN TRACK

HIS FAMILY background and early education had a profound influence on the career of Alexander Graham Bell. His mother, an accomplished musician, began to lose her hearing when he was twelve. His father, a teacher and author of textbooks on speech, had invented a code of symbols known as "Visible Speech." Thus the boy grew up in an environment where sound and speech were important.

Alexander Bell had talent for music and at one time planned a musical career, but finally decided to follow in his father's footsteps. His inventive ability appeared before he was fifteen. He and his brother made a model skull and fitted it with a device to reproduce the human voice. It wailed "ma-ma" in such realistic manner that the neighbors began searching for a child in distress.

As young Bell started his career, his talents and training combined to bring success. He had a creative mind, a sensitive ear, and soon became expert in the use of his father's symbols. The school for the deaf which later became the Horace Mann School invited him to Boston to demonstrate the use of the symbols in teaching the deaf to speak. Carrying on similar work at other schools he was able to teach children in a few weeks to use more than four hundred syllables.

Bell's work brought him in contact with others interested in helping the deaf. A friendship grew up between him and Gardner Hubbard, a Boston attorney whose daughter had lost her hearing at an early age. Thomas Sanders, a wealthy merchant of Salem, was another friend who had a son who was deaf. These friends helped Bell to finance his experiments, and Thomas A. Watson helped by making the instrument according to Bell's instructions.

The telephone was an accident. Bell was not trying to invent a device for long-distance conversation. He was attempting to send telegraph messages over a wire with a device which he called the "harmonic telegraph." On June 2, 1875, while he and Watson were working, he heard a tone over the wire that was different. Quickly he ran to Watson in another room, saying, "What did you do then? Don't change anything. Let me see."

Bell knew that the "break" had come. He gave Watson instructions for making the first telephone. The next day the sound of the human voice was heard, not in clear words but enough to know that success was assured. The experiments continued; and in September, Bell applied for a patent. On his twenty-ninth birthday, March 7, 1876, the inventor received his patent, the most valuable one ever issued in any country. Three days later the telephone talked, and in June, when it was shown at the Philadelphia Centennial Exposition, the judges declared that it was the most wonderful thing in America.

A year later Bell married Hubbard's daughter and sailed for England to introduce the telephone there. However, a rival company, using largely his ideas, already had the business there. During this visit the idea came to him that cables of telephone wires could be laid underground, or suspended overhead, and messages could be exchanged within a city and between different cities. The mind that invented the telephone was imaginative enough to foresee how wide might be its use to people everywhere.

Returning to America, Bell lived in Washington, where he was called upon frequently to defend his patent. In 1880 the French government awarded him the Volta prize, which he used to make the first phonograph records on wax discs. The income from this project was used to carry on his work with the deaf. He founded and financed the American Association to Promote the Teaching of Speech to the Deaf, giving many years of service to this work.

In other fields in which Bell experimented, he merely supplied the idea. His inquiring mind and pioneering spirit led the way while others carried the idea to completion. In 1908 he predicted that before long a man could take dinner in New York and breakfast the next morning in Liverpool. In a magazine article he described a device which had the same purpose as the iron lung, and several years before the Xray was discovered he perfected an electric probe which was used in surgery.

To young people everywhere who are interested in making their lives count, Alexander Graham Bell's career offers special inspiration. His name is written high on the roll of American geniuses who have contributed to the welfare of mankind. His work for the deaf hastened the development of enlightened methods for their education, and inspired the improvement of institutions devoted to their care. His telephone has largely shaped the whole pattern of modern life. It is an indispensable tool for living—in business, in social contacts, and in maintaining family and community ties. Not only has it made the world smaller, but it can become an agency in the hands of man to bring about a better understanding among the nations of the world.

Bell was an enthusiastic and tireless worker. In his younger days he often awakened his friends in the middle of the night to share the excitement of some discovery or the progress on some experiment. His inquiring interest in the world about him at the age of seventy reveals how unusual were the powers of his mind. Those who knew him were impressed by his charming personality and his desire to serve others. He was kind, considerate, impulsive, and generous. He became a citizen of the United States in 1882, a fact of which he was proud. But he was more than that: he was a citizen of the world who left an invaluable legacy for all mankind.

The spirit of the inventor may be seen in the following statements which he made to the youth of his day: "Don't keep forever on the public road, going only where others have gone. Leave the beaten track occasionally and dive into the woods. You will be certain to find something you have never seen before. Of course, it will be a little thing, but do not ignore it. Follow it up, explore all around it; one discovery will lead to another; and before you know it you will have something worth thinking about to occupy your mind. All really big discoveries are the result of thought." [1]

STORY 6

APPRECIATION THAT CAME TOO LATE

In the quaint old city of Salzburg, Austria, there was born a child prodigy whose development is one of the unique stories in the history of music. Wolfgang Mozart began to show his passion for music at the age of three. One afternoon at the close of his sister's music lesson, he went to the piano and played her exercises perfectly. At a time when other children were interested only in play, his mind was on music. He would sit at the piano for hours at a time.

His father, a musical director, taught the boy, and at five the boy not only played well but composed a number of short selections. Two years later the father took him on a tour of the chief cities of Europe, where he played in concerts before large groups. When presented at the royal court in Paris, he played the great organ in the King's Chapel and did it so well that he won the praise of the king and queen. But in spite of all the attention that was given to him he remained unspoiled.

Later, when the lad played in Buckingham Palace, to test his skill the king placed before him difficult compositions by Bach and Handel which he played correctly at sight. His genius was recognized at once, for he played with the skill of musicians many times his age. Even greater acclaim was given to him in England than in France. In fact he was given praise everywhere, and presented with enough gold snuff-boxes to set up a shop, but in money he remained poor. During his stay in England he composed ten sonatas for piano and violin, six of which were published.

At thirteen years of age Mozart was taken to Rome, where he listened to the organs in the great cathedrals. During Holy Week he visited the Sistine Chapel and heard the famous *Miserere* of Allegri, which had not yet been published. This selection was considered so sacred that it was not allowed to be taken from the chapel, and those who had tried to reproduce it from memory had failed. But after hearing it once the youthful musician wrote it entirely from memory. However, he went to hear it again so that he might correct any possible mistakes.

A few days later when the lad played this selection in the chapel, the master of the choir asked for the name of the person who had secretly given the boy a copy of the music. The master was astonished when the boy showed the copy of the music that he had made, and it was found to be identical with that used by the choir members. At this time the pope conferred upon the lad the Order of the Golden Spur, making him a knight. While in Milan the boy composed the opera, *Mitridate,* which was sung for twenty nights in succession.

At the age of twenty-five Mozart left Salzburg to live in Vienna, a center of culture where he hoped his music would be better appreciated. A year later he married Constance Weber, and the struggle for a living became ten times harder; however, during the next nine years he produced his finest compositions. He was appointed to a court position by the emperor, but at a low salary. To support his family Mozart took pupils and wrote numerous compositions, all the while filling his court position.

Mozart's wife did everything within her power to stretch their income, but there were limits beyond which she could not go. In extremely cold weather when there was no money for fuel a friend called and found Mozart and his wife waltzing to keep warm. Under this strain of poverty Mozart's health began to fail. But the hardships and the suffering did not affect his creative power or crush his spirit; he continued to write his matchless music. He did not mind his own suffering. He could endure that. The hardest part was to see his wife suffer and to be unable to do anything about it. However, she bore it courageously and without complaint.

On one occasion when Mozart was already at the breaking point his publisher called to say, "Mozart, your music is too difficult for the people to understand or to appreciate. If you do not write in a popular style, I will neither print your music nor give you a penny for it." Though at the time Mozart was without money and suffering from hunger and cold, he replied, "Then, my good sir, I have only to resign and die of starvation. I cannot write as you demand." It was during these lean years that he composed three of his greatest symphonies.

A mysterious stranger came to Mozart asking him to compose a requiem, but did not say for whom it was intended. In his weakened condition Mozart imagined that he was writing it for his own funeral, and so he was, for just before it was completed he died, apparently from typhus. There were debts, his wife was ill, and his friends did not come to his aid, so Mozart's body was hastily buried in a pauper's grave in a cemetery in Vienna.

The weather was so disagreeable that no one except the attendants at the cemetery stood at the grave during the ceremony. His wife, too ill to attend the funeral, returned later and found that a new grave digger was unable to identify her husband's grave. All her efforts to locate it proved fruitless, and so it happens that one of the greatest musicians of all time lies in an unknown and unmarked grave. Half a century later Salzburg erected a bronze statue in his honor, and seventy years later Vienna built a monument to his memory.

Mozart wrote over eight hundred works, which include eighteen operas, forty-nine symphonies, fifteen overtures, and seventy-eight sacred compositions. For this prodigious amount of creative work he did not receive enough money to pay for the bare necessities of life, but through all his suffering there was no sign of abatement in the flow of his musical ideas. His body, weakened by a meager diet, became susceptible to the disease which caused his untimely death at the age of thirty-five. The great musician died before he reached the summit of his genius.

Throughout his lifetime Mozart was burdened with debt and suffered from privations and overwork; he died in want and sorrow, and through sheer neglect was buried in a pauper's grave. His music brought joy to countless thousands, but during his lifetime the sale of it did not bring him the ordinary comforts of life. The world is slow to show gratitude to those of its own time who contribute much to humanity.

The people of his day did not recognize the greatness of Mozart's music, but a later generation acclaimed him a genius and spoke of his music as having a message for people of every age. It is a black mark on society when it does not recognize greatness in the gifted people of its own generation. We as members of society carry our part of the burden of that guilt, for we participate in it. Scientific truths are accepted immediately today, but the world is still slow to accept truth in other fields.

STORY 7

HEROINE IN BUCKSKIN

THE VAST Pacific Northwest belongs to the United States today because of a slim young Indian squaw. Without Sacajawea, the heroine who guided the Lewis and Clark expedition, these rich lands west of the Rockies might have become British.

In 1804 Lewis and Clark were encamped on the lower Missouri River with orders from President Jefferson to explore and claim the Northwest Territory in the name of the United States. Before them lay a wide expanse of mountains and hostile Indian country. The hand-picked party consisted of twenty-nine seasoned woodsmen and Clark's Negro servant, York. They picked up along the way a half-breed interpreter named Charbonneau, who insisted that he be allowed to take his wife on the trip.

Charbonneau's wife was a Shoshone Indian. The explorers knew that when they reached the Far Northwest they would have to deal with the Shoshones. These Indians had horses which the party would need to cross the Continental Divide. The journey had hardly begun when Sacajawea, the squaw, earned the respect and gratitude of Lewis and Clark.

One day the exploring part arrived at the upper reaches of the Missouri River. Charbonneau was steering the forward canoe—a dug-out with sail in which Sacajawea and her baby always rode. In it were stored the expedition's instruments, maps, medicine, and vital supplies. Lewis and Clark had agreed that one of them would always remain in this boat, but on that morning both leaders had gone ashore while the others continued upstream.

Suddenly a squall blew up and keeled the leading boat half over. The frightened men began to shout, and the hysterical Charbonneau broke into a sobbing prayer. Sacajawea saw the supplies sliding overboard—the articles which were indispensable to the success of the enterprise.

With the agility of a wild creature she jumped forward and snatched them from the swirling current. Her presence of mind steadied the frightened men, who sprang into action and righted the boat.

As the journey continued, Sacajawea's resourcefulness and usefulness daily became more apparent. She repaired the men's frayed clothing with the crude instruments of the forest—needles of small bird bones and thread of fiber and hide. Later, as the men's shoes and garments began to give out entirely, she made new ones of buckskin. When colic and dysentery struck the company, Sacajawea showed them how to find wilderness foods to supplement their monotonous campfire meals of salt fish, jerked meat, and bread. She knew how to retrieve the delicious wild artichokes stored in the gophers' winter holes; she dug roots of wild carrots and fennel, from which she made nourishing soups for the men.

Finally the expedition approached its most crucial test—the first meeting with the Shoshone tribe, upon whom the leaders depended for guidance across the mountains into the broad Columbia River Valley. Lewis and Clark had only a rough elk-hide map of this country. Sacajawea had not seen the region since her childhood, yet she recalled immediately the passes through the mountains, which to the untrained eye were only row upon row of sharp ridges. She had an uncanny sense of direction, and Lewis and Clark soon learned to follow her without question.

One day the party waited tensely as a band of Shoshone horsemen approached. Lewis and Clark were astounded to see Sacajawea run forward, throw her blanket over the chief, and burst into tears of joy. The chief was Cameahwait, Sacajawea's brother. The chance meeting was the purest good luck.

Cameahwait was obviously proud of a sister who was treated with respect by the white chiefs. His pride changed to gratitude when she brought out a packet of marvelous new foods which the explorers had saved as a gift for the tribe. The white men knew that the Shoshones were a hungry people, so hungry that they often devoured their game raw. They had never tasted the squash, corn, beans, and sugar which were now laid before them. Cameahwait was so impressed that he not only promised to help the party, but he induced his people to postpone their annual buffalo hunt so that they could guide the expedition over the Great Divide. ..

In turn Lewis and Clark, using Sacajawea as interpreter, promised the Shoshones that the Great White Father, President Jefferson, would make it possible for them to hunt to the south without danger from other tribes. They would be taught to grow corn, beans, and squash, and to live in comfort and plenty. Trading posts would be established, and they would get guns which would make hunting easier.

Yet under the surface there was a hint of treachery. Certain members of the tribe feared that in guiding the whites they would miss the buffalo, so they plotted to lead the party into the mountains and abandon them. Sacajawea discovered the plot and reported it to Lewis and Clark. The two leaders at once staged further entertainment, pipe-smoking, dancing, and singing, supplemented with pledges of good will and gifts of medals and plumed hats for the leading members of the tribe. The Shoshones agreed to keep their word, and the expedition moved on across its most dangerous barrier.

From this time on Sacajawea was no longer the "squaw" but Janey, their friend. As the party encountered one hostile tribe after another, she preached the gospel of "trust the whites," and her eloquence overcame all distrust. She taught the white men how music and dancing could be used to reassure the tribes that they met along the way. A fiddler whom Lewis and Clark had brought along would play his familiar tunes, and York, the Negro, would clog and shuffle, delighting the red men who had never seen such a performance. The Indians danced, too, softly beating the earth with their moccasined feet.

For her services during the two and a half year's trip, Sacajawea asked for one favor—to be allowed to go with the men to view the Big Water, the Pacific Ocean. When she saw it, her awe at the sight of the ocean, however, was lost in her amazement at the size of a whale cast up on the beach. In later years when she told her fish story to hundreds of inland Indians, she saw them shake their heads and mutter, "Big lie."

Sacajawea crossed the country many times with free passes on the early stagecoaches, and wherever she went she spread good will between the whites and Indians. She lived to be one hundred years old. When the march of civilization westward made game scarce, she tried to persuade the northern Indians to learn agriculture and to adopt the ways of white men.

Since her death her fame has grown steadily. Historians agree that had the Lewis and Clark expedition failed, the English would have reached the northwest coast first and established their claim to this vast territory. On the hills above Portland, Oregon, now stands a majestic bronze statue to Sacajawea, who saved for America the great mines, forests, and agricultural lands of those states of incomparable beauty —Montana, Idaho, Washington, and Oregon.

When Lewis and Clark decided to take Sacajawea on the expedition, they did not know that she would win fame, and that a hundred years later the historian James Truslow Adams, an elector to the Hall of Fame, would choose her as one of the six most important American women.[1]

STORY 8

EACH BURNING STAR PROCLAIMS GOD'S GLORY

MICHAEL PUPIN's scientific career began in his boyhood when he spent part of his vacation watching his father's herd of oxen. He was one of a squad that was chosen to guard the cattle from the thieves. The pastures were not fenced in, and at night the peasants from neighboring villages would hide in the tall corn and capture an ox when he was drawn there by his appetite. The boys were warned of the movement of the cattle by a system of signaling which their parents had taught them.

The boys lay down, separated from one another and about twenty yards from the cornfield; then they put their ears close to the handles of knives which had been stuck into the ground, and "listening in" they heard the noise of the cattle's hoofs, which traveled through the ground and made the knives vibrate. It took days of patient listening to learn the trick, but once it was accomplished, it was easy to tell whether the oxen were far away or near the cornfield.

This was a great challenge to Michael; he wanted to know how things happened, and why. At night when the boys were telling stories he was often silent as he watched the stars. He knew they were far away, and yet light from them reached him. He asked, "What is this thing streaming out of them, something like fire, only it does not go out?"

Michael remembered the nineteenth psalm, which his mother had taught him: "The heavens declare the glory of God. . . . Day unto day uttereth speech, and night unto night sheweth knowledge." What was that speech? What were the stars trying to say to him? He imagined that the light from the distant stars was a message from God helping him to guard the cattle. In a search for an answer to these questions he began his scientific career.

Michael, born in Hungary, was descended from Serbs who had been guaranteed political freedom on condition that they defend Austria against Turkish invasion. They kept their contract, but the emperor broke his by turning them over to Hungary. Young Michael made up his mind that he would never serve in the emperor's army because of the broken contract.

From the neighborhood meetings held in his home during the winter evenings Michael learned that the noblest thing in the world was the struggle for right, justice, and freedom. He heard about Lincoln, a great man who kept his word, and about another American who had discovered that lightning is electricity and had got a spark from that mysterious power. He had a great desire to go to America and learn more about its great leaders.

Michael's mother could neither read nor write, but was determined that her son should have an education. One day she said to him, "I feel that I am blind—so blind that I dare not venture beyond the confines of my native village. If you wish to go out into the world, you must provide yourself with another pair of eyes—the eyes of reading and writing. There is so much wonderful knowledge in the world that you cannot know unless you read and write. Knowledge is the golden ladder over which we climb to heaven; it is the light which illumines our pathway through this life."

The boy noticed that his mother did not say that knowledge is a means of becoming rich and famous, but that it makes for a richer, fuller life. He went to school in Panchevo, where the teachers made a profound impression upon him because of their knowledge of the natural sciences. Later he enrolled in the University of Prague but was not satisfied, for the Czechs and Germans were always arguing about which language should be spoken.

It seemed to Michael that America offered greater opportunities. His desire to go to the new country was such that he sold his books, his watch, and his warm clothes to pay for his passage. The voyage made by steerage during the month of March when the sea was rough made a vivid impression upon the boy.

When Michael landed in New York, the immigrant authorities, finding him strong and healthy but with only five cents in his pocket, were doubtful about admitting him. When asked about his friends in America he replied that Franklin and Lincoln were his friends. He talked of his pride in the Serbs, how they stood at the edge of Western Europe, fought back the Turks, and kept them from destroying Serbian religion and civilization. The examiner decided to admit a boy who talked so well and used such judgment in the choice of his friends.

Michael's first job on a farm did not appeal to him, but the daughter of the farmer helped him to learn English, and in a short while he was able to get a better job. He went to New York, where he became a helper in a boiler room. Jim, the foreman, taught him how to fire the engine, but when the boy was ready to apply for a fireman's license, Jim advised against it, saying, "There are plenty of men with strong muscles to do this kind of work, but not many with a brain such as you have. Go to school; get out of the boiler room as soon as you can."

Michael enrolled at Cooper Union Night School, where he made good use of its splendid library. He became interested in scientific articles appearing in the New York papers, and decided to go further in his education and become a scientist. He knew that it meant hard work and sacrifice, but he did not hesitate. Five years after landing in New York he enrolled in Columbia University and graduated four years later with honors, receiving a scholarship to continue his study in Cambridge University. Later he studied at the University of Berlin, where he received his doctorate and at the same time an invitation to teach in America.

Returning to Columbia University he taught until he was appointed director of the Phoenix Research Laboratories. Later he was elected a member of the National Academy of Sciences. In his research he made discoveries upon which others have built. His device which made possible selective tuning was used by Marconi to receive messages of different wave lengths. Pupin's most important invention was bought by the Bell Telephone Company and used to eliminate the buzzing and clicking sounds on long distance calls.

In 1917 Pupin turned over to the United States government his invention which did away with static interference in wireless transmission. When Roentgen discovered the X ray, it was Pupin who made the first X ray for surgical work. Many honors came to him: an honorary degree from Johns Hopkins University, the Hebert prize of the French Academy in Physics, and the gold medal of the National Institute of Science.

When Pupin died in 1935, he was world-famous. It was a long journey from the immigrant boy with five cents in his pocket to the great teacher and renowned scientist. Along the way there was hard work, many difficulties to overcome, but by seizing every opportunity for advancement he finally reached his goal. His thirst for knowledge led him to find out the why of things. His religious background led him to believe that science is leading man closer to God, and will make better Christians of all who try to understand God's simple and beautiful laws.

During his youth while working as a herdsman, Pupin said, "I watched the stars and felt that their light was a language proclaiming the glory of God. I did not know how that language reached me, but I hoped that someday I might find out. Today science tells us that the stars themselves bring it to us. Each burning star is a focus of energy, of life-giving activity, which it pours out lavishly into every direction of the energy-hungry space; it pours out life in order to beget life. . . . The light of the stars is a part of the life-giving breath of God. I never look upon them without feeling this divine breath and its quickening action upon my soul, and I am sure that scientific research will bring us closer to this divinity." [1]

A NEGRO WAS ALSO THERE

THE HARDSHIPS which he withstood in his childhood and youth gave Matthew Henson the physical stamina which he needed for a still more hazardous undertaking. When left an orphan at eight years of age, Matthew made his home with an uncle in Washington who lived in sight of the Potomac River. As he watched the ships go by from every part of the world, an intense desire came over him to embark on one of these vessels and learn something of the country beyond.

Slipping away to Baltimore one day he watched the boats that docked there. Without stopping to consider the country from which they came, he boarded a vessel that was about to sail for China, and asked for a job. Signing up as a cabin boy, he spent the next four years at sea traveling between North America, the Orient, France, Spain, and Russia.

In 1888, returning as an experienced seaman, Henson met the man with whom he was to make a trip of great significance. Immediately he felt drawn to this man who commanded respect and admiration. Robert E. Peary, a civil engineer in the United States Navy, was ready to sail on a mission to Nicaragua, and he invited Henson to go with him. Naturally, Henson was delighted to embark on a mission with a man whom he so thoroughly admired.

Upon his return to the United States after an absence of three years, Peary invited Henson to join him on an expedition to northern Greenland, and perhaps to the North Pole. In spite of the dangers involved, Henson eagerly accepted the invitation. Peary equipped himself and his men for the enterprise and set out with great expectation. Their personal risks were great as they fought their way nearer and nearer to the goal. Seven attempts were made, and seven times they turned back in failure, but they did not give up in defeat.

Henson worked in any capacity in which he was needed: as carpenter, cook, blacksmith, or navigator. When called upon to treat frozen hands and feet, he thawed them out with the warmth of his own body. He learned the language, the customs, and the skill of the Eskimos. With his own hands he built the sledges which took them on the last lap of their final journey.

On July 6, 1908, they sailed on the "S.S. Roosevelt" on their eighth trip, and after fighting through almost impassable ice they anchored at Camp Sheridan in northern Greenland, and from there made their way on sledges pulled by dog teams to their final base. On March 1, 1909, they started from this point on sledges and on foot for the four hundred miles of frozen ocean between them and the North Pole.

Progress was difficult, for the wind was blowing a gale and the temperature was 57 degrees below zero. In this day of radio and airplane we can hardly visualize the dangers and obstacles which they encountered on this expedition. When the sledges broke down and their feet were frozen, the weaker men turned back until, at last, only Peary and Henson with four hardy Eskimos were left. With dogged determination they pushed on and on until they were almost dead from exhaustion. Henson had the courage and hardihood to stay with Peary, and together they persevered until the goal was reached.

On one occassion the ice was so rough and jagged that they had to use their pickaxes to cut a trail. Once the runner of a sledge cut through the "young ice," but two Eskimos acted quickly and saved the sledge and dogs from being submerged. This averted a very serious accident, for that particular sledge contained the Commander's sextant and other instruments which were essential to the success of the expedition.

Ten months had elapsed since the expedition had started. At last, on April 6, 1909, Peary took his observation, calculated his position, and found that the goal had been reached. When they halted and started to build the igloos, Commander Peary unloaded his sledge and unpacked several bundles of equipment. He pulled from under his thick fur outer garment a small folded package and unfolded it. It was his old silk flag which he fastened to a staff and planted firmly on the top of his igloo. For several minutes it hung limp and lifeless in the dead calm of the haze, and then a slight breeze, increasing in strength, caused the folds to straighten out, and soon it was rippling out in sparkling color. The Stars and Stripes was "nailed to the Pole." [1]

On their return to New York City, Henson was given great acclaim and presented with a gold watch by his many admirers. The Geographic

Society of Chicago awarded him a gold medal forty years later. After a quarter of a century of adventure on the high sea Henson was content to enjoy the ease and comfort of civilian life. In 1913 he entered the United States Postal Service and served until he reached the age of retirement. He is now living quietly in New York City, and has the distinction of being one of the few men alive today who have been to the North Pole.

Peary considered Henson more than a personal attendant. He was a helper and trusted friend in whom the explorer placed a great deal of confidence. He paid this tribute to his faithful companion: "Matthew A. Henson, my Negro assistant, has been with me in one capacity or another since my second trip to Nicaragua, in 1887. I have taken him with me on each and all of my northern expeditions, except the first, in 1886, and almost without exception on each of my 'farthest' sledge trips. This position I have given him primarily because of his adaptability and fitness for the work; secondly, on account of his loyalty. He has shared all the physical hardships on my arctic work. He is now forty years old, and can handle a sledge better, and is probably a better dog-driver, than any other living person, except some of the best of the Eskimo hunters themselves. I congratulate the Negro race upon Matthew Henson. He has driven home to the world your adaptation and the fiber of which you are made. He has added to the moral stature of every intelligent man among you. His is the hard-earned reward of tried loyalty, persistence, and endurance." [2]

Every time a member of a minority race makes a worth-while contribution, he makes it in the name of his race. Not only does he add prestige to his race, but he opens doors and increases the chance for further development for other members of his race.

STORY 10

FRIEND OF PRISONERS

"You should not see such sights," cautioned the tutor.

"If the prisoner can endure it, I'm sure that I can bear to see it," replied Mathilda Wrede, daughter of the governor of the Vasa district in Finland. The incident about which the tutor spoke was the fitting of a red-hot iron to a prisoner's ankle.

Prison labor was frequently used about her home; the furniture in her room had been made by prisoners. On one occasion when a prisoner came to mend a lock on her bedroom door, Mathilda talked with him and learned something of life inside the prison, the kind of treatment the prisoners received. She was quite sure that she had discovered much that was good in the man. In turn she told him of her recent dedication to the service of others. Before they separated she promised to visit the jail on the following Sunday.

Her father was amazed when Mathilda told him of her plan to visit the jail. He advised her to control her feelings concerning the prisoners and to stay away from the jail. She protested saying, "But, Father, I have promised."

Her father agreed with her that a promise must be kept. Thus, at nineteen years of age, Mathilda Wrede began the prison work which continued throughout the remainder of her life. However hard she tried, she could not get away from the idea that this was the work to which she was called.

The horror of the Finnish prison system in the nineteenth century is revolting to most people. Men and women were beaten for minor offenses; they were underfed; they were herded into small unventilated rooms, and all kinds of indignities were heaped upon them. It was commonly believed that such treatment was necessary. Since most prisoners were of the poorer classes, the prison system was a threat held over them to keep them in their places.

Mathilda Wrede believed that prisons were actual schools of crime, judging from the high percentage of second offenders. When she started her movement to help prisoners, she was called an enemy to society; but she believed that all men, regardless of race or station, were children of God and should be given a chance. She contended that kind treatment would encourage them to become better citizens.

During a visit to the capital she obtained from the Chief Inspector of Prisons a permit to visit all the Finnish prisons. In the largest of them she found five hundred prisoners who were in for life. Seeing them chained by their necks, or wearing belts and collars which crossed back and forth, was a grueling experience. She was convinced that such treatment made them hard and bitter.

One man, haunted by his evil deeds, remarked to her, "If I could look back upon one good deed in my life, it would help." Mathilda's ready response was to ask for a drink. As she quenched her thirst from a drink which he offered, his face lighted up as he said, "This has been a great day for me." To others she gave encouragement and urged them to express their talents by making useful objects. Her friendship brought all of them new hope and courage, and helped to remake thousands of them.

Miss Wrede showed no fear in the presence of the most violent criminals. She was calm as she talked in the cell with a man who had forfeited his right to work as a carpenter because he had thrown his ax at a warden. He questioned her, "You surely know that I am the worst prisoner in Kakola. Aren't you afraid?"

To which she replied, "No, I am not in the least afraid, for I am sure that you would not harm me."

At another time a desperate criminal slipped his wrist chains about her neck, but her quick comment caused him to release her. Touched by her confidence in him, he remarked, "I thought there wasn't a person anywhere who cared about me, but now you come and show kindness. I suppose you are a Christian. I should like to be one, too, if that is possible."

Reassuring him that God is always ready to forgive when one repents and tries to lead a new life, she brought from him this response, "If it is true that God forgives, why don't men forgive, too? In these chains I'll grow worse day by day until I am a demon." She assured him that God cares, and he promised to co-operate in the prison to which he was doomed to spend the remainder of his days.

In addition to her work in the prisons Mathilda visited hospitals, preached, and ran a farm for discharged prisoners. There were times, however, when she was disappointed in those who appealed to her for help. A released prisoner who begged for money to go to America that he might start life over again, failed her. She had sold her horse, her most prized possession, to pay for the man's passage. But when he squandered the money in a drunken brawl, she did not lose faith in mankind.

During World War I, when the prisons were closed to her, she continued her work with released prisoners and the families of those still in prison. When permission was again granted for her to take up her work, an illness had sapped her strength, and it was impossible for her to continue her work. On her sixtieth birthday the women of Finland gave her a home which was furnished largely with prison-made furniture. In this home she lived four years, until her death on Christmas Day, 1928.

Mathilda Wrede saw something good in every person, and it was her faith in them that restored many to society again. Like the Master of men, she saw something of infinite worth in the thief and the murderer; her faith and confidence in them challenged them to make the effort to become worthy citizens. She bore the burdens of the poor and the friendless; she championed the cause of the minority groups. People in all walks of life were her friends—high officials as well as hardened criminals. Like another woman of whom Jesus spoke, it might be said of her, "She hath done what she could." [1]

STORY 11

THE MIRACLE OF "THE MESSIAH"

ONE night in 1741 a bent old man shuffled listlessly down a dark London street. George Frederick Handel was starting out on one of his aimless, despondent wanderings which had become a nightly ritual. His mind was a battleground between hope, based on his past glories, and despair for the future. For forty years Handel had written stately music for the aristocracy of England and the Continent. Kings and queens had showered him wth honors. Then court society turned against him; jealous rivals put rowdies to breaking up the performances of his operas. Handel was reduced to penury.

Four years before, a cerebral hemorrhage had paralyzed his right side. He couldn't walk, move his right hand, or write a note. Doctors held out little hope for his recovery. Handel went to Aix-la-Chapelle to take the healing baths. The doctors warned that staying in the scalding waters longer than three hours at a time might kill him. He stayed in nine hours at a time. Slowly strength crept back into his inert muscles. He could walk, move his hand. In an orgy of creativeness he wrote four operas in quick succession. Honors were again heaped upon him.

When Queen Caroline, a staunch patroness, died, Handel's income was reduced. A frigid winter gripped England, and there was no way of heating the theaters, so engagements were canceled. As Handel sank deeper and deeper into debt, he lost his creative spark. Nearly sixty, he felt old and hopelessly tired.

Now as he walked alone on the London street the façade of a church loomed dimly in the dark, and he paused before it, bitter thoughts welling up in him. "Why did God permit my resurrection only to allow my fellow men to bury me again? Why did he vouchsafe a renewal of my life if I may no longer be permitted to create?" And then that cry from the depths: "My God, my God, why hast thou forsaken me?"

Hopeless, he returned to his shabby lodgings. On entering he saw a bulky package on his desk. He broke the seal and clawed off the wrappings. So, a libretto: "A Sacred Oratorio." Handel grunted. From that second-rate, pampered poet, Charles Jennens. There was also a letter expressing the wish that Handel start work immediately on the oratorio, adding: "The Lord gave the Word."

Handel grunted again. Did Jennens have the effrontery to think he was inspired by God? Handel was not a pious man. He was always helping unfortunates, even when he could ill afford it, but he had a violent temper, was domineering, and made enemies right and left. Why hadn't Jennens sent him an opera instead of this religious stuff?

Listlessly Handel leafed through the oratorio and a passage caught his eye: "He was despised and rejected of men. He looked for someone to have pity on him, but there was no man; neither found he any to comfort him." With a growing sense of kinship, Handel read on. "He trusted in God. . . . God did not leave his soul in Hell. He will give you rest." The words began to come alive, to glow with meaning. "Wonderful Counselor" . . . "I know that my Redeemer liveth . . . Rejoice . . . Hallelujah."

Handel could feel the old fire rekindling. In his mind wondrous melodies tumbled over one another. Grabbing a pen, he started writing. With incredible swiftness the notes filled page after page.

Next morning his manservant found Handel bent over his desk. Putting the breakfast tray within easy reach, he slipped quietly out. At noon, when he returned, the tray had not been touched.

There followed an anxious time for the faithful old servant. The master would not eat. He'd take a piece of bread, crush it and let it fall to the floor—writing, writing all the while, jumping up and running to the harpsichord. At times he would stride up and down, flailing the air with his arms, singing at the top of his lungs, "Hallelujah! Hallelujah!"

"I've never seen him act like this before," confided the servant to a friend. "He just stares at me and doesn't see me. He said the gates of Heaven opened wide for him and God himself was there. I'm afraid he's going mad."

For twenty-four days Handel labored like a fiend, with little rest or food. Then he fell on his bed exhausted. On his desk lay the score of *The Messiah*—the greatest oratorio ever written.

Handel slept as though in a coma for seventeen hours. His servant, thinking he was dying, sent for the doctor. But before the doctor arrived, Handel was up and bellowing for food. He laughed heartily and joked with the doctor. "If you've come for a friendly visit, I like it, but there's nothing the matter with me."

Since London would have none of him, Handel took *The Messiah* to Ireland. The Lord Lieutenant had sent him a cordial invitation to come there. He would not accept a shilling for this work; the proceeds of its performance must go to charity. It was a miracle that had lifted him from deepest despondency; now let it be the hope of the world.

In Dublin he merged two choirs and rehearsed the work. Excitement mounted as the date of the first performance neared. All the tickets were quickly sold, and, to make more room, ladies were requested to come without hoops, gentlemen without swords. On April 13, 1742, crowds waited at the doors hours before the opening. The response of that first audience was tumultuous.

After that triumph London was anxious to hear the work, and during the first performance a dramatic incident occurred. At the Hallelujah Chorus the crowd, following the king's example, surged to its feet and remained standing until the conclusion—a practice that has persisted to this day.

While Handel lived he presented *The Messiah* yearly, the proceeds going to the foundling hospital. In his will he gave the royalties from this work to the same charity. Later he was beset with many difficulties, but he never again succumbed to despair. Age sapped his vitality. He went blind. But his undaunted spirit remained to the last.

On the evening of April 6, 1759—Handel was seventy-four—he was present at a performance of *The Messiah*. At the beginning of "The trumpets shall sound," he felt faint and nearly fell. Those near by steadied him. Friends helped him home and to bed. A few days later he said, "I should like to die on Good Friday." And on April 13, the anniversary of that first presentation of *The Messiah,* true to his wish, the soul of George Frederick Handel departed his body. But his spirit goes marching on in *The Messiah,* the triumph of hope over despair. Its performance in London's Albert Hall on Good Friday is today a traditional part of the celebration of Easter.

In *The Messiah,* Handel lit a torch that has been carried around the world to light the dark places of the earth as long as there are voices to lift in song, eyes to look to the hills, hearts to hope.[1]

A MODERN ITALIAN MADONNA

MARIA shuddered as the storm beat again upon the thatched cottage so that it trembled, and through the little window she could see a livid flash of lightning that rent the clouds. On the shore of the Mediterranean storms are not rare, but storms such as this do not occur every day even on the Italian coast. Maria winced at the lightning and thunder. Though she was thirteen and large for her age, she was afraid. Never before had she been alone in the house during a storm. She wondered if her father was safe.

There was a knock at the door. With trembling hands she unbolted and opened the door. As if the lightning had thrust him in, a man fell over the threshold and into the room, a cold blast blowing behind him. She helped him to a place beside the fire and brought food to him. He drank the wine and ate the cheese offered to him. When rested he related the story of his life in the monastery. As he spoke his face was no longer that of a tired man but of a prophet, and his voice was like a bell.

"Blessed shalt thou be, Maria, above all women because thou hast given food and shelter to a servant of God. Many shall be blessed because of thee." And then he was gone.

Maria asked, "Who was this man—a saint, an angel? One hears of such things in legends."

When her father returned, Maria told him of the visit of the monk but not of the blessing. Like another Maria of old, she pondered that in her heart. What did the monk mean? Perhaps she was to be a great lady and give alms to all the poor folks in the parish—to the crippled boy who begged, to the old market woman. So she continued to dream and to work, too, for Maria was a peasant and life was not easy.

One day, when she was about sixteen, something finer than fame came to her. It was the love of a good man, Pietro, the cooper, who lived on the other side of the hill and whose vineyard was the most prosperous in the entire countryside. They were married, and as the years went by two children came to them—boys with great brown eyes like their mother's. Now indeed there was work to do, caring for two boys who grew so fast. Sometimes at night she would recall that she had once dreamed of being a great lady, and she would laugh to herself, saying, "I do not look like one now—with my homespun dress and hardened hands. 'A blessing to the world,' the monk said. Well, if I can be a blessing to my husband and children, that is all I will hope for now."

One sunny afternoon she sat in the little dooryard watching Pietro at his work, holding the baby in her lap. The older boy held up a cross made from scraps of wood his father had left from making the casks. Just then a stranger entered the dooryard, evidently a man from the city. Maria gathered her child in her arms to rise and make him welcome.

"No," he said, "please sit just as you are with the little one at your knee. There. I should like to sketch your picture. I am a painter by trade." The man took one of the cask heads from the ground and began to make lines upon it with charcoal. Maria smoothed her hair as she thought of her rough dress. But after all, what matter how she looked. It was her boys' pictures which counted. She looked at their shining eyes, and her heart swelled with pride that they should have been entrusted to her keeping.

As the artist worked, he talked to himself: "Perfect! That expression—motherhood incarnate! What a Madonna!" When finished, he tossed a piece of silver to Pietro, said a hurried "Thank you," and strode from the yard, the cask head under his arm.

The visit of the artist was only an incident in the life of the busy mother. There was much work to be done in the home on the hillside. When Maria thought of the old monk and the promised blessing, it was with a wry smile. A blessing to the world—she! Nothing for her now but to minister to those she loved. But they were dear to her, and she was happy with her work.

Years later word came to their village of a wonderful painting by an artist named Raphael. The picture would hang in the Cathedral of Florence until everyone had a chance to see it; then it would be taken away to hang in one of the great galleries of the world. Rumor said that it was a picture of the Madonna—the most beautiful that had ever come from the brush of an artist.

Pietro and Maria planned a trip to the city to see the painting. They could hardly wait to reach the cathedral. What would the Holy Mother and the Baby be like? From the glare of the street they passed into the dimly lighted church, and inquired the way of an attendant. A moment later they stood looking at the wonderful picture in the great gold frame.

Maria's eyes were shining. Then she gasped, "Pietro! The artist—the cask head—our boys! It's our baby and little brother with the cross made from scraps of wood. Don't you remember?"

Pietro was gazing too. "Maria! That other figure—that is you—with the smooth hair and the wonderful eyes. That is you—you are the Madonna!"

Maria's heart stood still. Suddenly the old monk's words came back, and she could hear him speaking as if he were by her side: "Happy shalt thou be above all other women, and many shall be blessed because of thee." Maria bowed her head in prayer, realizing that the monk's prophecy had been fulfilled in her in the humble tasks of motherhood.[1]

STORY 13

A PICTURE FOR TRINITY

SLOW poisons were seeping through the congregation at Trinity—the poisons of labor-management bitterness and hatred. Sitting alone in the auditorium that afternoon I looked up at the painting, Dürer's "Praying Hands," newly hung in the recessed space behind the chancel. Footsteps interrupted my thoughts. Looking up I saw Sandy, the tall, red-haired janitor, who had come from the church-school room below. He walked in front of the picture and studied it a long time.

In the few months I'd been at Trinity I had come to realize that Sandy was more than a janitor. He was a real part of Trinity. It was Sandy who wanted a picture for that space in the front of the auditorium. It was he who selected it and bought it out of his small salary.

"Folks think that's a queer picture to hang in a church," he explained. "Fingers with big joints like that must have done hard work."

"Yes," I said. "There's a story behind the hands in that painting."

Sandy nodded. "I wanted that picture for Trinity on account of the story. It kind of belongs here."

"In a way, Sandy," I added, "it belongs anywhere because all of us—in one way or another—work with our hands. I am going to use the story of that picture as a part of Sunday's sermon."

"I'm glad you want to make a sermon about it. I was hoping you would, Pastor. I had a special reason for wanting a picture for Trinity—not just any picture, but that 'Praying Hands' picture. Things here at Trinity aren't good."

In my study half an hour later the phone rang. Sam Sherwood, president of the Sherwood Limestone Company was calling. He wanted to talk to me in his office at the plant. "I'll come out," I promised, but I was wishing I could have refused him. I was being pulled into the vortex of this labor-management dispute.

Later I faced the executive across the top of a desk. As I sat down my gaze found a pair of tense hands gripping the edge of the desk, the large-jointed fingers twisted nervously over the top. The resemblance to the hands in the painting was unmistakable, I thought, and no wonder, for I had heard the story of Sam Sherwood and of his boy-out-of-the-quarries career. Until a few years before he was often in overalls, working beside his men. Little wonder that his hands should look like those of a workingman.

Sam Sherwood went right to the point. "When my men went on strike, the pastor at Trinity then seemed to have all the answers."

"All the answers?" I repeated, smiling dubiously.

"What did I do?" he continued. "I gave in to their demands. I raised their wages and recognized their union. The Christian thing to do, he said."

My gaze followed that pair of hands as they fell back on the desk. "In a way, perhaps, I was wrong then," the president admitted frankly. Suddenly his jaws tightened. "But now, with their wages more than doubled, throughout my entire plant there is only grumbling. My men hate me. Production has fallen off so that I can no longer meet competition."

I knew all of these things when I had been at Trinity less than a week. Trinity was the only church in this limestone town. It ministered to Sam Sherwood, president of the corporation, and to Bill Lester, president of the union, as well as to each of the other members.

"Bill Lester—" I said, leading into the subject. Bill, as president of the union, was the key to the whole situation.

"Bill Lester!" Sherwood's fist hit the desk. "That trouble-maker! If only I could get rid of him."

"You don't understand Bill," I said quickly. "Bill's a crusader. He feels he's leading your men in a cause. When Bill feels that he's in the right, he'll fight. You can't stop him. Nothing can."

"When he feels he's in the right!" Sherwood shouted at me. "Then show him he's wrong. A crusader! That constant sketching of his maddens me."

"Bill's clever with a pencil," I explained.

There was a brief silence. The flush of fury in Sherwood had spent itself. "Sit down with your men once more. Talk things over with them," I suggested.

"With Bill Lester?" he demanded sharply. "No."

"Do this then," I continued. "Sunday we are dedicating the picture that Sandy bought. We'd like to see you at the service."

"I heard about the selection he made. Why didn't you make him put something better there?"

"It was Sandy's project. I can't interfere."

On Saturday I called a list of people I had seen only once or twice. As I sat at my desk, the telephone in my hands, I had Bill Lester on the phone. To him I could be frank, for he was intelligent. "We must check this virus of bitterness that is seeping through Trinity. Get your men together with Sam Sherwood. Sit down and talk things over."

"Get Sam Sherwood to send away those men with their stop watches. They check every move, as if we were criminals," Bill snapped.

I felt I understood how working under conditions like that could be exasperating; but had the men ever tried to see Sherwood's point of view? Competition in his business was keen. With the high wages he was paying, he had to watch everything.

"Sherwood is a slave driver," Bill added. "Sit down with him? Never!"

"Bill," I asked, "will you come to the service in the morning? That picture that Sandy worked so hard for has been put up."

"I've heard about it," Bill explained. "With all the fine paintings to select from, why did you let Sandy pick that one?"

"Because," I explained, "it's Sandy's picture for Trinity."

Sunday morning as I sat in the chancel looking at the faces before me, I felt very small. Sam Sherwood was on my right, Bill Lester on my left—both professed to believe in the teachings of Jesus, but here in a common worship service they were thinking bitter thoughts. Much of the sermon was the story of Dürer, the artist who painted the "Praying Hands." I directed my listeners to the hands in the picture. "Those hands in prayer are the hands of a friend who made the great sacrifice."

When the service ended, I hurried to the door to shake hands. The building emptied quickly; then I walked toward the front of the room to gather up my sermon notes. Suddenly I saw Sherwood sitting on a front pew studying the painting on the wall. As I gathered up my notes, Sherwood said, "I've changed my mind about that painting. All the money Dürer could ever give his friend would never repay him for the great sacrifice."

"That is true," I nodded.

"Hands." He spoke the words as if he had been pondering it a long time. "In a way hands are doing for me, too. Does my weekly check relieve me of all further obligation?"

Then suddenly, as if embarrassed by the frankness of his own words, Sam Sherwood rose and left the room. As I stood there, Bill Lester walked up the center aisle and stopped to look at the painting on the wall. He jerked a scratch pad from his coat pocket, studied something on it, then looked back at the painting.

"It's uncanny," he muttered. "The resemblance."

"The resemblance?" I repeated.

Bill showed me the pad. "It's a sketch of Sam Sherwood's hands," he explained. "I made it once while I was sitting in a conference."

"There is something . . ." I admitted.

"Maybe it was the story about that picture that made me think all these things," Bill continued. "Still it was Sam Sherwood's own hands that built the business which provides the rest of us with a job." He stopped, put the pad back in his pocket, and turned to go. "Forget what I did," he said over his shoulder and hurried toward the door.

When I turned to go, I saw that I was not alone. Sandy was there gazing at his beloved picture. Not wishing to disturb his meditations, I started to go, but he stopped me. "Look," he exclaimed. "They're hands like mine . . . like yours." Walking back, I watched his intent face. His eyes never left the picture. "I don't know where a man's soul abides, but it must be close to his hands." He turned to look at me. "I've got a feeling that's the way it is, Pastor."

I nodded. Sandy had preached an eloquent sermon. If only Sam Sherwood and Bill Lester had been there to hear it. "When a man does things with his hands, he puts some part of himself into it."

"Yes, Sandy," I agreed. "If only Sam Sherwood—"

A smile spread over Sandy's face. "That's what I wanted to talk to you about, Pastor. Sam Sherwood told me a minute ago he'll call his men together again to talk things over."

"But—" I interrupted. "How about Bill Lester? He wasn't in a compromising mood."

"It's different now," Sandy pointed out. "Bill promised me last night he'd come any time Sam Sherwood says."

There was an awkward silence. I did not know what to say. Sandy, the janitor at Trinity, had helped to draw the two men together with his picture. Only Sandy seemed to have words for the occasion. "Folks think that's a queer picture to hang on the walls of a church," he said. "But things here at Trinity are going to be better from now on." [1]

STORY 14

PIERRE'S PART

IN THE great studio, under the supervision of the master glazier, many workers were constructing the parts of a new window to be placed in the cathedral at Easter. Some were washing the glass with various tints and carrying the sheets to the kiln for burning; some were cutting the glass sheets into small pieces to be fitted into the different parts of the window. Other workers had fragments of pasteboard patterns, all of one color, which they arranged on a sheet of glass of the same hue and cut into the desired shapes. In the master's private room was a great cartoon, or colored pasteboard picture, of the window. There was also another complete pattern on which some of the most skillful men were fitting the mosaic, as the glass was brought from the shop.

Among the cutters was a youth, Pierre, who was working on an untinted glass of gray, greenish white. As he worked, he thought: "This plain glass is dull work. Jean there, who cuts the deep red, must enjoy his heap of jewels which glow like garnets and rubies. And Jacques yonder has amber and topaz. Guillaume has turquoise; Louis, sapphire; and Denis, beryl and aquamarine. They are like rich misers turning over their heap of gems. My work is cutting plain glass to fill the spaces about the picture. I suppose no one will notice my work, but the window is for God's glory, and the spaces must be filled. I as well as another may do it, and in the best way that I can.

"I wonder what the picture will be like when it is finished. The master is keeping it a secret, but I suppose that it will be a grand picture of saints and angels. Jean's ruby will make, perhaps, the shining satin and rich velvet of their robes; and Jacques's yellow their crowns and halos, and emerald will be the green grass and budding trees; and the others will be the azure sky and bright flowers, and I must fill the spaces. Yet, unless they are well filled, the picture will not be complete," mused Pierre as he measured and cut with greatest care.

"Well, my lad!" cried the master, coming to the bench at that moment. "I am glad that you are doing your part so well."

"So," said Pierre, "the master notices the plain glass which fills the spaces!"

As the winter days slipped by, the shop was bright with the colors of the glass. Pierre in his corner measured and cut the plain glass into pieces large and small—mere slender needles and bits almost too tiny for a man to hold between his fingers. As he worked he thought of the spaces of life, unnoticed and yet to be filled by the services of humble workmen.

Thinking along this line he began to notice some of these small services. It was he who often quietly found the missing bits of pattern and the borrowed tools in the workshop, when the men were beginning to fly into a rage over these things. He went on doing small services of which most of the workmen never thought. During Holy Week the men who did the final fitting of the mosaic and the setting into leaden frames were busy, but Pierre and the other cutters were having a holiday.

During these days Pierre walked in the forest and by the river, noticing the early wild flowers with their stars of rose, yellow, and white. He observed that their little disks made the forest floor into a beautiful mosaic. He dipped his hand into the river which was blue with the azure of the sky, and as the drops trickled off each one caught the sunshine and flashed with the colors of the rainbow. "Scarce anyone would notice a drop of water," he thought, "yet each single one is a thing of beauty."

Before Easter came, the covering and the scaffolds were taken from the wall, and the new window was revealed with all of its glowing colors. The fragments which Jean, Jacques, and the others had cut into meaningless pieces were now in their places, and full of meaning in the perfect window. Pierre noticed the rich ruby of the robes, the jeweled crowns, and the emerald grass, starred like the forest floor with rose and violet blossoms. In the highest medallion was the ascending Lord with two adoring angels.

Pierre forgot the rest of the beautiful window when he saw the highest group. Gazing at the winged angels and the holy face, he knelt and worshiped like the pictured angels. At that moment the master glazier came near and said, "Well, Pierre, do you like the window?" When he saw the look of reverence on the boy's face, he continued, "Oh, do you indeed find it so beautiful? You have the soul of an artist, and you have done your part well."

"My part!" exclaimed Pierre, surprised. He had not once thought of his own plain cutting, as he looked at the splendid window. "My part! Where is it?"

"There, on high in the last medallion," answered the master, "in the wings of the adoring angels and in the holy face."

"But the wings are not of dull, gray glass," said Pierre. "They are shining white, and the face is radiant and full of beauty."

"True," the master replied. "I touched all with my brushes at the last. The shining radiance comes to the plain glass when the work is quite finished and the sun is shining through, but the cutting and and the fitting were your work."

"Oh," murmured Pierre, "is that what happens to the bits of plain, colorless glass? At the end does the master touch and transform it, so that it seems no longer the work of the humble worker?"

The master understood Pierre in part and replied, "Nay, you know not, nor I, what is the highest nor the lowest, for every part is needed for the full beauty of the design. He who does well, the lowest, if such there be, is so much more fit to do the highest, if such there be. In God's mosaic there is neither high nor low." [1]

HEAVEN STOOPS LOW

A MILE and a half, it may be two miles, southeast of Bethlehem there is a plain separated from the town by an intervening swell of the mountain. At the side farthest from the town, and close under a bluff, there was an extensive sheepcote, ages old. In some long-forgotten foray the building had been unroofed and almost demolished. The inclosure attached to it remained intact, however, and that was of more importance to the shepherds who drove their charges thither than the house itself.

There were six of these men, omitting the watchman, and after a while they assembled in a group near the fire. They rested and talked, and while they talked, and before the first watch was over, one by one the shepherds went to sleep, each lying where he had sat.

The night, like most nights of the winter season in the hill country, was clear, crisp, and sparkling with stars. There was no wind. The atmosphere seemed never so pure; the stillness was more than silence; it was a holy hush, a warning that heaven was stooping low to whisper some good thing to the listening earth.

By the gate, hugging his mantle close, the watchman walked. The midnight was slow in coming to him; but at last it came. His task was done; and now for the dreamless sleep with which labor blesses its wearied children! He moved toward the fire, but paused; a light was breaking around him, soft and white, like the moon's. He waited breathlessly. The light deepened; things before invisible came into view; he saw the whole field, and all it sheltered. A chill sharper than that of the frosty air—a chill of fear—smote him. He looked up; the stars were gone; the light was dropping as from a window in the sky; and as he looked it became a splendor; then, in terror, he cried, "Awake, awake!"

Up sprang the dogs, and, howling, ran away. The herds rushed together, bewildered. The men clambered to their feet, weapons in hand. "What is it?" they asked in one voice.

"See!" cried the watchman. "The sky is on fire!" Suddenly the light became intolerably bright, and they covered their eyes and dropped upon their knees; then as their souls shrank with fear, they fell upon their faces, blind and fainting, and would have died had not a voice said unto them: "Fear not!"

And they listened. "Fear not; for behold, I bring you good tidings of great joy, which shall be to all people. For unto you, this day, in the city of David, is born a Saviour, which is Christ the Lord! And this shall be a sign unto you. Ye shall find the babe wrapped in swaddling clothes and lying in a manger."

The voice in sweetness and soothing more than human, and low and clear, penetrated all their being and filled them with assurance. They rose upon their knees and, looking up, beheld the appearance of a man, clad in a robe intensely white; above its shoulders towered the tops of wings shining and folded. A star over its forehead glowed with a steady luster, brilliant as Hesperus. Its hands were stretched toward them in blessing; its face was serene and divinely beautiful.

The herald spoke not again; his good tidings were told; and yet he stayed awhile. Then suddenly the light, of which he seemed the center, turned roseate and began to tremble; and then up, as far as the men could see, there was a flashing of white wings, and a coming and going of radiant forms, and voices as of a whole multitude chanting in unison, "Glory to God in the highest, and on earth peace, good will toward men!" Not once the praise, but many times.

Then the herald raised his eyes as seeking the approval of one afar off; his wings stirred, and spread slowly and majestically, on their upper side white as snow, in the shadows vari-tinted, like the mother-of-pearl. He rose lightly and, without effort, floated up out of sight, taking the light up with him. And long after he was gone, down from the sky in measures mellowed by distance fell the refrain: "Glory to God in the highest, and on earth peace, good will toward men."

Then the shepherds said to one another, "Come, let us take a wee ewe lamb from the fold, and go yonder into Bethlehem, and see this thing which has come to pass. The priests and doctors have been a long time looking for the Christ. Now he is born, and the Lord has given us a sign by which to know him. Let us go and worship him."

And they followed the light until it came and stood over where the young Child lay. And they went in, and found Mary and Joseph and the Child, asleep in the sweet-smelling hay. And they worshiped him, leaving the wee ewe lamb without spot or blemish as their offering; and returned again to their flock on the hillside, believing anew the words of their prophets.

"For unto us a Child is born. Unto us a Son is given. And the government shall be upon his shoulders; and of the increase of his Kingdom there shall be no end. And his name shall be called, 'Wonderful Counselor, the Mighty God, the Everlasting Father, the Prince of Peace.' " [1]

STORY 16

THAT SECOND MILE

Nimrod the shepherd came down a lonely hill road on one of his rare journeys to his home in the little town in the valley. He was walking steadily with a light foot and a light heart, thinking of the welcome that awaited him at the little square house in the corner of the olive grove at the end of the village. With easy stride he swung round a sharp bend in the road and had to pull himself up to avoid colliding with a tall soldier in the armor of a Roman guard, who carried a heavy pack upon his shoulders.

"Hold," the soldier cried in an instant. "In the name of the Emperor, carry my pack for a mile, for, verily, I am weary of the burden of it, in this heat."

Nimrod looked longingly at the little white house among the olives. He could see it from this point, and he was sure that yonder patch of blue against the green was little Rachel keeping watch for him. But what use to protest? Rome was Rome, and in Judea you must do as Rome commanded.

A mile and a heavy load—it was no easy thing in the mid-day heat. With a shrug of the shoulders, Nimrod picked up the soldier's pack and trudged along behind him over the road he had come. There was little but bitter resentment and hot anger in his heart at first. Then, in some way he could not explain, he began thinking of Jesus of Nazareth. One night in the hills Jesus had come out of the darkness and stood in the red light of the shepherds' campfire and wished them peace. He had sat down with them and talked of sheep and lambs as though he had been a shepherd himself all his days. Then he had gone on to talk of his new law, the law of love, the law in the heart that would always make a man do a little more than he was compelled to do. "Whosoever shall compel thee to go one mile with him, go with him twain." Strange that it should come back to him

—194—

now. Stranger still that all bitterness and anger seemed to have passed from his mind.

The voice of the soldier, speaking Aramaic dialect brokenly, broke in upon Nimrod's thoughts: "You have gone a mile. Put down the pack."

Nimrod looked up with a quiet smile. "I will go a little farther," he said.

The Roman stared. Frowns and curses he was accustomed to. This was something strange and new. "As you will, but the law says only one mile."

The soldier stalked on again, and behind him Nimrod plodded beneath the pack. They reached the second milepost.

"I will take the pack myself now," the soldier said, "but what made you come a second mile?"

Nimrod told him of the Stranger who had talked by the campfire. The soldier listened intently. "I have never heard teaching like that before."

"Nor I," Nimrod the shepherd answered, as he turned away to go home. "Nor I. Never man spake like this man." [1]

STORY 17

WITH ME THIS DAY

THE THIEF groaned and balanced the weight on his body upon the footpiece of his cross to ease his agony.

"Curses upon Jehovah and his creation!" His feet slipped upon the narrow foothold and a scream tore from his twisted lips.

"King of Israel!" he shouted to the man who hung upon the center cross with his white face uplifted to the sky. "A fine king you are! Jehovah is your God—if he be so mighty, come down, then, from your cross! Come down, I say—come down!"

Pagiel, whose name meant "Intervention of God," brought his pain-glazed eyes from the mocking crowd to look upon his friend Cephas.

Pagiel did not fight death. He hung almost as motionless as the man upon the center cross, whom they called the King of the Jews. And he was very still. One could scarcely tell if he still lived or not. Drops of blood clung upon the crown of thorns pressed upon his head. Their red stain matted his hair darkly against his white cheeks.

Pagiel knew men. This man was no wrongdoer. Hate burned in Pagiel's outlaw heart against the powers that could hold life and death in their hands. He had heard of the new prophet. He had never thought to find time to speak with him. Here was time.

"Master," he said, and he looked at the still face.

But the prophet did not hear; he seemed already withdrawn from the world.

"Hail him who is King of the Jews!" the crowd shouted.

"If thou be Christ," the thief Cephas mocked, "then save thyself and us!"

Pagiel looked again upon his old companion. Cephas had lived many years, yet he still clung to life. Pagiel felt, through the numbing pain of his own agony, pity for the other. It was a strange emotion; it had been long since he had felt pity for any other than himself.

"Dost thou not fear God?" he called to Cephas. "We are condemned justly, you and I. But this man has done nothing amiss."

The effort of the words brought weakness; his chin sank upon his breast with their speaking. His mind slipped from the torture of his body and went back to a day he remembered.

He had been only a lad upon this day. Slipping among the market stalls in Nazareth, his quick fingers had reached for a bracelet in a merchant's booth, when a brown boyish hand had stopped him.

"No," a voice had spoken softly so that none might hear, "it is written, 'Thou shalt not steal.'"

Pagiel wheeled angrily, jerking his wrist from the other's grasp. Facing him, he saw a boy his own age, a rugged brown-skinned lad with clear eyes. His own fell before them.

"That," the boy pointed to the bracelet, "is not so beautiful as many things I could show you."

Pagiel dug his toe into the dirt. "I will be beaten," he muttered, "if I come back to my master empty-handed."

That strange boy still held his arm.

"Must you go back?" he asked earnestly. "It is bad to have to serve such a master. But you have no father or mother—is it not so?"

"I have no father—or mother," Pagiel answered shortly. He looked about for an escape. There was the day's work to be done, and as yet he had accomplished nothing. He had no mind for a beating from old Horam, in whose house he lodged, for such pay as this.

This boy seemed kind, and remarkably understanding, yet what could he know of the need for working? What did he know of hunger and beatings and cursings! He had both father and mother; that was plain to be seen. His tunic was bright and clean and his sandals were whole. Pagiel's heart was filled with bitterness. His own father had passed upon his vagrant way before his son's baby eyes had ever opened upon the Judean hills. His mother had died before he was out of swaddling clothes. He had been taken from the streets by Horam, master thief, and taught the only means of livelihood he knew.

And he had been taught well. His sly fingers could go beneath the very girdle of the old wine merchant, undiscovered. The men who gathered at the house of Horam after dark praised him until he held his head high with pride.

"That is a lad!" they would say to Horam. "We watched him at work today. Give him two more years and there will not be his equal—no, not even in Jerusalem!"

When Pagiel listened to their praise, he forgot the beatings Old Horam had given him for his clumsiness while he learned his trade. He held his head high and swaggered when he walked in the streets, for praise is sweet when one's heart is hungry. Now came this gentle-faced lad with his sandals and his striped robe, saying, "Thou shalt not."

The strange lad laid his hand upon Pagiel's shoulder.

"Thou hast no home?" he asked again.

Pagiel shook his head. He felt a lump rising in his throat that made him angry. He knew that if he answered tears would come to his eyes. He had no mind to cry like a child, he whom the men at Horam's accepted as one of themselves. He tried to draw away, but the lad held him fast.

"This day," he said, "thou shalt be with me—this one day thou shalt be with me in my home. My father shall be as your father, and thou shalt know my mother."

Against his will, Pagiel had gone. Something compelled him. He put from his mind all that his empty-handed return to Horam would mean, and went where his new friend led. The home was in a carpenter shop, and there among the bright clean blocks and crisp curled shavings the two talked together while the sun climbed the sky. Pagiel wished that he might stay forever.

At noon a woman came, bearing in her hands a wheaten loaf in a napkin and a pitcher of milk. When she smiled at her son, Pagiel forgot his hunger for food. This was a new hunger! This, then, was what a mother was!

"Mother," the lad drew Pagiel forward. "This is my friend—I have brought him home with me!"

The woman smiled at Pagiel. He blushed to the roots of his hair and looked at the ground. Women were accorded scant respect in the house of Horam, and Pagiel had never known such a woman before. But when he raised his eyes timidly, she was looking at him no longer. Her eyes rested upon her son, who was fashioning two pieces of wood together, in the shape of a cross.

"Oh!" she cried sharply. "Make not a cross, my son!"

After that, she smiled no more, and soon she left them. When the long, beautiful day drew to a close, the two boys helped the carpenter close the shutters of his shop, and Pagiel went back to Horam and took his beating manfully, without whimpering.

Sometime, he thought, he would see the boy again. But there was never time. Soon he moved with the old man, his master, to Jerusalem, where their trade was better, and with the years coming and going Pagiel forgot that morning in the carpenter shop.

Now there was time to remember. This crucifixion was a slow business; it ended more quickly if one fought as Cephas fought. By the power of his will Pagiel held his numbing body still. Death was darkness—and the ending of all things. Pagiel, who had loved both dawns and starlit nights, clung with his dimming sight to the sunlight that was turning the clouds to copper and gold.

That crowd swam dizzily before his eyes. It was thinning now. There was scant sport in reviling a man who had met their baiting with silence. Also, a storm threatened. A rumble of thunder circled the hill. The sunlight faded beneath the clouds that rolled higher and higher.

A few stopped before they turned to go down into the city, to hurl their last abuse.

"If thou be the Son of God, come down from the cross!"

Soon these would be beyond abuse!

"Yes," they wagged their heads, "if he be the King of Israel, let him come down!"

Pagiel fought to conquer the waves of nausea that swept over him. He would not die until these curious ones had departed! And they were already going—hurriedly, because of the storm. All that remained were those from the Temple whose business it was to see that the imposter died, a few soldiers, and a little group of the prophet's followers who knelt, weeping.

They were so close that Pagiel could look down upon their bowed heads. His lips twisted in a wry grimace. No one waited to see him die.

The prophet stirred and groaned. Pity moved Pagiel's heart again. The thief wished that he knew what it was that this man's followers believed, that he might comfort him now by saying, "I believe."

"Surely this was a righteous man," a soldier said uneasily.

Pagiel opened his eyes at the words. The sky was black. Those from the Temple moved closer together uneasily.

"He would have done no harm," another answered; "he was a humble fellow—his father is a carpenter at Nazareth."

A carpenter—Nazareth—Pagiel strained his ears to hear.

A woman at the foot of the cross raised her tear-wet face. Beneath its suffering Pagiel knew her—she was the boy's mother! This was no ordinary prophet. Suddenly the thief knew what he wanted to say.

"Lord," he gasped, "remember me when thou comest into thy kingdom!"

The man on the cross raised his head and looked at him. Pagiel's body sank with the weakness that rushed over him at that look.

"Verily—" certainty was a deep note beneath the smouldering pain in the voice— "verily I say unto you, this day shalt thou be with me in Paradise."

"With him—with him!" the thief whispered.

Suddenly he whom they called the King cried out with a loud voice, "Father, into thy hands I commend my spirit!"

He was gone. The darkness deepened and the thunder beat upon the edge of it. Below in the city untimely lights glimmered and hurried here and there. The people were afraid.

But Pagiel was afraid no longer. Remembering the boy's arm about his shoulders, he believed. Peace lifted him high above pain.

"He took me home with him before," he whispered, and waited for the end.[1]

WHAT IF THEY HAD QUIT?

Twenty years after the Day of Pentecost a group of men met by appointment to talk over a crisis in their lives. Peter, Andrew, Matthew, John, and Paul were seated on a hillside, looking out over the Sea of Galilee. Their work was going hard with them. Paul had suffered the loss of all things; Peter had left all to follow Christ and was finding it hard to support his family; and Matthew had just had a flattering offer at a large salary and an interest in the business to return to his old place in the customs house.

Peter, as usual, opened the discussion, saying, "I have a chance to buy back my interest in the fishing business. I can make a good living by fishing five days in the week, and I will have my Sundays for evangelistic work in the cities around the lake. I am getting along in years and am afraid that I can't stand the pace at which I have been working. And then, too, I need the money."

Paul said, "Aquila and Priscilla, who have prospered in the tent-making business in Ephesus, have offered me a position at a good salary to open a branch business in Philippi, and from there to establish and supervise the business of the principal cities in Macedonia. I can do this work; it will not be any harder for me than the care of all the churches. I will have my Sundays for Christian work, and can lay by something for a rainy day, which I can see is coming."

Matthew said, "My story of the life of Christ is having a large sale, and is bringing me enough to pay my expenses, but my business experience tells me that I ought to have a larger margin. Persecution may come and sales would drop off. I have a chance now to take my old position, and I know that I can make enough out of it not only to support myself and family, but to take care of the rest of you if you should need it. And then, too, I will have more leisure for writing and can probably help the cause more in this way than by traveling about over the country."

Andrew said, "Peter, do you see that sand beach over there? That is the very spot where we beached our boat after the miraculous haul of fish, and where we quit the fishing business when the Master said, 'Fear not; from henceforth thou shalt catch men.' How long is 'henceforth'? Do you see that hillside over there? That is where the Master fed the five thousand, and I can see the very spot where the lad stood when I asked him to give up his lunch for the Master. Do you remember the look of compassion on the Master's face when he looked out over the multitude and asked us to pray that laborers might be thrust forth in his harvest?"

Paul's jaw set; the old fire came back into his eyes, and a determined look in his face, as he said: "If we are going to continue to pray that other men rise up, leave all, and follow him, can we do less? Men, I don't think we need to talk about this any more; let us pray."

As they prayed, the things of time and sense receded; a light breeze rustled in the near-by treetops, reminding them of that "rushing mighty wind" on the Day of Pentecost and of the marvelous power with which Peter had preached the gospel on that day. They seemed also to see the Master himself standing on the shore just a few rods away, and to hear him saying to them again, "Launch out into the deep and let down your nets for a draught; fear not, from henceforth thou shalt catch men."

They looked, and the evening caravan for Tyre was coming into sight. "Good-by," said Paul. "I must catch the next boat for Ephesus, and I will get Aquila to put up the money for a campaign in that old city that will shake the whole of Asia."

"Good-by," said Peter. "Andrew and I will say good-by to the folks, for we must join the midnight caravan for Babylon and go on east as far as the land of Sinim."

"Good-by," said Matthew. "There is a group of publicans down in Jerusalem who were going in with me on this tax-gathering business, but I will get them to join me in financing a five-year campaign in Egypt and up the Nile as far as Ethiopia. I have heard from the Ethiopian treasurer that practically the whole country is open to us, and he believes that all Ethiopia will soon stretch out its hand to God."

"Good-by," said John, and he sat there alone till the stars came out and the waves on the beach, impelled by the rising wind, sounded like the voice of many waters, and he said to one whose presence he felt,

"Lord, do not charge this thing against them. I have felt that way myself at times. I would have left this work but for the fact that thou didst prevent and strengthen me. They are ready to live and die for thee, as I am. Lord, let me see thee ever before us, hear thy voice, feel thy presence, and we shall not fear what men can do unto us." [1]

STORY 19

GETTING BY

"PIERMONT COLLEGE is going to lose its most brilliant student. Julia Archer will be a tradition. She never seemed to study at all, yet she is graduating with marks about the average. The instructors could not catch her napping. Do you remember that oral test in Roman history when she hadn't opened the book the whole term and Dr. Greer asked her: 'What was the principal occupation of the inhabitants of the Po basin during the reign of Tiberius?' She replied, 'Agriculture,' and when he asked her to name the crops she said, 'Grain and olives.'"

"Do you remember the day she headed off Dr. Jenkins from calling on her in English by volunteering an answer to a general question about Tennyson's dramas which she had never read? He asked why they were better read than performed, and she replied, 'Because they have so little action.' What a wonderful position she is going to—research for a new encyclopedia."

Such comments as these were made by Julia's classmates.

Julia Archer was at work on the first section of the encyclopedia in the office of Mr. Hartley, the editor. She had finished a piece of French biographical translation which the typist expected to copy that morning. She enjoyed searching through reference books and combining her choice of facts into striking paragraphs; her keenness and good memory for general information won her favor with Mr. Hartley, who appreciated well-educated assistants.

"I've finished my assignment," said Julia to Mr. Hartley.

"Did you have any difficulties?"

"No," replied Julia. She never had difficulties.

"Then the first section of the work is completed," said Mr. Hartley.

Julia was surprised when the editor looked up from the typewritten pages to ask her, "Miss Archer, did you ever hear of General San Martín?"

"I think not," she replied.

"But you seem to have heard of Bolívar. Perhaps that accounts for this item in your article: 'Only one military commander, Bolívar the Liberator, was able to scale the almost impassable summit of the Andes with an army—a feat that was accomplished in 1819.' Did you look up these facts?" asked Mr. Hartley.

"No, I knew them," replied Julia.

"The statement is true only in part. In 1817 General San Martín, the national hero of Argentina, led an army across the Andes into Chile with strategy so extraordinary that it is still studied in military schools. You made an offhand statement without looking up the fact. Had you done so, you would have found references to the Argentine general, San Martín, for he and Bolívar were closely associated."

"I am sorry that I made a slight mistake," said Julia defiantly.

Mr. Hartley turned to her French translation. "Listen to this sentence, 'The vessel commanded by the merchant-captain Vidal was proceeding upstream after having taken on a cargo from Saindoux.' What does merchant-captain mean?"

"Literally it means 'long-voyage captain,' so I decided that 'merchant-captain' was as good English as I could get."

"It will pass. You guessed fairly close to the mark. I see that this vessel was proceeding up the Loire River. There's a large map of France in that atlas yonder. Will you please find Saindoux?"

Several minutes passed while Julia searched in vain for the city. Finally she said, "It isn't here."

"Try looking in the dictionary," directed Mr. Hartley.

As Julia gave one glance at the word and closed the book, Mr. Hartley said, "Saindoux is the French word for lard, isn't it? I think the vessel had a cargo of lard. Why did you suppose that it was the name of a place?"

"It looks like a French proper name, and I thought it was mis-printed without a capital."

"Why didn't you find out? Is that the way you studied? I'm afraid that you have that American ideal which is decidedly not one of the best—the ideal of 'getting by,'" said Mr. Hartley.

Julia was embarrassed, but was confident that she had made no more errors, when Mr. Hartley began again, "What is all this about 'shat-tered destinies, ensuing cataclysms, and hope of the first magnitude?' A connecting paragraph, I presume? Were you ever ordered to leave out facts from connecting paragraphs? These are showy, meaningless phrases. People are not going to pay fifty dollars to read about 'shattered destinies,' Miss Archer. You will have to give up your work."

Julia looked so utterly bewildered that Mr. Hartley was sorry for her, though he continued, "I am sorry, Miss Archer, the more so because you seemed full of promise. But I've suspected for some time that you were not dependable. You refuse to think honestly, and you want to write an encyclopedia, but you won't look up a word in the dictionary. You need to wake up and stop bluffing! Mentally honest people do not want merely to 'get by.' They want to enter in triumph. You may stay until the end of next week and copy figures. That will give you time to look for another position."

Though no one mentioned her coming departure, Julia felt as though she had been publicly humiliated. Her first reaction was wounded vanity; her second was a disbelief in Mr. Hartley's criticism. She determined to go where she would be better appreciated. Literary work was not the only career in which she could succeed.

Immediately she wrote to the dean of Piermont College asking for a recommendation as a leader of club work. The reply which came astounded her: "I cannot recommend you for club work because you made your way in college by means of devices rather than by honest work. The faculty passed you because of your marks, but the college was not satisfied with your influence."

Julia sought the typist to tell her of the editor's criticism of her work, the dean's reply, and her own bitter discovery that in no relationship of life was she thoroughly acceptable. The typist heard her with sympathy.

"Because you lost your first job," she said, "it is not the end of everything. But you must make up your mind to think straight. I have a plan if you are interested. The first of September a number of typists will be employed to rush the copy. I happen to know because I am to oversee their work. If you will start at once at a business school and learn typing, then take our typing test, I'll give you a job."

"But Mr. Hartley will not want me," said Julia.

"Oh, yes, he will if you pass all the requirements."

"Then I could still work on the encyclopedia. I hate to be let out of here as a failure."

"With your ability if you will work hard you may get your former position again," said the typist.

"Thank you," said Julia with renewed confidence in herself.[1]

STORY 20

WORTHY OF TRUST

ANNE GRENFIELD, a nurse in training at the Norfolk City Hospital, had been appointed to night duty to nurse a personal friend of Dr. Endicott, chief of the medical staff. Immediately after her nineteenth birthday she had entered the hospital to begin her training. During the eleven weeks' stay she had been reproved again and again for the blunders she had made when she was merely trying to finish a task in the alotted time.

Yet in spite of chapped hands, swollen feet, and aching back, in spite of frequent corrections and scant praise, Anne never wavered in her determination to become a nurse. Now an honor had come to her. Out of twenty-four nurses in training, she had been selected for night duty on a case in the influenza wing of the hospital, and the patient was Mr. Stanton, a personal friend of Dr. Endicott. Miss Price, the superintendent of nurses, urged her to do her best on the case.

"Miss Grenfield," she said, "this is your chance to prove that the time we have spent in trying to correct some of your careless ways has not been spent in vain."

"But I have tried so hard," faltered Anne.

"Yes, I know," Miss Price interposed, "but in hospital work it is not trying hard that counts, but trying successfully. With the hospital filling with influenza patients, you probationers must be trusted to do some of the work."

"I'll follow directions exactly as you give them, for I want you to trust me," Anne promised.

"Very well," she said, "take your hours off now and get as much rest as you can. You will go on duty at seven o'clock tonight."

Anne went to her room and wrote to her mother, telling her of the good fortune that had befallen her. She said, "All of the girls like to work with Dr. Endicott. Not that he is easy on the nurses, but he is so fair to them. I am very anxious that everything go right on my first private case."

Anne's roommate, who was also a nurse, came in later to report, saying, "I have some news for you. Miss Price put Mr. Stanton in the sunroom. His temperature went so high today that he was delirious and disturbed the others in the ward. He kept shouting for someone to help him kill those Germans. Did you know that he had been shell-shocked last year?"

"No," answered Anne. "Do you think that Miss Price will trust me to take care of him now that his temperature is so high?"

"Of course she will; I saw the directions. You are not to leave Mr. Stanton alone one second. She underscored those words in two different places."

"But why should I leave him alone? Did she think I would choose that time to go to the movies?"

"Every one of us admits that Miss Price was right in selecting you first for private duty, even if you have knocked over everything in the hospital that wasn't nailed down."

Dr. Endicott waited at the hospital to speak to her, saying, "I have given him his quieting medicine. You will see by the chart that it must be repeated at midnight. He seems quiet now, but don't leave him alone. If you want anything, ring the bell and the ward nurse will bring it. Good night."

The early hours of the night passed quietly. Mr. Stanton stopped his muttering and seemed to be asleep. The ward nurse said, "His temperature is coming down. Don't ring if you can help it, for the next fifteen minutes. We have two nurses off the floor, helping in an emergency upstairs."

Anne looked at her watch—midnight—time for the second powder. She rang the bell for water to dissolve the powder. No answer. With a start she remembered that the ward nurse had told her not to ring for a few minutes. She went to the door to see whether by chance a nurse was passing through the corridor, but no one was in sight. She glanced at Mr. Stanton, who was sleeping quietly.

Anne hesitated a moment. What should she do? She had been told not to leave the patient alone, and yet she had been told to give him a powder at midnight. She looked at the sleeping patient and darted into the hall and ran to the service room, where she quickly filled the glass with water. In her hurry her hand struck the edge of the shelf, and the glass fell with a crash into the bowl. Gathering up the pieces she started back with the water. The door of the sunroom was open, and as she approached it she could look directly into the room.

There was no head on the pillow. Rushing into the room, she closed the door with her heel. Mr. Stanton sat astride the low window sill; one foot was swinging in the rain outside, the other was resting on the floor of the room. His face was fiery red, and his eyes were blazing.

"They threw a hand grenade at me!" he shouted. "Did you hear it smash the windows outside?"

"I heard glass breaking," Anne replied, setting down the glass and moving toward him quietly, but with anxiety.

"Better get out of here," he warned.

"Yes, but wait a minute for me."

Just then someone upstairs let a door bang. With a look of terror Mr. Stanton swung his other foot over the sill. With one spring Anne caught him round the waist and drew him, kicking and shouting, back into the room.

"You're a German spy!" he muttered and grappled with her. They whirled around the room; Anne tried to force him near the bell, so that she could ring for help, but he kept her away from that side of the room. Should she scream for help? The door was closed, and to make the nurses hear she must frighten some patients who were seriously ill.

Suddenly she felt the grasp on her arm relax. The man swayed unsteadily. With a quick shove Anne pushed him toward the bed. He fell with a thud on the bed, and ceased to struggle. Quickly she felt his pulse. It was rapid, but gave no sign that his condition was serious. Even as she watched, he turned on his pillow as if to go to sleep.

Hurriedly she prepared the powder. After taking the powder the patient slept for hours. When he woke, he seemed rational and apparently remembered nothing unusual that had occurred during the night. When Anne joined the other nurses for breakfast, she was greeted with a chorus of questions: "Did you get along all right? Did Miss Price say anything to you this morning? Why don't you tell us about it?"

Anne looked at the eager faces and said, "Do leave me alone." The girls looked at her in amazement, and one of them said, "Anne is too tired to talk."

Alone in her room Anne reviewed the events of the night. First, she had disobeyed an order; second, she had dropped a glass and frightened her patient into delirium again. And it was owing to good luck rather than to good care that at the end of her first night on private duty she had a live patient and not a dead one.

"I don't care," she muttered. "Whose business is it anyway what went on during the night, so long as my patient is all right this morning?"

"Tell the whole truth and take the consequences," urged a voice within.

"I can't. If I tell the whole truth, I shall be sent home in disgrace," argued Anne.

"All right then, don't tell, and have it to remember that you deceived people who trusted you."

Anne was unhappy as she went about her tasks on the following week. On the last morning she was sent to Miss Price's room with the requisition slips, which she laid on her desk. Anne looked steadily at the back of her head as she said in a queer voice, "I disobeyed orders the night that I took care of Mr. Stanton. I left him alone a minute and he nearly got out of the window, but I dragged him back. I didn't tell because I thought you would send me home."

At that instant Dr. Endicott entered. "Tell Dr. Endicott what you have just told me," said Miss Price as she left the room.

"I left Mr. Stanton alone that night," Anne began.

"I know all about it," said Dr. Endicott, "Mr. Stanton told me the next morning, but I told him not to speak of it until you made your report."

"You knew all about it!" asked Anne.

"Yes. Mr. Stanton remembered everything perfectly. That often happens when a delirious person becomes rational again. Why didn't you make a full report the next morning?"

"I was afraid that you would send me home," Anne answered.

"You nurses seem to think that we are watching for a good chance to send you home. On the contrary, we are very anxious to keep you. Nothing happened that night for which we should think of expelling you, except that you did not make a full report of it." Anne lifted her head in astonishment.

"You were told to not leave the patient alone and to give the medicine at midnight. You did not use good judgment in deciding which order should take precedence, but an error of judgment is not criminal. To offset that, you showed remarkable coolness and presence of mind in an emergency. Mr. Stanton feels that you saved his life."

"Saved his life! I nearly killed him!" Anne replied.

"He doesn't feel that way. But at any rate the incident in itself was not just cause for refusing your promotion. The quality that is indispensable in a nurse is a certain staunchness of moral fiber. A nurse must be trustworthy. Miss Price and I hated to lose such all-round good material for a nurse as we found in you, but if you had failed to make full report of what happened that night we should have had to send you home. Take this slip to Miss Price," he said abruptly.

Anne glanced at the slip and read, "Anne Grenfield, recommended for promotion into regular training. Dr. Endicott." [1]

HOLY BREAD

DONLEY had spent half an hour resolving to speak to the next man who stopped at the door. He had never begged before; begging came hard. "But I might as well get used to it," he reflected grimly. "Looks like the only way for me now."

A man came to the door, fumbling for a key. He'd be a rich man, belonging as he did to this exclusive club and having a key to enter by the side door. The woman who had got out of the car with him waited at the bottom of the steps.

Donley came close, muttering in a shamed voice: "Could you stake me to the price of a meal, sir? I've not eaten today."

"Sorry, fellow, but I've no change with me," the man said crisply. Donley shrank back and hung over the railing with his back turned, until they should go.

"I didn't bring the right key," said the man to his companion. "We must go to the other door."

"What did he want?" the woman asked, nodding toward Donley as they turned to the street.

"Price of a meal. Said he was hungry."

"Oh, Larry! We can't go in and eat a meal we don't need, and leave a hungry man out here."

"There's one of them begging on every corner now. Likely he wants the money for drink. Anyway, I have nothing less than ten dollars, and I don't see myself handing that to a bum."

"He looks hungry. I couldn't eat for thinking of him. You know what Christ says to the unrighteous in the day of judgment: 'I was hungry, and ye did not give me to eat.' Wait a minute. I have something in my purse. I'll have to give him something."

Donley, with his back turned in shame, could hear it all. An electric shock passed through him. She was talking about Christ, just as his mother used to do. His mother had read that very same verse to him more than once. He had supposed vaguely that rich people didn't think about Christ, didn't need him with all the other things that they had. But here was this woman, beautiful and dressed in luxurious clothes, talking about Christ as if he were a real person, to be met any moment.

She touched his arm, and he turned around. "Here is a dollar; buy yourself some food. And don't lose courage, even if things look hard. There's a job somewhere for you. I hope you'll find it soon."

He could only stammer pitifully: "Thanks, lady, thanks. I'll sure buy food, not drink. You've given me a fresh start, lady. I'll never forget your kindness."

"You'll be eating Christ's bread. Pass it on," she said, and smiled at him in a friendly fashion, as if he were a man, not a bum. Then she was gone to join her escort, who waited at the steps.

Donley started toward the region of cheap eating houses. His head was up. A good meal would enable him to try again. He could get a meal for fifty cents. There would be half of his dollar left for food tomorrow. He would be eating Christ's bread two days, but one could not save up Christ's bread just for oneself.

An old man was shuffling along just ahead of him. Donley had seen him before at two places where he had asked for work. It was hard, looking for work when one got to that age. Maybe he was hungry too. Christ's bread must be shared. Suddenly Donley felt a great uplifting of the heart. He too could give! A dollar was enough for both of them. But what about tomorrow? Christ was never short of bread. Donley felt an amazing sureness about that.

"What do you say to going in and having a good meal?"

The old man turned, his watery eyes blinking up at Donley. "You wouldn't fool me?" he quavered. But he couldn't believe it until he was seated at the oilcloth-covered table with a bowl of hot stew before him. They ate with concentration. Presently Donley noticed that the old man was wrapping up his buttered bread in a paper napkin.

"Saving some for tomorrow, eh?" he asked genially.

"No. There's a kid down here whose Dad is on a drunk. He was crying a little when I passed—hungry, I guess. I want to give him the bread."

"Let's both take him our bread. We've got plenty without it. I'll wrap up my pie, too." They wrapped the food and carried it out with them. The old man led the way to where the boy stood with a few papers that he was trying to sell.

"Here, kid, eat this," said the old man proudly.

The boy began to eat greedily. Then he stopped, and called a dog that hung back in the alley, a frightened, lost dog, as one could see at a glance. "Here, Jack, you can have half," he said. The boy stood up gamely now and began to cry his papers. He sold three while they watched him.

"Good-by," said Donley to the old man. "There's a job for you somewhere. You'll find it soon; just keep on. You know this that we've eaten is Christ's bread. A lady told me so when she gave me the dollar. We're just naturally bound to have good luck."

"Yes," agreed the old man. "I've thought of a new place where maybe they need a night watchman. I wouldn't ask much pay—a warm place to stay and enough to buy my eats. Yes, we're bound to have good luck."

Donley parted with the old man and went his way. He too had thought of a new place to ask for a job. He was turned down, but somehow it didn't hurt so much this time. As he turned away from the shop, he noticed that the lost dog was following him. In fondling the dog he felt a narrow strap around his neck, and found a license tag and an address.

"You're in luck," he said to the dog. "Someone wants you. Guess you'll eat tomorrow, all right. Come along, I'll take you home."

It was a long walk uptown, but after a while the dog was barking madly at a door, which was opened by a maid. "Come in," she said to Donley. "The master will see you. He told me to bring in the person who brought the dog home."

A keen-eyed man looked Donley over. "Why did you bring the dog home?"

Donley hesitated. He could hardly say to this stranger that he had to do it because he had eaten Christ's bread. "He followed me from down in the market district. I stopped to pat him, and found the tag. I wanted to bring him back to his folks."

The keen-eyed man had meant to say, "Didn't you steal him for the sake of reward?" But he didn't say it, for there was something of dignity about Donley. Instead he said, "I advertised in last night's paper—ten dollars reward."

"I didn't know—I didn't see the paper. It wasn't for the reward—"

"I can see that. I'm glad it came to you. Thanks, and good luck to you."

HOLY BREAD

Donley looked at the bill in his hand and said, "I don't like to take it. I just wanted to do a good turn."

"Take it along. What you did is worth more than that to me. Come to my office tomorrow. I may have a job for you."

Donley was walking along, the bill clutched in his hand. A miracle! He had been down and out—hopeless. Then there was Christ's bread. It had multiplied like the loaves and fishes that he had read about in the country Sunday school long ago. Once he had eaten it, he didn't need to be afraid of going hungry any more. There was enough of that bread for all. Here were courage, a job, a new chance, and always something to pass on to others who were hungry. And something more than the bread that one could see! The world could not beat the man who had eaten holy bread! [1]

STORY 22

AN ILL WIND

INSIDE the manager's office Mr. Gregory was giving Tommy Reynolds his instructions. "Go to the bank at once and cash this check," he said.

Tommy paused at his desk, slipped one corner of the check under the wire basket, and began to put on his overcoat. At that moment Miss Babcock opened the window for fresh air, and a tremendous blast of air rushed into the room. Confusion reigned among the employees near the window as the air was filled with fluttering papers and wildly grabbing hands.

"Shut the window, please!"

Tommy's desk near the window suffered the most. His basket, piled high, contributed a deluge of sailing papers which slowly settled to the floor when the window was closed. The paper hanger returned from the telephone in time to prevent his freshly pasted strip of paper from slipping to the floor. Since it was ready to go on the wall, he caught it, slapped it against the plastered surface, and quickly brushed it into place.

Tommy's first thought was of the check that he had put under the wire basket. It was gone. He gathered all the papers on the floor and went through them several times, but the check was not among them. He examined the contents of the wastebasket and dragged his desk from its position to see whether the check could have blown under it. The situation was becoming desperate. The bank would close in eleven minutes. Tomorrow would be Christmas—and the next day Sunday. Whatever Mr. Gregory's reason for wishing the check cashed immediately, it would soon be too late to get it cashed before Monday.

Tommy appealed to his fellow employees, and they joined in the search. He told Miss Greene, the cashier, of his predicament. "I'll have to go in and tell Mr. Gregory about it before long," he said.

"It's too bad, Tommy," said Miss Greene. "It was a careless thing to let the check get out of your hands, especially after it had been endorsed. That check came in the mail this afternoon from a man who has been owing the bill a long time. Mr. Gregory called the bank, and they told him to get it cashed immediately. Go and tell Mr. Gregory about it—the sooner you have it over with the better—or the firm will lose ninety-eight dollars."

Sick with apprehension Tommy went to the manager and explained the matter.

"You haven't been to the bank yet, and you've lost that check!" cried the manager. "You don't mean to tell me. Go find that check, and don't come in here again until you do."

Tommy realized that he must postpone further search for the check until his work was finished. On this last day of the holiday rush he knew that he could not expect any more help from the other employees. As the hour grew late, one after another left the office with a cheery "Merry Christmas!" Tommy's spirits sank lower and lower. Christmas indeed! He glanced at the cashier's office and saw that Miss Greene was still there, and then her light went out and she came to Tommy's desk.

"Tommy," she said, "I know how you feel. I'm going to tell you something which might encourage you. Robert, the young fellow who used to have your job, was a great tease. One afternoon he was waiting outside the window while I finished counting a pile of bills. The last bill happened to be a new one-hundred-dollar note.

" 'Whew!' Robert exclaimed. 'You're not going to faint at the sight of so much money, are you? Allow me to give you some fresh air.' And before I knew what he was doing he had grabbed an electric fan and switched on the current so that the sudden blast of air came across the shelf and almost directly into my face. That bill went up in the air, to the wall at the back of my cage, and then shot downward toward the floor.

"I was annoyed because I couldn't find the missing bill. Robert offered to help, but I wouldn't let him. When he returned later and learned that I hadn't found it, he was scared, for he knew that it was his fault. The next morning he failed to appear for work, and we have never heard of him since.

"Mr. Gregory was very kind and exonerated me of all blame, but I felt that next to Robert I was responsible for losing that bill, and I made it up to the firm. It's two years now since it happened, and I don't want you to make the mistake Robert did. Whether you find that check or not, you stick."

"Miss Greene, you've helped me a great deal, and I want you to know I appreciate it. It's when a fellow is down and nobody seems to care that it's hard."

A few minutes after Miss Greene left, Mr. Gregory came by and said, "Well, my boy, how are you coming on? Found that check yet?"

"No, I haven't. I've only finished my other work, but I'm going to find it if it's in this office."

"That's right. Go after it now, while there's nobody round to bother you. Report to me the first thing Monday how you come out. Good night."

Tommy began his search. He pulled out every desk and searched thoroughly every wastebasket, and finally entered Miss Greene's cage, and with a movable electric light began to peer between the tubes of the radiators from end to end. He moved the filing cabinet and noticed that the baseboard behind it was warped by the steam, and with a strip of stiff pasteboard he examined the crack behind the baseboard. Presently he struck some object and worked to bring it in view, but it proved to be only an old envelope.

Continuing his search, he reached the partition that separated the cashier's office from the outer office, and going to the inner office he investigated the crack. He had scarcely gone three feet when his strip of paper struck another object. The next instant he brought into view Miss Greene's long-lost hundred-dollar bill!

As Tommy rose to his feet he thought, Miss Greene will have a happy Christmas now. Then, with a rush, a startling temptation assailed him. No one could possibly ever know! He could make good the lost check and probably keep his position. But no—Miss Greene was the best friend he had; she had tried her best to hearten him when things looked hopeless. And he was thinking of stealing a hundred-dollar bill that she probably needed a great deal more than he!

Tommy hurried to the desk and scribbled a note to her and enclosed the bill. He returned to his task of probing the remaining length of the crack until he came to the place where the new wallpaper had been put on that afternoon. He saw a dark brown rectangular outline on the paper, and with his knife cut it around two sides, bent it back, and there was the missing check, somewhat blurred but otherwise unharmed.

Pressing back the flap of paper against the wall, Tommy smoothed it into place. Then placing the check beneath a blotter and a heavy weight, he sat down to let it dry. Glancing at the clock, he saw that it was 2:30. As he was speculating on the extraordinary place in which he had found the check, the telephone rang. To his astonishment it was Mr. Gregory.

"Is that you, Tommy? How are you coming on? Found the check yet?"

"Yes, sir, I have. Under a strip of wallpaper that the paper hanger put on. It must have blown down and stuck on the freshly pasted strip of paper, and he put it on without seeing the check. I happened to notice the dark spot on the wall where the paste wet through the paper. But, Mr. Gregory, I found something else! I found that hundred-dollar bill that Miss Greene lost two years ago. It was down in a crack between the baseboard and the wall at the back of her office. And I'm going to give her a Merry Christmas with it tomorrow."

"Well, Tommy, if Miss Babcock hadn't opened the window and the wind hadn't blown in and—well—you know the old proverb, 'It's an ill wind that blows nobody good.' You go home now, quick, and go to bed. But listen. Before you leave, go into my office and raise the top to my desk—it's unlocked—and you'll find an envelope there for you—your envelope! Good-by and Merry Christmas to you!" [1]

STORY 23

SENSITIVE TO THE NEEDS OF OTHERS

"PLEASE see the girl in the reception room for me. She's probably a struggling young artist. Be nice to her but tell her that we are over-supplied with illustrators as it is," said Mrs. Lloyd, the editor, to her assistant, Marian Lamar.

"Isn't it a shame the hard times these young artists have getting a start?" Miss Lamar remarked.

Mrs. Lloyd nodded. "When you have been on a magazine as long as I have, you will hear many pathetic stories. At times it's a real struggle between pity for someone who needs the work and my duty to the magazine, but I can't run the department on sentiment. I can't accept work that isn't good, no matter how hard it is to say no. That is why I am sending you to see Miss Wing. You were wise to choose a steady job, and, because of your experience here, you'll be a better artist later."

Marian Lamar had come to New York with ambitions to be an il-lustrator and was earning her living by working for the magazine dur-ing the day and studying at the art school in the evening. Struggling with her art she was sympathetic with youthful artists who came to the office day after day making vain attempts to establish themselves in their profession.

On the way to the reception room the thought came to her, "Oh, if her work will only be good. It's so discouraging when one knows that it isn't good and perhaps never will be. Somehow, I haven't the courage to tell her she is wasting her time and should try something else. I suppose I should. It would be kinder in the long run."

There was only one person in the room, a small, thin, poorly dressed girl with dark shadows under her eyes. Smiling in her friendliest man-ner, Marian said, "Mrs. Lloyd asked me to see you. I'm Marian Lamar, her assistant. Have you some sketches that you want to show us? Though I must say that we are not in need of any at the present."

"Oh," said Miss Wing.

The sketches proved to be much better than Marian had expected. Although they showed that the girl had talent, she would have to devote herself to years of hard work if she wished to succeed.

"I like this one especially," said Marian. "But you should study a while longer, I think. I'd like to talk to you about your work. Could you have lunch with me today?"

"Yes. You're very kind. I'd appreciate any suggestions that you would give me."

As they talked Marian learned a number of things about Miss Wing, one of which was that her funds were running low. As they rose from the table, Marian said, "I have your address, and you can count on my doing anything for you that I can. Come in and see me once in a while. Perhaps I might hear of something. If I were you, I would keep on studying. Here is the address of an art class that I attend in the evening."

Marian returned to her work and for several days was so busy that she did not think of Miss Wing. One morning she hurried to the art manager's office with a sketch to be rushed through, and he inquired, "Do you know of a young man I could get as an assistant? I haven't been able to find anyone since Jimmy left."

"I'm sorry," replied Marian. "I don't know of one. How about trying a girl instead?"

"Meaning you?" he inquired.

"No, thank you," Marian laughed. "I like my job so well, or I would be tempted. But I know a girl whose work is good, for she has talent. The experience she would get here would be worth many months of study elsewhere. She could do Jimmy's work and a great deal more. She worked on a newspaper one summer, filling in during a vacation."

"Since you recommend her, I'll give her a chance. Do you think that you could get her here by tomorrow?"

"I'll do my best," Marian replied.

At lunch hour she went to the address that Miss Wing had given, and after climbing three flights of stairs came to a gloomy hall. Marian found the door with Miss Wing's card, and under it these words, "Will return at 2:00 P.M." She decided to wait even if she missed her lunch, but after a few minutes she heard a sound in the room. She knocked but there was no reply. Then turning the doorknob, she swung the door open. In a heap on the floor by the easel was a pile of sketches, and the girl was huddled beside them. Her face was pressed against the seat of a chair, her shoulders shaking in sobs.

Miss Wing raised a tear-stained face, and the two girls stared at each other. Marian spoke first, "I know. Your money is running low and you're discouraged."

The girl sobbed, "I'll have to spend my last dollar if I eat today. My room rent is paid until Saturday. If I had a home to go to, I wouldn't mind; but Aunt Jane did not want me to come to New York. I suppose she would send money for my return, and let me have the maid's place. I might as well wash dishes. I've failed here. How did you happen to come today?"

"If I were you," Marian said, "I shouldn't go back to Aunt Jane's. I'd get a job that would pay for your room, board, and clothes, and leave the evening free for art classes. I know that it is possible, for I am doing it myself."

The girl looked up hopefully, inquiring, "But could I? I've never had any experience except one summer on a newspaper that I told you about."

"Put on your hat and come with me," Marian said. "I happen to know where there is a perfect job for you." When told about the opening in the art manager's office, Miss Wing could not find words to express her gratitude.

"What have I done?" Marian protested, cutting short the girl's attempt to express her thanks. "Now it's up to you to make good. You will have a grand opportunity here. We'll have fun lunching together and studying art in the evenings. It's a splendid job, and I know you will like it."

"What makes you do so much for me?" the girl inquired.

"I enjoy doing it, and it wasn't any trouble," replied Marian. "So many times I've wanted a chance to help. Perhaps sometime you will have a chance to help someone and pass it on. It's worth doing."

"I know it is worth doing," the girl remarked. "Stepping forward to lend someone a hand, going out of one's way to give a lift, is the thing that makes life worth living." [1]

STORY 24

QUICK THINKING

"COME on, fellows, snap into it," called Whitfield, athletic director of Danby High School. "Ten minutes scrimmage between the first and second teams. Let's go!"

Ten of the dozen or more boys who had been half-practicing on the floor of the gym took their places. The coach tossed a ball up between the opposing centers, and the game was on with the thud of racing feet and sharp calls as the ball passed from one player to another.

Stanley Adams, forward on the first team, momentarily forgot his troubles in the excitement, for he loved basketball. A clever bit of play swept the ball down toward the scrubs' goal, where Stanley received it from the center.

"Shoot, Stan!" yelled one of his mates.

The basket was only fifteen feet away, but even as Stanley started his shot, Bill Peck, the other forward, broke from his guard and flashed swiftly down under the goal. It seemed as if the ball had started for the basket, yet it ended in Peck's hands, and he shot the goal.

"Time out!" called Whitfield. "That's basketball. Stan had a good shot, and no one could have blamed him for taking a crack at the basket, but he saw that Bill was in a better position and changed tactics in about one fifth of a second, willing to let another player have the glory. I like to see a chap pass the ball instead of shooting at the ring himself. That's the kind of stuff that wins a game. Let's go."

Stanley felt a warm glow of pleasure as the game was resumed, but the feeling soon left him. He had never played basketball until this season, and at first he was mentally slow, but he snapped out of it. The boy was an orphan and had been brought up in the home of an uncle, Joseph Bently, a plain austere man who did not consider basketball an essential part of a boy's education. He was not a wealthy man, and he felt that any spare time left over from his nephew's studies should belong to him. He had a small stone quarry outside the city, where the boy worked during vacations.

Stanley knew that his uncle did not approve of his taking time for practice, and he felt that he should give up his basketball. So at the close of the practice he said to the coach, "I've decided to give up basketball."

"But you can't do that, Stan. You'll make a star player, and two years from now you will be practically sure of being captain. What makes you want to give it up?"

Stanley told the whole story—the debt of gratitude that he owed his uncle, and his uncle's disapproval of basketball. The coach replied, "I'll go to your uncle and see if I can bring him around."

Whitfield carried out his promise the next day when he found Mr. Bently at the quarry. "Stan told me that he intends to give up basketball. I think you are making a serious mistake allowing him to do it. Any boy will profit by the training and discipline that he gets on an athletic team. It develops self-reliance and quick action between the brain and muscles; it also builds character, for it inculcates high ideals of honor and clean sportsmanship. Haven't you seen how Stanley has benefited by his basketball experience? All his mental processes have quickened tremendously. But he will not play without your approval."

"I don't know about that," said Bently. "At any rate, I think I'm right, but I'm going to leave the whole matter to Stanley. I shan't forbid his playing."

"Which of course means that he won't play. I'm sorry both for Stan and for myself. He really needs the game. And I'll admit that I need him, for he is a player of unusual promise."

Stanley turned in his basketball uniform and began spending his afternoons at the quarry, driving a truck over the quarry road. It was work that he enjoyed, for he liked the feeling of importance and responsibility that it gave him. Mr. Bently admitted that his nephew had skill and judgment in driving that were far beyond his years.

One afternoon shortly after Whitfield's visit to the quarry, Stanley drove the truck to the derrick for two huge blocks of granite that the stonecutters had already shaped. The derrick hoisted the rough blocks out of the quarry pit. The horizontal arm of the machine was an eight-inch timber more than forty feet long and weighing fully twelve hundred pounds. And whenever necessary shaping had been done, the derrick was again called upon to hoist the block to the truck.

On that particular afternoon Stanley stopped the truck not far from the base of the derrick and left the engine running while he waited for the dressed granite that would presently be swung aboard.

"All right," Bently called, signaling to the man in charge of the steam engine that operated the hoist.

The rattle of machinery sounded as the big beam swung round high in the air before being lowered to receive its load. Stanley watched indifferently while the chains were attached to a great block of granite; the working of the apparatus was an old story to him.

Suddenly there was a hoarse cry of warning, and Stanley was horrified to see that the wire cable was giving way under the weight of the load. Mr. Bently, who was standing a few feet from the truck, glanced upward and saw the beam was straight over him. He started to run to a place of safety, but as he did so his foot slipped on a rounded rock fragment, and he pitched forward, struck his head on a small stone, and sprawled at full length, helpless in the path of the huge timber. He lay perhaps eight feet beyond the radiator of the truck and a little to the right.

Stanley saw all of this in a brief glance. His reactions were instinctive, instantaneous—just as they had come to be on the floor of the gym during a basketball game. He reasoned that the thing to do was to break the fall of that beam with his truck. He worked both feet and his right arm simultaneously—clutch out, gears into low, accelerator wide open, clutch in—all in the fraction of a second. With a roar from the motor the huge truck leaped forward.

Stanley knew that the chances were that he would be crushed, even though he did succeed in saving his uncle. As he shot forward he realized dimly that the enormous timber was just above his head. Then all thought was blotted out in a reverberating crash, and he was hurled violently from his seat. He recovered consciousness sometime later to find himself looking at his uncle, who bent over him. He looked at the big bruise on his uncle's forehead where he had fallen on the stone. Then he turned toward the truck; the huge beam was lying across it, just behind the driver's seat. He struggled to his feet.

"I never thought I would make it!" he muttered.

"Are you hurt?" his uncle demanded anxiously.

"Not a bit," the boy said. "The wind was knocked out of me for a minute. Are you all right?"

"Yes, thanks to you, Stanley. That was a wonderful thing you did, my boy. Nothing but your quick thinking and quick action saved me from a horrible death under that beam. Quickest bit of thinking I ever saw."

"I'm afraid the truck is ruined," said Stanley.

"Never mind the truck. Tell me, Stanley, did playing basketball make such a quick thinker of you?"

"I guess it did. I know my brain seems to work much faster than it used to."

"Um!" mused Mr. Bently. "Training like that is too valuable for you to miss. Reckon you are worth more to me playing basketball than working here in the quarry. Report to Mr. Whitfield again, starting tomorrow."

"Yes, Uncle Joe," Stanley answered.

"When will you be playing in a game?" the uncle asked.

"We're scheduled to meet Middletown High on Friday night."

"I'm coming to that game, and don't you dare let those fellows beat our team!"

And when Friday night arrived, Stanley followed his uncle's instructions.[1]

APPENDIX

BUILDING WORSHIP SERVICES

EVERY CHURCH, whether large or small, is responsible for leading its youth into vital worship experiences which will help them to know God and to find guidance for the problems they face. The task of the church is to provide a setting which is conducive to worship, and to provide leaders to train youth in worship. Young people worship easily and with a sense of reality when trained in the art of worship, but if this training has been neglected they will need additional help to make up for this neglect.

It is possible through fellowship with God for young people to become integrated personalities, to meet whatever comes—reverses, frustration, disappointment, or other difficulties—in such manner as to contribute to their growth and development. This is, in part, Paul's meaning when he said, "I can do all things through Christ which strengtheneth me." He had lived in such fellowship with God that he could say, "For me to live is Christ;" he had surrendered his life to God, and had gained inner peace and harmony. He lived radiantly and victoriously in any circumstance; he met defeat courageously without resentment or bitterness, and success without vainglory.

As young people learn to know God, become aware of his presence, new insight comes to them, and there is an inner drive or incentive to live by God's will. Evidently God is not real to some persons, for they live more or less as if God does not exist. But when God is a reality and one is conscious of his presence, he tries to adjust his life according to God's will or purpose.

There are definite results which may be expected from worship, and it is well to check up occasionally to determine whether these changes are taking place in the lives of the young people. The following test questions may help:

Is God real to the young people? Are they growing in their knowledge of him?

Are they improving in their ability to participate in worship? Are they natural and sincere in their expressions?

Are they learning to use devotional material to advantage?

Are they learning to pray and to seek God's guidance in matters that vitally concern them? Are they finding a Christian solution for their problems?

What changes for the better are noticeable in their lives? Are they becoming more Christlike in their attitudes and behavior?

Are they taking part in Christian service and helping to build a better world?

The steps in a complete worship experience are as follows: One approaches God humbly, feeling his need of God; he turns his thoughts toward God, confessing his sins; he seeks to know God's will and accepts Jesus' way of life; he enters into Christian service and shares his experiences with others.

Principles for Building Worship Services

Lack of variety in worship, using the same leaders and the same type of material, will cause the interest to lag and the attendance to fall off. No service is entirely original, but variety and balance will bring favorable results. The following questions suggest some principles which will improve the quality of worship:

Are the worship themes selected with the interests and needs of the young people in mind? Are the themes related to the entire program for youth?

Is each worship service built around a central theme? Are all elements of the service focused upon this theme?

Are announcements and other irrelevant items omitted from the worship?

Are the various elements arranged in a logical order, and do they lead to a climax?

Is there a proper balance of material? Is sufficient time allowed for meditation without too much talking or singing?

Is there a definite aim or purpose for each service? Is a record kept of the services? Are the results evaluated?

Is provision made for group participation early in the service through responsive readings, litanies, hymns, and the like?

Is quiet music used to provide a mood for each service?

Is there an appropriate setting for worship—the room clean and orderly, hymnals in place, and so forth?

Are the services planned far enough ahead of time to allow ample time for preparation?

Are young people used in the planning and leading of worship? Are persons selected because of their fitness for certain parts?

Are the ideas that are expressed in worship clothed in good English?

Is the service dignified? Does it move smoothly without distracting pauses?

MATERIALS FOR WORSHIP

The youth leader has the opportunity to bring to the attention of the worship committee the books and magazines which will supplement and enrich the worship services in the denominational periodicals. There is a vast storehouse of material available if the leader will spend sufficient time to become familiar with it and assemble it in usuable form. In addition to private and church libraries, public libraries contain a wealth of religious material, and more would be added if church workers made wider use of it. In addition to the biographies there are the works of Tolstoy, Van Dyke, Hawthorne, Whittier, Longfellow, Tennyson, and others which would enrich the worship of any group.

The Bible, the hymnals, and the periodicals of one's denomination furnish the main source of devotional material. These may be supplemented by the inspirational books and magazines available. A splendid magazine is the *International Journal of Religious Education,* which has worship services for all age groups, except adults. The services are dated a month ahead of time, allowing ample time for preparation.

If a leader is searching for devotional material, he may frequently find it in current magazines. The *Christian Herald* and *Christian Century* furnish inspirational poems, stories, and articles. *Christian World Facts,* published annually, carries outstanding stories of the work in the mission fields of the various denominations. This digest of the stories which have appeared in the denominational publications should be available to every youth worker. Another annual publication, entitled *Christmas,* presents a variety of seasonable stories.[1] Secular magazines also carry inspirational material, especially at Easter, Christmas, and other holidays.

Those who collect devotional material may sometimes find it difficult to locate the story or poem needed at a certain time. A simple and inexpensive system of filing would save time and make the material accessible. Poems may be clipped from magazines or copied from anthologies and pasted one on a page in a loose-leaf notebook and arranged alphabetically by title or subject. Such a collection gathered over a period of years becomes valuable and will enrich the worship.

Stories may be clipped from magazines and filed alphabetically in a letter file, or a commercial expanding file, bought at an office supply store. An index may easily be prepared from the file. If the titles of the stories are listed alphabetically, any story may be found immediately when needed. Stories which are too long for worship services may be condensed, copied, and filed. Occasionally a chapter or a portion of a book will contain a complete worship story. For example, in Victor Hugo, *Les Miserables,* may be found the story of the bishop and the candlesticks, and in Van Dyke, *The Story of the Other Wise Man,* the last chapter is a splendid Christmas story.

An interesting project for a worship committee would be to collect, adapt, and file devotional material. With a little practice young people can condense and adapt worship stories, making them available for their use. As the collection grows, it is advisable to have separate files for biographical stories, for Easter and Christmas stories, and for hymn and picture interpretations. The youth publications of the various denominations furnish a vast amount of stories, poems, and interpretations which should be clipped and filed, even after they have been used.

An experienced leader who is sensitive to the quality of material would not need criteria for judging material, but a younger leader may find the following test questions helpful:

Is the material graded to suit the age and experience of the persons in the group?

Is it based upon their interests and needs?

Is the message specific, easily understood, and meaningful to the group?

Is the message positive? Does it have definite religious value and make clear the Christian way of thinking and acting?

Does it give guidance to a Christian solution of the problems of youth?

Is the message self-centered, or is it concerned with service to others?

Is the material clothed in beautiful language and of high literary quality?

In order to work efficiently each local group should have its own library, or have access to a library containing worship material. A minimum library would include the following books or their equivalent:

Bartlett, Robert. *They Dared to Live.*

———. *They Did Something About It.*

Bible (King James Version, also a modern version).

Bowie, Walter Russell. *Lift Up Your Hearts.*

Clark, Thomas C. and Clark, Robert E. *Poems for the Great Days.*

Clark, Thomas C. and Gillespie, Esther A. *1000 Quotable Poems.*

Eastman, Fred. *Men of Power.* Vols. I-V.

Erdman, Walter C. *Sources of Power in Famous Lives.*

———. *More Sources of Power in Famous Lives.*

Hoyland, John S. *A Book of Prayers for Youth.*

Hymnal for Youth or *American Student Hymnal.*

Lantz, J. Edward. *Best Religious Stories.*

Lotz, Philip Henry. *Creative Personalities.* Vols. I-III.

Morrison, James Dalton. *Masterpieces of Religious Verse.*

Oxenham, John. *Gentlemen, the King!*

———. *Hearts Courageous.*

Pease, Dorothy Wells. *Altars Under the Sky.*

Rauschenbusch, Walter. *Prayers of the Social Awakening.*

Reid, A. C. *Invitation to Worship.*

Smith, Henry Augustine. *Lyric Religion.*

Wallace, Archer. *In Spite of All.*

———. *One Hundred Stories for Boys.*

———. *Overcoming Handicaps.*

———. *Stories of Grit.*

Worship is a two-way proposition in which each person makes his own contribution or response. A well-prepared service led by a capable person is of no value to the young person who does not give attention or make his own contribution to the service. A leader cannot make worship for the listener, but he can set the mood and make it easier for the worshiper to contact God.

A leader should keep in mind the nature and meaning of worship and strive to improve his skill as a leader. He should dress for the occasion in an inconspicuous manner and avoid calling attention to himself. He should strive to develop poise, a pleasing voice, and the ability to express himself clearly. He should attempt to be in a mood for worship and conscious of the presence of God as he leads others. He should not allow the technique of leading to interfere with his worship. Before the service begins, he and those who assist him might withdraw from the group to pray for guidance.

Through discussion a youth leader may help a group to realize some of the conditions which need to be met in order to achieve worship. The following questions might help to guide the discussion: Is God real to me, and am I in a mood for worship? Do I have an expectant attitude? Is it possible for me to lead others into an awareness of God unless I am also worshiping?

Do I have a definite purpose or aim for this service? Have my plans been approved by the worship committee?

Do all who assist me understand the parts they are to take and the time available to them?

Have I given sufficient time to prayer and the preparation for this service?

Have I been resourceful in discovering the most appropriate material for this service? Does it contain a message for me?

Does my life conform to the things that I shall say? Am I sincere and reverent in the presentation of the material?

Have I put myself in the background and centered my thoughts upon the message which I wish to convey?

The Worship Room

A correct setting for worship depends not so much upon the amount of money expended as upon the imagination, good taste, and ingenuity of the workers. The worship room is the place around which young people weave memories of high moments. It should be kept clean and orderly; old periodicals and discarded objects should not be allowed to accumulate; banners, mottoes, bulletin boards, and cheap pictures should not clutter up the walls; symbols, empty vases, and other objects not in use should be kept in a storeroom.

The worship room should resemble a chapel as much as possible. The walls, if painted, should be in a soft, restful tone, and the entire color scheme should be harmonious. If the library of worship material is kept in the room, the books should be neatly arranged in a bookcase.

A beautiful worship center relating to the theme of the service will help to secure a proper setting. When the worship center is arranged in a dimly lighted room with a strong light thrown upon it, it serves as a focal point to hold the attention of the group, helping them to concentrate on the message.

A worship center may be built by hanging on the wall a background of dark velvet or velour, and placing in front of it an improvised altar or table which is covered with the same material. On the altar or table may be placed symbolic objects—such as a cross with lighted candles, or an open Bible and candles, or a globe of the world with small flags of various countries set in standards around it—or a beautiful painting may be hung on the wall above the table with a low bowl of flowers placed beneath it. The use of too many objects at a time in a worship center makes it difficult for the worshipers to concentrate on the message. If additional suggestions are needed for building worship centers, write to the Interdenominational Bureau of Architecture, 297 Fourth Avenue, New York, N. Y.

MUSIC IN WORSHIP

Music in worship is used not for entertainment, but to convey a message. Musicians are invited to assist because of their ability to help the group to worship, and never to show them off. Orchestras, except when composed of string instruments, are out of place in worship. Occasionally a trumpet or a trombone may be used with a large group. Soloists are invited when they can help to carry forward the central message of the service and aid the group in worship.

Since music helps to set the mood for worship, every service should begin with religious music. Secular tunes are out of place in a worship service. A pianist may help to maintain a reverent mood by playing while the group is arriving, and also by playing short interludes between the elements of the service. A prayer hymn played during the meditation helps the group to concentrate on the prayer.

The singing will have more meaning if the hymns relate closely to the message of the service. Hymns should be read through carefully before they are included in a service. Learning new hymns from time to time makes it possible for the leaders to choose hymns with appropriate messages for each service. When the group is learning a new hymn, an entire service might be planned around the hymn: one speaker might give the setting out of which the hymn grew, another the story of the writing of the hymn, and another the interpretation of the hymn, and a choir member might teach the group to sing the hymn.

The following questions may help the group to evaluate the hymns which are selected for use:

Are the words of the hymn within the understanding of the group? Are they within the range of normal experiences of young people?

Are the thoughts and ideals expressed natural to young people?

Are the ideas expressed elevating and conducive to the development of Christian character?

Are the words of the hymn in beautiful English, and easily understood by the group?

Does the hymn give a correct impression of God? Is the theology up to date?

Does the hymn carry forward the central message of the service?

Is the tune suitable to the words and within the range of the voices of the group?

PRAYER IN WORSHIP

Prayer is one's response to God, and it is addressed, not to the group, but to God, and should not be used to instruct the Lord or the group. Prayer is to be used for praise, adoration, confession, thanksgiving, petition, dedication, and submission. The classic prayers of the past are a part of our religious heritage, but as a rule a sincere, dignified prayer by a young person has more meaning to a youth group. It is advisable always to use the expressions in prayer that are natural and normal to the group.

When a young person finds it difficult to pray in public, he might write his prayer and read it. A written prayer expressing the sentiment of the group may be read in such manner that no one need be aware that it is being read. Directed meditation is helpful when the leader suggests ideas which are normal for the group and leads in an unhurried manner.

The great religious poems help one to express thoughts that are difficult to express otherwise; they color the thinking and have a great influence upon the lives of young people. Simple poems which are easily understood are more effective in worship than complex poems. Since poems are used widely in worship, one should guard against frequent repetition of certain poems. When they become shopworn, they tend to lose some of their meaning and significance to the group.

THE WORSHIP COMMITTEE

The chairman of the worship committee and those who work with him have an opportunity to help young people to appropriate spiritual resources for living. If the church fails at this point, it fails in its most important mission. Every member of the youth group should share the responsibility for worship at some time. Those who have not been trained and refuse to speak in public may be asked to prepare the worship center or arrange the room for worship.

Plans for organizing the worship committee will vary with the size of the group and with the various denominations. In a small group one person may serve as the worship committee, and he will select from the entire group the leaders for the various services. These leaders will plan in detail the services assigned to them, calling on others to help if needed.

For a larger group the chairman of the worship committee is elected by the entire group, and the members of the committee are appointed because of their fitness for the task. There should be three or more young people appointed, also an adult counselor who is prepared to guide in planning and leading the worship, The counselor works in the background, gives suggestions, but refrains from dominating the group.

The chairman calls the committee together to elect the officers needed and appoint the necessary subcommittees. The following officers may be needed in a large group: chairman, vice-chairman, secretary, treasurer, counselor (an adult). The subcommittees are as follows:

Usher Committee: welcomes strangers and members, receives the offering, and holds latecomers until a time when they will not disturb.

Room and Equipment Committee: responsible for room being clean, orderly, properly heated and lighted, hymnals in place, flowers arranged, pictures hung, and so forth.

Worship Center Committee: works with leader of each service and arranges worship center suitable for the theme of the service.

Resource Material Committee: collects devotional material; culls and files the best of poetry, meditations, and interpretations; classifies, condenses, and files inspirational stories suitable for youth worship.

The worship committee meets every two or three months and chooses the themes for the services, using the suggestions of its own denomination, appoints leaders for each service, and supplies them with additional worship material. After this the work is turned over to the leaders selected, who complete the details and lead in the services. In some groups two leaders are appointed for each service. It has been found that the service is smoother when an experienced person shares the task with an inexperienced person. This encourages the beginner to make an effort at leading and does not overwork him in his first attempt. They plan together. One of them will lead the service, and the other will bring the special message.

ORDER OF SERVICE

Worship tends to become monotonous if it is not varied from time to time. Changing the order of service, introducing new and timely material, and urging speakers to give more time to preparation will help to improve the worship. The order of service may vary according to the type of service and the time available. A simple order for a short service is as follows:

PRELUDE
CALL TO WORSHIP
SCRIPTURE
PRAYER
HYMN
SPECIAL MESSAGE (story, talk, interpretation)
PRAYER
HYMN
BENEDICTION

For a longer service the following is suggested, but some parts may be omitted:

PRELUDE
CALL TO WORSHIP (scripture, short poem, or a stanza of a hymn)
HYMN
SCRIPTURE (in unison, or responsively, or by an individual)
PRAYER OR LITANY
PRAYER RESPONSE
POEM
SPECIAL MUSIC
SPECIAL MESSAGE (story, talk, meditation, interpretation, or dramatization)
PRESENTATION OF CHRISTIAN ENTERPRISE
OFFERING
HYMN
PRAYER
BENEDICTION

When a young person gives himself to a study of literature suitable for worship, not only will his own life be enriched, but his efforts will stimulate thought, awaken interest, and lead to dedication and high resolves on the part of others.

NOTES

SERVICE 1, TO RENOUNCE SELF

1. Matt. 10:37-39; John 12:24-26.
2. By Augustine.
3. By John Ladd. From *Highroad,* June, 1946. Copyright 1946 by Stone and Pierce. Used by permission of the author and the publisher.
4. Adapted from Richard K. Morton, *A Book of Prayers for Young People.* Copyright 1935 by Whitmore and Smith. Used by permission of Abingdon-Cokesbury Press.

SERVICE 2, TO MASTER SELF

1. Gal. 5:26; 6:1-10; I Cor. 13:9-12. From Edgar J. Goodspeed, *The New Testament, an American Translation.* Used by permission of University of Chicago Press, publisher.
2. From *Doctrines and Discipline of The Methodist Church,* 1944. Used by permission of The Methodist Publishing House.
3. "Up and On." From *All's Well.* Used by permission of Miss Erica Oxenham.
4. Adapted from the story by Lloyd C. Douglas in the *American Pulpit Series.* Copyright 1945 by Whitmore and Stone. Used by permission of Abingdon-Cokesbury Press.
5. "Mixed." Used by permission of Charles Scribner's Sons, publishers.

SERVICE 3, TO SHOULDER RESPONSIBILITY

1. "At the Day's Beginning." Used by permission of the author.
2. Ps. 8.
3. From *The Book of Worship for Church and Home.* Copyright 1944, 1945 by Whitmore and Stone. Used by permission of The Methodist Publishing House.
4. "There Is a Life Above Your Own." Used by permission of the author.

5. Adapted from the story by Marian Goodnow in the *Youth's Companion,* July 12, 1917. Used by permission.

SERVICE 4, TO ACCEPT DISCIPLINE

1. Prov. 16:32; Ps. 143:10; Prov. 4:23; Ps. 141:4; Prov. 4:24; Ps. 141:3; Jas. 1:2-4; Rom. 5:3-4; Eph. 6:10-11; Phil. 4:13.
2. Glenn Cunningham in *Classmate,* Oct. 22, 1944. Copyright 1944 by Whitmore and Stone. Used by permission of the publisher and Allied Youth.
3. "Carry On!—And Make It So." From *Hearts Courageous.* Used by permission of Miss Erica Oxenham.

SERVICE 5, TO DISCOVER LIFE THROUGH SERVICE

1. Hag. 1:7; Prov. 3:1-6; Josh. 24:14-15; I Cor. 12:31; Matt. 20:26-27.
2. "Things That Abide." Used by permission of the author.

SERVICE 6, TO SEARCH PATIENTLY FOR TRUTH

1. "Invocation." Used by permission of the author and the Bethany Press.
2. Ps. 43:3; John 16:13; 18:37; 8:32.
3. From *The Kingdom, the Power, and the Glory.* Copyright 1933 by Oxford University Press, Inc. Used by permission.
4. From Archibald Rutledge, "Better—Or Just Better Off?" in *Classmate,* March 25, 1945. Published by Whitmore and Stone. Used by permission.
5. "The Patient Scientists." From the *Congregationalist.* Copyright, The Pilgrim Press. Used by permission.
6. From Walter Rauschenbusch, *Prayers of the Social Awakening.* The Pilgrim Press. Used by permission.

SERVICE 7, TO MAKE PRAYER EFFECTIVE

1. Matt. 6:5-8; 7:7-11; 21:22; John 15:7.
2. From Ralph S. Cushman, *Practicing the Presence.* Copyright 1936 by Ralph S. Cushman. Used by permission of Abingdon-Cokesbury Press.
3. "Talking to God." Used by permission of the author.
4. From *The School of Prayer* by Olive Wyon, p. 15. Copyright 1944 by the Westminster Press. Used by permission.
5. "Luminous." Used by permission of the author.

SERVICE 8, TO LIVE BY ONE'S CONVICTIONS

1. Dan. 1:8, 21.
2. Hymn No. 183 in *New Hymnal for American Youth,* or the words may be sung to tune No. 267 in the *Methodist Hymnal.*
3. Adapted from the story by Lida Lisle Molloy in *Classmate,* Aug. 11, 1946. Copyright 1946 by Stone and Pierce. Used by permission.
4. From *Classmate.* Used by permission.
5. By Paul Worley. Used by permission.

SERVICE 9, TO CO-OPERATE WITH GOD

1. John 15:1-8.
2. From Walter Rauschenbusch, *Prayers of the Social Awakening.* The Pilgrim Press. Used by permission.

SERVICE 10, TO FULFILL GOD'S APPOINTMENT

1. Used by permission of the author.
2. I. Cor. 13:4-8. From *The New Testament in Modern Speech* by Richard Francis Weymouth. The Pilgrim Press. Used by permission.
3. "Eternal Love." Used by permission of the author.
4. From Walter Rauschenbusch, *Prayers of the Social Awakening.* The Pilgrim Press. Used by permission.
5. Adapted from the story by Robert B. Gilbert in *Classmate,* Aug. 10, 1947. Used by permission.

SERVICE 11, TO ANSWER THE CALL OF CHRIST

1. Mark 2:17; John 10:10; 18:37; Matt. 4:18, 19.
2. "Morningstar." From *Highroad,* April, 1943. Used by permission.
3. Matt. 16:24.
4. Adapted from the story by Eleanor B. Stock in *Classmate,* Aug. 8, 1931. Used by permission.

SERVICE 12, FEAR NOT

1. "A Christmas Prayer." Used by permission of the author and the Bethany Press.
2. Luke 2:1, 4-14.
3. "Western Christmas." Used by permission of the author.
4. By Glora M. Wysner. From *The Church Woman,* Dec., 1946. Used by permission.
5. "The Forgotten Star." From *Poems for the Great Days,* Thomas Curtis Clark and Robert E. Clark, compilers. Copyright 1948 by

Stone and Pierce. Used by permission of Abingdon-Cokesbury Press.
6. Adapted from J. Emerson Ford, "Bethlehem and Calvary," *The Christian Home,* Dec., 1945. Copyright 1945 by Whitmore and Stone. Used by permission.

SERVICE 13, ACCEPTING CHRIST AS MASTER

1. Mark 16:1-9. From *The New Testament in Modern Speech* by Richard Francis Weymouth. The Pilgrim Press. Used by permission.
2. "Legend of the Bells." Used by permission of the author.
3. Reprinted from *Hymns of the Spirit* by permission of the Beacon Press.
4. By Roy L. Smith. From the *Christian Advocate,* April 2, 1942. Used by permission.
5. "He Lives in Love Victorious." Used by permission of the author.

SERVICE 14, HONORING A GREAT MOTHER

1. Prov. 31:10-12, 25-31.
2. From *The Home in a Changing Culture* by Grace Sloan Overton. Used by permission of the author and Fleming H. Revell Co., publishers.
3. Based on John Kirk, *The Mother of the Wesleys,* and Halford E. Luccock and Paul Hutchinson, *The Story of Methodism.*
4. "Mother." From *Poems for the Great Days,* Thomas Curtis Clark and Robert E. Clark, comps. Copyright 1948 by Stone and Pierce. Used by permission of Abingdon-Cokesbury Press.

SERVICE 15, ATTEMPT GREAT THINGS FOR GOD

1. "Far Through the Night." Used by permission of the author. May be sung to the tune "Pilgrims," No. 532, or "Ancient of Days," No. 59, in the *Methodist Hymnal.*
2. Matt. 9:37-38; John 10:16; Matt. 28:18-20.

SERVICE 16, SPREAD THE LIGHT

1. Matt. 10:5-7; Mal. 1:11; Ps. 98:2; Isa. 60:3.
2. "Spread the Light." Used by permission of Miss Erica Oxenham.
3. "The Gleaming Wings." Used by permission of the author. This hymn may be sung to the tune "Sheltered Dale," No. 455 in the *Methodist Hymnal.*
4. From Walter Rauschenbusch, *Prayers of the Social Awakening.* The Pilgrim Press. Used by permission.

SERVICE 17, NOT WHERE YOU LIVE BUT HOW

1. Acts 17:24-27; Luke 13:29; Rom. 10:12; Luke 6:31; Matt. 25:40.
2. From Richard K. Morton, *A Book of Prayers for Young People.* Copyright 1935 by Whitmore and Smith. Used by permission of Abingdon-Cokesbury Press.
3. "Brother." Used by permission of the author and the Bethany Press.
4. Send offering to your denominational headquarters for the support of projects set up to build better relations between the races.
5. "If Every Christian Were Christlike" from the *Christian-Evaneglist,* Feb. 18, 1949. Used by permission of the author and the Christian Board of Publication.
6. By Ina E. Lindsley. Used by permission of the Religious Press Committee.
7. "How—When—Where" from *Hearts Courageous* by John Oxenham. Used by permission of Miss Erica Oxenham.

SERVICE 18, MAKING THE BIBLE KNOWN

1. Poem from hymn No. 392 in the *Methodist Hymnal.*
2. By P. R. Hayward from the *International Journal of Religious Education,* Nov., 1944. Used by permission.
3. Adapted. By James R. Joy from the *Bible Society Record,* Sept., 1947. Used by permission.
4. Adapted. By Robert Root from the *Christian Herald,* Jan., 1948. Used by permission.
5. Send offering to American Bible Society, Bible House, 450 Park Ave., New York 22, N. Y.
6. II Cor. 9:7.

SERVICE 19, HE BUILDED BETTER THAN HE KNEW

1. Ps. 86:11; II Tim. 2:15; Ps. 90:12. The poem may be repeated or sung to the tune of No. 218 in the *New Hymnal for American Youth.*
2. By Thomas Aquinas.
3. "We Would Be Building" from the *Hymnal for Youth.* Copyright 1936 by Purd E. Deitz. Used by permission. Tune "Finlandia."
4. Adapted from the story by O. K. Armstrong in the *Christian Advocate,* June 10, 1948. As condensed in the *Reader's Digest.* Used by permission.
5. "Braving the Wilds All Unexplored" from the *Church School Hymnal for Youth.* Copyright 1928, Board of National Missions of the Presbyterian Church, U.S.A. Used by permission.

SERVICE 20, REMEMBERING JESUS

1. From *Doctrines and Discipline of The Methodist Church,* 1944. Used by permission of The Methodist Publishing House.
2. Mark 14:12-15, 17; John 13:4-9, 12-16; Matt. 26:21-23, 26-28. From Edgar J. Goodspeed, *The New Testament, an American Translation.* Used by permission of the University of Chicago Press, publisher.
3. Luke 22:19.
4. Based on Clarence Tucker Craig, *We Have an Altar.* Copyright 1934 by Clarence Tucker Craig. Used by permission of Abingdon-Cokesbury Press.
5. From the *Christian Century,* Feb. 14, 1940. Used by permission.
6. By Lola P. Acuff. Used by permission.

STORY 1, STALWART SON OF SCIENCE

1. Adapted from the story by John Ladd in *Classmate,* May, 1948. Copyright 1948 by Stone and Pierce. Used by permission of the author and the publisher.

STORY 2, PADEREWSKI, PIANIST AND PATRIOT

1. Quotation is from Charles Phillips, *Paderewski, the Story of a Modern Immortal.* Copyright 1933 by the Macmillan Co. and used with their permission.
2. Story by Mary S. Starr. Based on Charles Phillips, *Paderewski, the Story of a Modern Immortal.*

STORY 3, WALTER REED, DOCTOR IN UNIFORM

1. Reprinted by permission of Julian Messner, Inc., from *Walter Reed: Doctor in Uniform* by Laura N. Wood, copyright by Julian Messner, Inc., June 11, 1943.
2. *Ibid.*

STORY 4, HE GAVE THEM WINDOWS

1. Adapted from the story by J. Alvin Kugelmass in the *Christian Herald,* Nov., 1948. Used by permission.

STORY 5, AVOIDING THE BEATEN TRACK

1. Quotation is from "Observation: Twin Brother to Invention," *Youth's Companion,* Feb. 7, 1918.
   This story is based in large part upon information furnished by the American Telephone and Telegraph Co.

STORY 7, HEROINE IN BUCKSKIN

1. From Nancy Wilson Ross, *Westward the Women*. Copyright 1944 by Nancy Wilson Ross. Used by permission of Alfred A. Knopf, Inc., and *Reader's Digest*, from whose condensation the story was adapted.

STORY 8, EACH BURNING STAR PROCLAIMS GOD'S GLORY

1. Adapted from Michael Pupin, *From Immigrant to Inventor*. Used by permission of Charles Scribner's Sons, publishers.

STORY 9, A NEGRO WAS ALSO THERE

1. From Matthew A. Henson, *A Negro Explorer at the North Pole*. Used by permission of the author.
2. From Robert E. Peary, *The North Pole*. Used by permission of J. B. Lippincott Co.

STORY 10, FRIEND OF PRISONERS

1. Adapted from D. M. Gill and A. M. Pullen, *Adventures of Service*. Used by permission of the Friendship Press.

STORY 11, THE MIRACLE OF "THE MESSIAH"

1. From the story by Doron K. Antrim in the *Christian Herald*, April, 1948, as condensed in the *Reader's Digest*. Used by permission.

STORY 12, A MODERN ITALIAN MADONNA

1. Adapted from the story by Velma Bell in the *Epworth Highroad*, Dec., 1933. Copyright 1933 by Whitmore and Smith. Used by permission.

STORY 13, A PICTURE FOR TRINITY

1. Adapted from the story by Ben F. Sheetz in *Classmate*, Aug., 1947. Copyright 1947 by Stone and Pierce. Used by permission.

STORY 14, PIERRE'S PART

1. By S. Alice Ranlett in *The Use of Stories in Worship*, published by the Board of Christian Education, Canadian Girls in Training, The United Church of Canada. Used by permission.

STORY 15, HEAVEN STOOPS LOW

1. Adapted from Lew Wallace, *Ben-Hur*.

STORY 16, THAT SECOND MILE

1. Author unknown. From *The Use of Stories in Worship,* published by the Board of Christian Education, Canadian Girls in Training, The United Church of Canada.

STORY 17, WITH ME THIS DAY

1. By Rhoda Nelson from the *Haversack,* April 12, 1936. Copyright 1936 by Whitmore and Smith. Used by permission.

STORY 18, WHAT IF THEY HAD QUIT?

1. By C. K. Ober from the *Missionary Intelligencer.*

STORY 19, GETTING BY

1. Adapted from Agnes Miller, "Julia Wideawake," in the *Youth's Companion.* Used by permission.

STORY 20, WORTHY OF TRUST

1. Adapted from Ann Skinner, "Kate Grenfield, Probationer," in the *Youth's Companion,* Jan. 8, 1920. Used by permission.

STORY 21, HOLY BREAD

1. Adapted from the story by Zelia M. Walters. Used by permission of Unity School of Christianity.

STORY 22, AN ILL WIND

1. By Frederick William Roe. From the *Youth's Companion,* Jan. 2, 1919. Used by permission.

STORY 23, SENSITIVE TO THE NEEDS OF OTHERS

1. Adapted from Marguerite Aspinwall, "Rose Lends a Hand," in the *Youth's Companion,* Aug. 25, 1921. Used by permission.

STORY 24, QUICK THINKING

1. Adapted from George M. Johnson, "Quick Thinking," in the *Youth's Companion,* Nov. 29, 1923. Used by permission.

BUILDING WORSHIP SERVICES

1. *Christian Century,* 407 S. Dearborn St., Chicago 5, Ill.
   Christian Herald, 27 East 39th St., New York 16, N. Y.
   Christian World Facts, 156 Fifth Ave., New York 10, N. Y.
   Christmas, Augsburg Publishing House, 425 S. Fourth St., Minneapolis 15, Minn.

SOURCES FOR HYMNS

CODE: The letter refers to the hymnal, and the number to the page on which the hymn is found in the hymnal.

A . . . New Hymnal for American Youth
B . . . Broadman Hymnal (Southern Baptist Convention)
C . . . Common Service Book (Lutheran)
D . . . Church School Hymnal for Youth (Presbyterian U.S.A.)
E . . . American Student Hymnal
F . . . Hymnal for Youth (Presbyterian U.S.A.)
G . . . Abingdon Song Book (Methodist)
H . . . Presbyterian Hymnal (U.S.)
I . . . Worship and Praise
J . . . Hymnal for Christian Worship (Presbyterian U.S.)
M . . . Methodist Hymnal
N . . . Pilgrim Hymnal (Congregational, now United Church of Christ)
P . . . The Hymnal (Presbyterian U.S.A.)
R . . . Devotional Hymns
S . . . Great Songs of the Church (Disciples)
T . . . New Baptist Hymnal (Southern Baptist Convention)
W . . . Christian Worship (Northern Baptist Convention and Disciples)

Above the Hills of Time
G—41; M—145; W—236

A Charge to Keep I Have
B—157; C—376; E—379; G—186; H—289; I—196; J—161; M—287; N—500; R—240; T—203; W—373

A Glory Gilds the Sacred Page
C—170; M—388; R—107; T—74

Another Year Is Dawning
B—275; D—6; H—476; J—291; M—534; T—311; W—587

Are Ye Able?
A—205; B—396; E—174; G—184; J—189; M—268; W—360

As with Gladness Men of Old
A—95; C—38; D—96; F—77; G—259; J—79; M—90; N—84; P—135; W—196

Believe Not Those Who Say
A—183; F—227

Beneath the Cross of Jesus
A—120; B—234; D—186; E—105; F—173; G—39; H—95; I—176; J—91; M—144; N—125; P—162; R—242; S—351; T—110; W—235

Be Strong
A—182; D—214; E—185; F—229; M—300; N—253; P—488

Book of Books
A—69; E—337; M—390

Break Thou the Bread of Life
A—71; B—192; D—157; E—101; F—133; G—235; H—381; I—243; J—132; M—387; N—412; P—216; R—199; S—354; T—81; W—461

Breathe on Me, Breath of God
A—61; B—417; D—152; E—98; F—130; G—76; J—123; M—180; N—201; P—213; T—146

Come, Ye Faithful, Raise the Strain
C—108; F—108; J—101; M—151; N—134; P—168; S—363; W—242

Dear Lord and Father of Mankind
A—152; B—401; D—236; E—80;
F—150; G—137; H—242; I—238;
J—202; M—342; N—224; P—302;
R—280; S—366; T—63; W—411

Dear Master, in Whose Life I See
M—376; N—265; P—507; W—318

Draw Thou My Soul, O Christ
A—149; D—234; E—370; F—164;
G—151; H—250; J—160; M—297;
N—232; W—299

Fight the Good Fight
A—207; B—270; D—212; E—158;
F—288; G—204; H—299; J—201;
M—286; N—255; P—270; R—261;
S—375; T—200; W—376

Give of Your Best
B—366; F—176; G—189; I—32;
T—375

God of Grace and God of Glory
F—236; G—115; M—279; W—378

Go Forth to Life
M—296; N—474; W—319

Go, Labor On
F—249; H—285; J—198; M—292;
N—330; P—376; S—381; T—206;
W—473

Happy the Home When God Is There
G—242; M—428

Heralds of Christ
A—258; F—235; G—181; H—407;
J—264; M—482; N—375; P—379;
W—533

He Who Would Valiant Be
A—204; E—169; F—233; J—193;
M—265; N—250; P—276; W—364

Holy Spirit, Truth Divine
A—60; D—146; E—100; F—128;
M—173; N—496; P—57; W—274

In the Cross of Christ I Glory
A—124; B—180; C—62; D—117;
E—377; F—95; G—43; H—94; I—210; J—94; M—140; N—127; P—154;
R—86; S—412; T—113; W—237

It Came upon the Midnight Clear
A—78; B—141; C—29; D—76;
E—245; F—64; H—58; J—73;
M—92; N—73; P—127; R—56;
S—416; T—85; W—191

I Would Be True
A—177; B—368; D—225; E—180;
F—180; G—119; I—23; N—469;
R—134; W—361

Jesus Christ Is Risen Today
A—129; B—32; C—111; D—129;
E—331; F—103; G—48; H—118;
I—212; J—102; M—155; P—163;
R—94; S—358; T—115

Jesus, Kneel Beside Me
E—107; G—146; M—308; P—494;
W—328

Just as I Am
A—145; B—162; C—337; D—180;
F—170; G—144; H—174; I—127;
J—150; M—198; N—483; P—230;
R—176; S—131; T—169; W—295

Just as I Am, Thine Own to Be
B—411; D—181; E—136; F—171;
G—143; H—280; J—310; N—428;
R—68; W—297

Life Is Good
M—160; W—248

Lift Up Our Hearts
A—3; E—176; G—180; J—253;
M—472; N—154; P—405; W—372

Lord, for Tomorrow and Its Needs
A—317; B—259; G—156; H—360;
J—222; M—314; T—197; W—327

Lord of All Power and Might
C—221; M—392

Lord of Life and King of Glory
C—418; M—426

Lord, Speak to Me That I May Speak
A—251; C—212; D—293; E—216;
F—196; G—175; H—279; I—222;
J—248; M—460; N—339; P—399;
S—438; T—211; W—470

Love Divine, All Loves Excelling
A—67; B—19; C—276; D—231;

E—356; F—153; G—111; H—21; I—2; J—176; M—372; N—270; P—308; R—81; S—440; T—183; W—379

Love Thyself Last
A—239; D—276; G—218

March On, O Soul, with Strength
A—184; D—220; E—110; F—234; G—192; H—300; M—264; N—247; P—273; W—359

'Mid All the Traffic of the Ways
A—159; F—165; G—165; H—237; J—204; M—341; P—322

More Love to Thee, O Christ
B—218; D—200; F—191; G—110; H—224; I—240; J—168; N—146; P—315; R—283; S—148; T—195; W—390

My Faith Looks Up to Thee
A—155; B—209; C—360; D—190; F—211; G—103; H—194; I—236; J—211; M—213; N—498; P—285; R—270; S—445; T—168; W—355

My Jesus, as Thou Wilt
B—178; C—395; F—172; H—247; J—214; M—330; N—494; P—280; S—446; T—222; W—408

My Soul, Be on Thy Guard
B—247; C—272; E—378; H—295; I—245; M—277; N—256; R—279; T—177; W—370

Now in the Days of Youth.
A—146; F—169; G—207; J—308; N—477; W—300

O Come, All Ye Faithful
A—83; B—143; D—89; E—298; F—74; G—30; H—56; J—69; M—96; N—105; P—116; S—452; T—90; W—205

O Jesus, I Have Promised
A—196; B—187; D—187; E—369; F—174; H—253; I—189; J—165; M—226; N—196; P—268; R—239; S—462; T—193; W—308

O Jesus, Master, When Today
E—212; H—278; M—470; N—307; W—517

O Jesus, Prince of Life and Truth
D—224; F—182; N—257; W—505

O Little Town of Bethlehem
A—82; B—144; C—31; D—78; E—330; F—66; G—31; H—55; I—281; J—64; M—100; N—74; P—121; R—57; S—464; T—82; W—184

O Love Divine
G—170; H—212; I—65; M—430; N—292; P—485; R—129; W—353

O Master, Let Me Walk with Thee
A—197; B—202; D—182; E—214; F—166; G—116; H—271; I—263; J—245; M—259; N—291; P—364; R—19; S—468; T—274; W—306

O Master Workman of the Race
A—98; D—106; E—74; F—85; G—59; H—82; J—86; M—118; N—328; P—140; R—62; W—210

Open My Eyes That I May See
B—351; D—192; F—189; I—34; R—251

O Perfect Love
C—415; H—484; J—296; P—484; N—430

O Young and Fearless Prophet
G—212; M—266; W—362

O Word of God Incarnate
A—68; B—75; C—169; D—155; E—364; F—132; H—134; J—131; M—386; N—421; P—215; T—75; W—434

O Zion, Haste, Thy Mission
A—306; B—157; C—224; D—308; E—270; F—240; G—222; H—395; J—257; M—475; N—372; P—382; R—131; S—474; T—264; W—529

Rejoice, Ye Pure in Heart
A—27; B—285; D—139; E—199; F—124; G—9; J—209; M—358; N—476; P—297; R—181; S—483; T—47; W—418

Rise Up, O Men of God
A—254; B—186; D—288; E—224; F—258; G—203; H—274; J—252; M—267; N—313; P—401; W—374

Saviour, Like a Shepherd Leads Us
B—13; C—565; H—323; I—12; J—218; M—337; N—492; P—458; R—157; S—490; T—377; W—401

Sing, Men and Angels, Sing
M—152

Spirit of Life, in This New Dawn
A—63; E—22; G—74; M—178

Sun of My Soul, Thou Saviour Dear
A—22; B—177; C—463; D—13; E—93; F—25; G—25; H—457; I—254; J—28; M—56; N—61; P—37; S—498; T—239; W—150

Take My Life, and Let It Be
A—198; B—174; C—382; D—221; E—142; F—175; G—131; H—268; I—83; J—166; M—225; N—195; P—242; R—244; S—501; T—329; W—296

Take Thou Our Minds, Dear Lord
D—11; F—168; G—276; J—311; P—245

Teach Me, O Lord, Thy Holy Way
D—199; F—188

Temper My Spirit
A—173; E—182; F—185; J—307

The Morning Light Is Breaking
B-12; C-230; D—307; F—239; H—406; J—260; M—487; N—364; P—389; R—132; T—271; W—524

The Voice of God Is Calling
D—284; E—235; F—202; G—205; M—454; N—337; W—490

Truehearted, Wholehearted, Faithful and Loyal
F—277; I—28; M—255; R—226; S—278; T—383

We Gather Together
E—29; G—12; M—20; J—10; N—29; W—117

We May Not Climb the Heavenly Steeps
M—120; N—148; R—268; T—178

We Thank Thee, Lord, Thy Paths
A—249; B—301; D—287; E—223; F—203; G—206; M—458; P—367; W—495

We've a Story to Tell to the Nations
A—302; B—379; D—306; F—238; G—215; I—146; J—261; M—501; N—374; R—124; T—261; W—530

We Would Be Building
F—204; G—113; J—313; W—489

When I Survey the Wondrous Cross
A—123; B—191; C—97; D—118; E—376; F—96; G—44; H—88; I—215; J—97; M—148; N—122; P—152; R—247; S—532; T—108; W—228

Where Cross the Crowded Ways of Life
A—265; B—405; D—268; E—60; F—253; G—214; H—330; I—230; J—268; M—465; N—140; P—410; R—24; S—536; T—276; W—519

While Shepherds Watched Their Flocks
B—147; C—28; D—79; F—67; G—32; H—50; I—282; J—80; M—88; N—83; P—120; R—58; S—537; T—89; W—185

Wonderful Words of Life
B—233; G—237; I—137; R—165; S—208

Work, for the Night Is Coming
B—243; M—293; N—502; I—235; S—538; T—272

SELECTED BIBLIOGRAPHY

WORSHIP FOR YOUNG PEOPLE

Bailey, Albert Edward. *The Gospel in Art*. Boston: The Pilgrim Press, 1916.

——. *The Arts and Religion*. New York: The Macmillan Co., 1944.

Bowie, W. Russell. *The Story of the Bible*. New York and Nashville: Abingdon-Cokesbury Press, 1934.

——. *The Story of Jesus*. New York: Charles Scribner's Sons, 1937.

Blackwood, Andrew W. *The Fine Art of Public Worship*. New York and Nashville: Abingdon-Cokesbury Press, 1939.

Cushman, Ralph S. *Practicing the Presence*. New York and Nashville: Abingdon-Cokesbury Press, 1936.

Herman, Nicolas (Brother Lawrence). *The Practice of the Presence of God*. London: The Epworth Press, 1933.

Hopper, Myron Taggart. *The Candle of the Lord*. St. Louis: Christian Board of Publication (The Bethany Press), 1948.

Jones, E. Stanley. *Abundant Living*. New York and Nashville: Abingdon-Cokesbury Press, 1942.

——. *The Christ of the American Road*. New York and Nashville: Abingdon-Cokesbury Press, 1944.

Jones, Rufus M. *New Eyes for Invisibles*. New York: The Macmillan Co., 1943.

Lotz, P. Henry. *The Quest for God Through Understanding*. St. Louis: Christian Board of Publication (The Bethany Press), 1937.

Luccock, Halford E. and Brentano, Frances. *The Questing Spirit*. New York: Coward-McCann, Inc., 1947.

McDormand, Thomas Bruce. *The Art of Building Worship Services*. Nashville: The Broadman Press, 1942.

McIlwain, Orene. *Worship God*. Richmond: John Knox Press, 1947.

Page, Kirby. *Living Creatively*. New York: Farrar & Rinehart, 1932.

——. *Living Triumphantly*. New York: Farrar & Rinehart, 1934.

Palmer, Albert W., ed. *Aids to Worship*. New York: The Macmillan Co., 1944.

Paulsen, Irwin G. *The Church School and Worship*. New York: The Macmillan Co., 1940.

Pease, Dorothy Wells, ed. *Altars Under the Sky*. New York and Nashville: Abingdon-Cokesbury Press, 1942.

Phillips, D. B., Nixon, L. M., Howes, E. B., eds. *The Choice Is Always Ours*. New York: Richard R. Smith, 1948.

Quimby, Chester W. *Jesus as They Remembered Him*. New York and Nashville: Abingdon-Cokesbury Press, 1941.

————. *The Jubilant Year.* New York and Nashville: Abingdon-Cokesbury Press, 1946.

Reid, Albert C. *Invitation to Worship.* New York and Nashville: Abingdon-Cokesbury Press, 1942.

————. *Resources for Worship.* New York and Nashville: Abingdon-Cokesbury Press, 1949.

Rice, Merton S. *My Father's World.* New York and Nashville: Abingdon-Cokesbury Press, 1943.

Sadler, Alfred J. *Out of Doors with God.* New York and Nashville: Abingdon-Cokesbury Press, 1940.

Seidenspinner, Clarence. *Our Dwelling Place.* New York and Nashville: Abingdon-Cokesbury Press, 1941.

Smart, W. Aiken. *The Contemporary Christ.* New York and Nashville: Abingdon-Cokesbury Press, 1942.

Smith, H. Augustine. *Lyric Religion.* New York: D. Appleton-Century Co., 1931.

Snowden, Rita F. *While the Candle Burns.* London: The Epworth Press, 1942.

Toner, Helen L. *When Lights Burn Low.* New York and Nashville: Abingdon-Cokesbury Press, 1942.

POEMS

Armstrong, O. V. and Helen, comps. *Prayer Poems.* New York and Nashville: Abingdon-Cokesbury Press, 1942.

Clark, Thomas Curtis, comp. *Poems of Justice.* Chicago: Willett, Clark & Co., 1929.

Clark, Thomas Curtis and Robert Earle, comps. *Poems for the Great Days.* New York and Nashville: Abingdon-Cokesbury Press, 1948.

Clark, Thomas Curtis and Gillespie, Esther A., comps. *1000 Quotable Poems.* Chicago: Willett, Clark & Co., 1937.

Cushman, Ralph S. *Practicing the Presence.* New York and Nashville: Abingdon-Cokesbury Press, 1936.

————. *Hilltop Verses and Prayers.* New York and Nashville: Abingdon-Cokesbury Press, 1945.

Cushman, Ralph S. and Cushman, Robert E. *More Hilltop Verses and Prayers.* New York and Nashville: Abingdon-Cokesbury Press, 1949.

Gibran, Kahlil. *The Prophet.* New York: Alfred A. Knopf, 1923.

Harkness, Georgia. *The Glory of God.* New York and Nashville: Abingdon-Cokesbury Press, 1943.

Hill, Caroline. *The World's Great Religious Poetry.* New York: The Macmillan Co., 1923.

Kagawa, Toyohiko. *Songs from the Slums.* New York and Nashville: Abingdon-Cokesbury Press, 1935.

Markham, Edwin. *Selected Poems.*

Morgan, Angela. *Selected Poems.* New York: Dodd, Mead & Co., 1926.

Morrison, James Dalton, comp. *Masterpieces of Religious Verse.* New York: Harper & Bros., 1948.

Mudge, James, comp. *Poems with Power to Strengthen the Soul.* New York: Abingdon Press. 1907, 1909.

Oxenham, John. *Gentlemen—the King!* Boston: The Pilgrim Press, 1928.

————. *Hearts Courageous.* New York: The Methodist Book Concern, 1918.

————. *Selected Poems.* New York: Harper & Bros., 1948.

SELECTED BIBLIOGRAPHY

Piety, Chauncey, R. *General Sam Houston.* Emory University: Banner Press, 1943.

Van Dyke, Henry. *Collected Poems.* New York: Charles Scribner's Sons, 1920-25.

STORIES

Bartlett, Robert M. *They Dared to Live.* New York: The Association Press, 1937.

———. *They Did Something About It.* New York: The Association Press, 1939.

———. *They Work for Tomorrow.* New York: The Association Press, 1943.

Bolton, Sarah. *Famous Men of Science.* New York: Thomas Y. Crowell Co., 1941.

By an Unknown Disciple. New York: Harper & Bros., 1927.

Cather, K. Dunlap. *Boyhood Stories of Famous Men.* New York: D. Appleton-Century Co., 1916.

———. *Girlhood Stories of Famous Women.* New York: D. Appleton-Century Co., 1924.

Eastman, Fred. *Men of Power.* Vols. I-V. New York and Nashville: Abingdon-Cokesbury Press, 1938-40.

Eliot, George. *Silas Marner.* New York: Dodd, Mead & Co., 1948.

Erdman, Walter C. *Sources of Power in Famous Lives.* Nashville: Cokesbury Press, 1936.

———. *More Sources of Power in Famous Lives.* Nashville: Cokesbury Press, 1937.

Gill, D. M. and Pullen, A. M. *Adventures of Service.* New York: Missionary Education Movement, 1938.

Griggs, Edward H. *Moral Leaders.* New York and Nashville: Abingdon-Cokesbury Press, 1940.

Henson, Matthew A. *A Negro Explorer at the North Pole.* New York: J. B. Lippincott Co., 1912.

Lantz, J. Edward, ed. *Best Religious Stories.* New York: The Association Press, 1948.

Lotz, Philip Henry, ed. *The Altar Hour.* St. Louis: Christian Board of Education, 1941.

———. *Creative Personalities.* Vols. I-III. New York: The Association Press, 1940-41.

Matthews, Basil. *Book of Missionary Heroes.* New York: Geo. H. Doran, 1922.

Oxenham, John. *The Hidden Years.* New York: Longmans, Green & Co., 1925.

Parkman, Mary R. *Heroines of Service.* New York: D. Appleton-Century Co., n.d.

Pupin, Michael I., *From Immigrant to Inventor.* New York: Charles Scribner's Sons, 1925.

Ross, Nancy Wilson. *Westward the Women.* New York: Alfred A. Knopf, Inc., 1944.

Sawyers, Mott R. *Famous Friends of God.* New York: Fleming H. Revell, 1933.

Snowden, Rita F. *Safety Last!* London: The Epworth Press, 1946.

Stidger, William L. *The Human Side of Greatness.* New York: Harper & Bros., 1940.

———. *There are Sermons in Stories.* New York and Nashville: Abingdon-Cokesbury Press, 1942.

———. *More Sermons in Stories.* New York and Nashville: Abingdon-Cokesbury Press, 1944.

Thomas, Henry and Lee, Dana. *Living Biographies.* Vols. I-XII. Garden City, New York: Garden City Publishing Co., 1942.

Turnbull, Agnes S. *Far Above Rubies.* New York: Fleming H. Revell Co., 1926.

Use of Stories in Worship. Toronto: Board of Christian Education, The United Church of Canada, 1947.

Wallace, Archer. *Overcoming Handicaps.* New York: Harper & Bros., 1927.

———. *Stories of Grit.* New York: Harper & Bros., 1930.

———. *In Spite of All.* New York and Nashville: Abingdon-Cokesbury Press, 1944.

————. *100 Stories for Boys.* New York and Nashville: Abingdon-Cokesbury Press, 1947.

Wallace, Lew. *Ben-Hur.* New York: Harper & Bros., 1880.

Wood, Laura N. *Walter Reed.* New York: Julian Messner, Inc., 1943.

PRAYER

Abernethy, Jean Beaven. *Meditations for Women.* New York and Nashville: Abingdon-Cokesbury Press, 1947.

Bowie, W. Russell. *Lift Up Your Hearts.* New York: The Macmillan Co., 1939.

Cavert, Walter Dudley. *Remember Now.* New York and Nashville: Abingdon-Cokesbury Press, 1944.

Fox, Selina F. *A Chain of Prayer Across the Ages.* New York: E. P. Dutton, 1943.

Harkness, Georgia. *Prayer and the Common Life.* New York and Nashville: Abingdon-Cokesbury Press, 1948.

Herman, Emily. *Creative Prayer.* New York: Harper & Bros., 1940.

Hoyland, J. S. *A Book of Prayers for Youth.* New York: The Association Press, 1939.

Lester, Muriel. *Ways of Praying.* London: Independent Press, 1931.

Luccock, Halford E. and Brentano, Frances. *The Questing Spirit.* New York: Coward-McCann, Inc., 1947

Morton, Richard K. *A Book of Prayers for Young People.* New York and Nashville: Abingdon-Cokesbury Press, 1935.

Phillips, D. B., Nixon, L. M., Howes, E. B., and others. *The Choice Is Always Ours,* New York: Richard R. Smith, 1948.

Rauschenbusch, Walter. *Prayers of the Social Awakening.* Boston: The Pilgrim Press, 1925.

The Kingdom, the Power and the Glory. New York: Oxford University Press, 1933.

Wyon, Olive. *The School of Prayer.* Philadelphia: Westminster Press, 1944.

INDEX OF STORIES

WORSHIP SERVICES FOR PURPOSEFUL LIVING